Names and Titles of Jesus

A Discipleship Study

for Personal Devotional Use, Small Groups or
Sunday School Classes, and Sermon Preparation for Pastors and Teachers

JesusWalk® Bible Study Series

by Dr. Ralph F. Wilson
Director, Joyful Heart Renewal Ministries

Additional books, and reprint licenses are available at:
www.jesuswalk.com/books/names-jesus.htm

Free Participant Guide handout sheets are available at:
www.jesuswalk.com/names-jesus/names-jesus-lesson-handouts.pdf

JesusWalk® Publications
Loomis, California

Paperback

ISBN-13: 978-0-9962025-2-7

ISBN-10: 0-9962025-2-8

Library of Congress subject headings:

>Jesus Christ – Name.

>Jesus Christ – Person and offices.

Suggested Classifications

>Dewey Decimal System: 232

>Library of Congress: BT590.N2

Published by JesusWalk® Publications, P.O. Box 565, Loomis, CA 95650-0565, USA.

JesusWalk is a registered trademark and Joyful Heart is a trademark of Joyful Heart Renewal Ministries.

Unless otherwise noted, all the Bible verses quoted are from the New International Version (International Bible Society, 1973, 1978), used by permission.

151212

Preface

I love Jesus as a Person, as my Lord and Friend. He's the "historical Jesus," yes, a human as he appeared on earth and walked the dusty roads of Galilee. But he is much more. He was with God at the beginning. All things were made through him. He is the Redeemer of mankind, the Shepherd of souls. He is the One by whom all will be judged. And he is the Coming Messiah who will wrap up the world and make it a place where, once more, righteousness dwells. He is God the Son.

I'd like to explore with you the various facets of Jesus' person, life, and mission. One way to do this is by carefully studying the Gospels and Epistles. But another way is to approach it topically – by Jesus' names, titles, descriptors and the metaphors.

I'll try to mention at least once all these names, titles, descriptors, and metaphors. But I'll concentrate on the ones most used in Holy Scripture. If you understand Jesus in these

Philip Handel (1931-2009), "The Good Shepherd," St. John the Baptist Anglican Church, Ashfield, New South Wales.

chief names and titles, then the seldom-used, but precious names will be icing on the cake for you.

What we're about to commence on is actually "theology," the study of God. I did this in relation to God the Father in my book *Names and Titles of God* (JesusWalk, 2010). But as the present study focuses on Jesus, a more precise word is "Christology," the study of Jesus Messiah and his various offices.

Of course there'll be some overlap and repetition, since these names and themes are interwoven, with several often mentioned in the same passage. But that's fine. We're going swimming together, and though we'll try to keep the study organized, the most important thing is to enjoy the water.

I don't want this to be a merely academic survey. My goal during this study is to help you enter into a deeper relationship with Jesus. I'll suggest songs for you to worship him with, and prayers to pray. I'll suggest some weekly exercises to help you know Him in these various ways. So by the end of our 10-week study, you'll not only know more *about* Jesus, but actually know Him better *experientially*.

Last weekend my wife and I enjoyed again a performance of Handel's "Messiah," and became aware afresh of the glorious names and titles by which Jesus has been called throughout the ages. The concert ended with joy on my face. Hallelujah!

I look forward to studying with you as we explore and revel in a study of Jesus Christ our Lord.

Yours in Christ Jesus,
Dr. Ralph F. Wilson
Christmastide 2015

Table of Contents

Preface 3

Table of Contents 5

References and Abbreviations 10

Reprint Guidelines 12

Introduction to the Names and Titles of Jesus 13
Why Study the Names and Titles of Jesus? 13
What Is a Title of Jesus? 13
Messianic References 14
Second Person of the Trinity 15
Features of This Study 15

1. Jesus the Nazarene Carpenter's Son 17
The Jesus of History 17
Early Historical References to Jesus 17
The Given Name of Jesus 18
Usage of the Name Jesus 20
Son of Joseph and Mary 20
Genealogies 21
Carpenter 21
Nazarene 22
Messianic Prophecy Concerning Galilee 23

2. Jesus our Rabbi, Teacher, Prophet, and Word 31
Jesus the Rabbi 31
A Rabbi and His Disciples 32
Jesus the Prophet 34
Jesus Is the Word, the Logos 36
Logos 37
Jesus Is the Faithful and True Witness 38
Jesus is the Truth 39
Jesus Is the Wisdom of God 40

Jesus and Lady Wisdom of Proverbs 8   41
Wonderful Counselor   42

3. Jesus the Son of Man   **45**
The Hebrew Idiom   45
Daniel's Heavenly Son of Man   46
Jesus' Use of Son of Man in the Gospels   48
The Man Christ Jesus   48
Two Natures in One Person   49
Man of Sorrows   50
Seed of the Woman, Seed of Abraham   50
The Last Adam   51
Mediator of a New Covenant   52
Jesus the Advocate and Reconciler   53
Consolation of Israel   54
Our Hope   55
Jesus, the Apostle of God   55
Jesus, the Indescribable Gift   56

4. Jesus the Messiah, Christ, and Son of David   **59**
Anointing   59
The Davidic Covenant   60
Messianic Prophecy   61
Jesus the Messiah   64
Titles as Christ   65
Son of David   66
Seed or Offspring of David   66
Root, Branch, and Shoot   67
The Lion of Judah   68
The Chosen One   69

5. Jesus our Lord, the Divine Son of God   **73**
Uses of Son of God   73
The Son in the Synoptic Gospels   75
Son of God in John's Gospel   76
Alternate Divine Titles   76
My Beloved Son   76
Jesus the "Only-Begotten"   77

The Only-Begotten God   79
Lord (and Master)   80
Lord and Rabbi   83
The "I Am" Sayings in John's Gospel   84
Jesus as God   85
Image of Invisible God   86
Emmanuel, God with Us   86

6. Jesus the Lamb of God, Holy and Righteous One   91
Holiness and Righteousness   91
Absolute Goodness   92
The Righteous One   92
Righteous Branch   93
Our Righteousness   94
Righteous Judge   94
The Holy One   95
The Lamb of God   96
Animal Sacrifice   97
Behold, the Lamb of God   98
Jesus the Servant   99
A Servant Mentality   100
Jesus our Priest   101

7. Jesus our Savior, Shepherd, and Redeemer   106
God My Savior   107
Prophecies of a Savior   107
Friend of Sinners   108
Rescuer, Deliverer   108
Combinations Using Savior   109
Redeemer   111
The Kinsman-Redeemer   111
Boaz the Kinsman-Redeemer   112
Jesus Our Ransom and Redeemer   112
Jesus Our Shepherd   114

8. Jesus our Head, Cornerstone, and Way   120
Jesus is Head   120
Head of the Body, the Church   121

God our Rock   122
Messianic Prophecies Regarding the Stone   122
Stone, Cornerstone, Foundation, and Capstone   124
Jesus the Way, the Door, the Gate   127
Banner for the Peoples   129
Jesus, the Great Physician   130

9. Jesus our Light, Life, Bread, and Bridegroom   **134**
Jesus the Light of the World   134
Messianic Prophecy of the Light   135
The Sun of Righteousness   136
Rising Sun, Dayspring   136
Morning Star   136
The Life-Giver   137
The Bread of Life   138
Jesus the Vine   139
The Resurrection and the Life   139
The True God and Eternal Life   140
The Author of Life   140
Christ Who Is Your Life   140
Husband and Bridegroom   141
The Covenant and Guarantor of the Covenant   142

10. Jesus the Risen King of Glory   **147**
God's Shekinah Glory   148
Jesus' Glory   150
Glory at the Coming of the Son of Man   150
Jesus the Beginning and the End, the Alpha and Omega   151
Author and Perfecter of Our Faith   153
Christ the Firstborn   153
Firstborn from among the Dead   155
Heir of All Things   156
The Desire of All Nations   156
The Messenger of the Covenant   157
Refiner and Purifier   158
Jesus the Judge   159
Messiah's Reign Will Have No End   160

Commander, Leader, Prince   161
King of Glory Enters Jerusalem   163

Appendix 1. Participant Handout Guides   **171**

Appendix 2. Names, Titles, Metaphors, and Descriptors of Jesus: A Comprehensive List   **172**

Appendix 3. Songs and Hymns Celebrating Names and Titles of Jesus Christ   **186**

Appendix 4. The Title Son of Man in the Gospels   **187**
Jesus' Use of Son of Man in John's Gospel   188

Appendix 5. Disputed Titles of Jesus   **190**
Titles from the Song of Solomon   190
Plant of Renown   190
Jesus as the Angel of the Lord   190

Appendix 6. Exercises to Help You Internalize the Names of Jesus   **191**

References and Abbreviations

BDAG   Walter Bauer and Frederick William Danker, *A Greek-English Lexicon of the New Testament and Other Early Christian Literature* (Third Edition; based on previous English editions by W.F. Arndt, F.W. Gingrich, and F.W. Danker; University of Chicago Press, 1957, 1979, 2000)

BDB   Francis Brown, S.R. Driver, and Charles A. Briggs, *A Hebrew and English Lexicon of the Old Testament* (Clarendon Press, 1907)

Brown, *John*   Raymond E. Brown, *The Gospel According to John* (Anchor Bible volumes 29A and 29B; Doubleday, 1966, 1970)

DJG   Joel B. Green, Scot McKnight, I. Howard Marshall (Editors), *Dictionary of Jesus and the Gospels* (InterVarsity Press, 1992)

DOTP   T. Desmond Alexander and David W. Baker (eds.), *Dictionary of the Old Testament: Pentateuch,* (InterVarsity Press, 2003)

DPL   Gerald F. Hawthorne, Ralph P. Martin, and Daniel G. Reid (eds.), *Dictionary of Paul and His Letters* (InterVarsity Press, 1993)

Fee   Gordon D. Fee, *Pauline Christology: An Exegetical-Theological Study* (Hendrickson, 2007)

France   R.E. France, *The Gospel of Matthew* (New International Commentary on the New Testament; Eerdmans, 2007)

Grudem   Wayne Grudem, *Systematic Theology* (Zondervan, 1994)

ISBE   Geoffrey W. Bromiley (general editor), *The International Standard Bible Encyclopedia* (Eerdmans, 1979-1988; fully revised from the 1915 edition)

Ladd   George Eldon Ladd, *A Theology of the New Testament* (Eerdmans, 1974)

NIDNTT   Colin Brown (ed.), *New International Dictionary of New Testament Theology* (Zondervan, 1975-1978; translated with additions and revisions from *Theologisches Begriffslexikon zum Neuen Testament*, Coenen, Beyreuther, and Bitenhard, editors)

TDNT   Gerhard Kittel and Gerhard Friedrich (editors), Geoffrey W. Bromiley (translator and editor), *Theological Dictionary of the New Testament*

(Eerdmans, 1964-1976; translated from *Theologisches Wörterbuch zum Neuen Testament*)

Thayer Joseph Henry Thayer, *Greek-English Lexicon of the New Testament* (Associated Publishers and Authors, n.d., reprinted from 1889 edition)

TWOT R. Laird Harris, Gleason L. Archer, Jr., and Bruce K. Waltke, (editors), *Theological Wordbook of the Old Testament*, (2 volumes, Moody Press, 1980)

Reprint Guidelines

Copying the Handouts. In some cases, small groups or Sunday school classes would like to use these notes to study this material. That's great. An appendix provides copies of handouts designed for classes and small groups. There is no charge whatsoever to print out as many copies of the handouts as you need for participants.

Free Participant Guide handout sheets are available at:

www.jesuswalk.com/names-jesus/names-jesus-lesson-handouts.pdf

All charts and notes are copyrighted and must bear the line:

Copying the book (or the majority of it) in your congregation or group, you are requested to purchase a reprint license for each book. A Reprint License, $2.50 for each copy is available for purchase at

www.jesuswalk.com/books/names-jesus.htm

Or you may send a check to:

Dr. Ralph F. Wilson
JesusWalk Publications
PO Box 565
Loomis, CA 95650, USA

The Scripture says,

"The laborer is worthy of his hire" (Luke 10:7) and "Anyone who receives instruction in the word must share all good things with his instructor." (Galatians 6:6)

However, if you are from a third world country or an area where it is difficult to transmit money, please make a small contribution instead to help the poor in your community.

Introduction to the Names and Titles of Jesus

Why Study the Names and Titles of Jesus?

Should we study the names, titles, metaphors, and descriptors of Jesus so we can impress others with our Jesus vocabulary? By no means. I believe there are three ways that a study of Jesus' names and titles can benefit us, all of them closely related:

1. Our prayer life is enriched by having meditated on Jesus' names, titles, and metaphors. For example, as I've studied about Jesus as my Shepherd, I find myself calling on Jesus in prayer as my Shepherd, trusting him to supply my needs and to guide me.

"Bread of Life" stained glass window (1911), First Congregational Church, Fremont, Michigan.

2. Our worship is enriched, as well. With a limited vocabulary of praise and a limited understanding of Jesus we are reduced to a kind of hobbled, truncated praise. But as we begin to know more of Jesus' facets, we are able to praise him better.

3. Our faith in and understanding of Jesus is increased. As I study how Jesus provides as a shepherd, I now am able to trust him more fully in this area of my life. Whereas I once had a lot of anxiety about making ends meet, now my trust in Jesus as my Shepherd and Provider bring me confidence, assurance, and joy that was missing before.

What Is a Title of Jesus?

Name. "A word or phrase that constitutes the distinctive designation of a person or thing." Let's use Billy Graham as an example. "Billy" is his first name, "Graham" is his surname, his father's name. Jesus was known by people in his village as "Jesus, son of Joseph" (Luke 3:23; John 1:45; 6:42).

Title. "An appellation of dignity, honor, distinction, or preeminence attached to a person or family by virtue of rank, office, precedent, privilege, attainment, or lands." When he is introduced in public he is often called "Reverend Graham" or "Doctor

Graham." If he had been a pastor, he might have been referred to as "Pastor Graham." He also might be titled "Evangelist." One of Jesus' titles is "Messiah" or "Christ."

Metaphor is "a figure of speech in which a word or phrase literally denoting one kind of object or idea is used in place of another to suggest a likeness or analogy between them." For example, Jesus is referred to as Shepherd, though he wasn't a literal shepherd for his living. But the metaphor of "shepherd" tells us something about his ministry.

Descriptor is "something (as a word or characteristic feature) that serves to describe or identify." Sometimes metaphors of Jesus could also be called descriptors. In English we have several grammatical constructs used to describe nouns. Descriptors can describe his functions, such as Savior, Redeemer, Healer.

One is an *adjectival phrase,* a noun together with an adjective modifying it. In Hebrew and Greek, this modifier often appears in the genitive, such as "Man of Sorrows" (Isaiah 53:3). Another is a *predicate adjective,* "an adjective which appears in the position of the predicate (i.e., after the verb) but which modifies the subject,"[1] such as "Jesus is hope." This describes a quality of Jesus, but is it a title? Probably not. But if Jesus is addressed in prayer as "Jesus, my Hope," perhaps we should consider it a descriptor. If the phrase is used often enough, it might even be considered a title.[2]

Perhaps this helps you see the fuzzy borders of determining what are the names, titles, metaphors, and descriptors of Jesus. Add to that different translations. So let's not be too dogmatic about precisely which are which. What we're really seeking to know is the Jesus who existed long before any names for him were even needed.

Messianic References

When we examine the names and titles of Jesus, we look back to the Old Testament, to messianic prophecies. Of course, not everyone agrees on whether a particular Old Testament passage refers to the Messiah. That's okay. But we'll be looking at the clearest ones, especially prophecies mentioned in the New Testament with reference to Jesus. For example, in Isaiah 53, Jesus is called "Servant" and "Man of Sorrows." In Isaiah 9 he is called "Wonderful Counselor."

---

[1] Albert H. Marckwardt and Frederic G. Cassidy, *Scribner Handbook of English* (Third Edition; Charles Scribner's Sons, 1960), p. 256.

[2] To make it even more complicated, Hebrew may omit the verb and put a noun side by side with Elohim or Yahweh. Does this make it a title? Maybe.

Second Person of the Trinity

In our study we'll consider Jesus as the Second Person of the Trinity. I won't spend time trying to prove the concept of the Trinity here. Rather see my article, "Four Reasons Why I Believe in the Trinity" (www.joyfulheart.com/scholar/trinity.htm). For many centuries Jesus' relation to the Father has been helpfully described by the Apostles' and Nicene Creeds:

> "I believe in God the Father Almighty, Maker of heaven and earth: And in Jesus Christ his only Son our Lord...." (Apostles' Creed, second century AD)

> We believe ... in one Lord Jesus Christ, the only-begotten Son of God, begotten of the Father before all worlds, Light of Light, very God of very God, begotten, not made, being of one substance with the Father; by whom all things were made...." (Nicene Creed, 325 and 381 AD)

Features of This Study

Hebrew and Greek Word Studies. Rather than relying on previous books about the names of Jesus, I've gone back to the original Hebrew and Greek languages and the conclusions of contemporary conservative scholars to determine the meanings of the words as precisely as possible. If you find Hebrew and Greek confusing, you're not alone. Please accept my condolences and just skip it. But for preachers, teachers, and small group leaders I've included this kind of information, as well as footnoting my sources, so that readers can assess the value of the information and not just pass it along blindly to their listeners.

Questions are included at various points in each chapter to help the reader pause and think more deeply. It's too easy for us to read unthoughtfully and assume that we understand what we are reading. The questions are designed to help readers articulate and apply what they are learning to their own lives and growing faith. Each question includes a hyperlink to the Joyful Heart Bible Study Forum where participants can share their answers to the questions and read what others have written.

Songs and Hymns are ways that we use the names and character of Jesus in our worship. To help those designing worship services around the names and titles of Jesus, and to facilitate personal worship, I have tried to include some of the more popular hymns and songs that I could find, among the many thousands in the CCLI Song Select and Cyber Hymnal databases. I've tried to include songs that actually include names and titles somewhat prominently, though that is a judgment call. These are included at the end of every lesson, and for all lessons in a separate Appendix 3 available online.

Lists of the Names and Titles of Jesus in each of ten categories are included too. Appendix 2 provides a complete listing of all the names, titles, descriptors, and metaphors of Jesus that I could find. I encourage you to try to use the various ways of addressing Jesus in your prayers for each week of the study. Your prayers will be richer for it, and so will your understanding of the great God whom we serve.

Be aware that the exact names and titles can vary a bit. I've used the NIV as the primary text for these lessons, but also show variations in the NRSV, ESV, and KJV.

I've also included Appendix 6. Exercises to Help You Internalize the Names of Jesus. These suggest ways to include a lesson's names and titles in prayer, meditation, worship, drawing or painting, composing a song, community involvement, and prayer for friends. I hope you'll take advantage of many of these ideas throughout the study.

Okay, we're about ready to begin. Don't be afraid to stretch yourself and do some things you've never done before. It is my joy to take this journey with you. Let's pray:

> Father, guide us as we learn about Jesus through his names, titles, descriptors, and metaphors that we find in your Word. I pray that you would change our lives, energize our faith, and make us more like Jesus in this process. Help us to know him more fully. In Jesus' holy name, we pray. Amen.

1. Jesus the Nazarene Carpenter's Son

Jesus first appears in the Gospels as Jesus of Nazareth, son of Joseph and Mary, who was born in Bethlehem, was raised in Nazareth, earned his living as a carpenter, and at age of about 30 began a three year ministry that ended in his death by crucifixion.

Sir John Everett Millais, 'Christ in the House of His Parents' (1850), oil on canvas, 30 x 55 in, Tate Britain, London

The Jesus of History

Unlike mythical figures unfettered by time and history – such as the gods of India, Rome, Greece, the Celts, and the Norsemen – Jesus' story is firmly set in history. Consider this passage:

> "In the fifteenth year of the reign of Tiberius Caesar – when Pontius Pilate was governor of Judea, Herod tetrarch of Galilee, his brother Philip tetrarch of Iturea and Traconitis, and Lysanias tetrarch of Abilene – during the high priesthood of Annas and Caiaphas, the word of God came to John son of Zechariah in the desert." (Luke 3:1-2)

Pretty specific!

Early Historical References to Jesus

A number of early non-Christian documents refer to Jesus as an historical person as well:

Jewish historian **Josephus** (early second century AD) has two mentions of Jesus, though the first appears to have been tampered with by later Christian scribes, since Josephus himself did not pretend to be a Christian.[3] The second quotation, however, is

---

[3] Josephus, *Antiquities of the Jews*, 18.3.3.

likely to be authentic regarding the stoning of "the brother of Jesus, who was called Christ, whose name was James."[4]

Pliny the Younger (c. 62 - c. 113 AD) was a lawyer, author, and magistrate of ancient Rome, known for his hundreds of surviving letters. In a letter to Emperor Trajan (ruled 98-117 AD), Pliny records his dealings as a magistrate in trials of Christians, who were already numerous enough to be common subjects of the Roman court system, since they refused allegiance to the emperor in favor of Christ.[5]

Tacitus (c. 55 - c. 117 AD), who was a Roman senator and historian, wrote of Nero blaming Christians for the burning of Rome, followers of "Christus, from whom the name had its origin, [who had]suffered the extreme penalty during the reign of Tiberius at the hands of one of our procurators, Pontius Pilatus."[6]

Suetonius (c. 69 - c. AD 140), in his *Lives of the Twelve Caesars*, describes Christian persecution in two passages "at the instigation of one Chrestus."[7]

Celsus, a second century pagan Greek philosopher attacked Christianity in his literary work, *The True Word* (c. 160-180 AD). The book was largely quoted and then refuted by Origin of Alexandria (c. 185-254 AD) in his major work *Against Celsus* (248 AD). Clearly, Celsus understands Jesus as an historical character, and attacks him as such.[8]

It becomes obvious that Jesus is not some first century myth, but an historical figure who by himself and through his followers affected the history of his period and even to our day. This is acknowledged by both Christians and fair scholars everywhere.

The Given Name of Jesus

The history of Jesus begins with his given name, told to Mary at his conception by an angel, and confirmed to Joseph in a dream.

In Greek, Jesus' name is *Iēsous*, but its origin is from Hebrew. In Hebrew "Jesus" is *Yēshūa'*, a shortened form of Joshua (*Yehôshûa'*), who was one of Israel's most celebrated heroes. Many Jewish boys in Jesus' day were named Jesus, as are many Hispanic boys today – after a hero.

---

[4] Josephus, *Antiquities of the Jews*, 20.9.1.
[5] Pliny, *Letters* 10.96-97.
[6] Tacitus, *Annals*, book 15.
[7] Suetonius, *Lives of the Twelve Caesars: Claudius*, sec. 25. Suetonius, *Lives of the Twelve Caesars: Nero*, sec. 16.
[8] Origin, *Contra Celsus*, 1:28. In one section Origin quotes Celsus, who denies Jesus' virgin birth, and then tells a corruption of Jesus' story. Origin then refutes this account.

Jesus' Hebrew name is a compound word which means "Yahweh Saves." "Saves" is from the verb *yāsha'*, "to save, deliver, give victory, help."[9] That he bears this name is no coincidence, but the plan of God. The angels direct both his earthly parents to name him Jesus:

> To Mary: "You will be with child and give birth to a son, and you are to give him the name **Jesus**." (Luke 1:31)

> To Joseph: "... You are to give him the name **Jesus, because he will save his people from their sins**." (Matthew 1:21)

To Joseph, the angel gives the reason. Jesus' name was to indicate his mission. Both Mary and Joseph were given this name by the angel so neither would ever forget who Jesus was – Yahweh's salvation embodied in human form.

As a little baby, "Yahweh saves" might have been born and raised in the humblest of circumstances, but that never diminished who he was. His destiny was to save. The Greek verb in Matthew 1:21 is *sōzō*, which means, "to preserve or rescue from natural dangers and afflictions, save, keep from harm, preserve, rescue," here, "to save/preserve from eternal death, bring Messianic salvation."[10]

Seeing the Messiah as Savior was the popular Jewish understanding of the Messiah's role at the time. But the angel made it clear to Joseph that this salvation would not be political or military. Jesus' mission was not to overthrow the Roman oppressors and reinstate the Jewish kingdom. His mission was to save his people from a far more insidious enemy – sin. Jesus came to destroy the power of sin.

To help you internalize and apply what you're learning from this study, I've included several Discussion Questions in each lesson. These are designed to help you think about and ponder the most important points. Don't skip these. It's best to write them out. You can post your answers – and read what others have written – by going to the online forum by clicking on the URL below each question. (Before you can post your answer the first time, you'll need to register. You can find instructions at http://www.joyfulheart.com/forums/instructions.htm

Q1. How is the meaning of Jesus' name linked to his mission? What is his mission?

---

[9] John E. Hartley, *yāsha'*, TWOT #929, Hiphil.
[10] *Sōzō*, BDAG 982-983.

How did he fulfill this mission? How did he fulfill his mission in *your* life?
http://www.joyfulheart.com/forums/topic/1597-q1-name-and-mission/

Usage of the Name Jesus

The name Jesus is used alone many times, but also in various combinations that we'll consider later:

- **Jesus** (Matthew 1:21, 25; 1 Thessalonians 1:10)
- **Jesus Christ our Lord** (Romans 1:3; Romans 6:11; Romans 6:23; 1 Corinthians 1:9; 7:25)
- **Jesus Christ our Savior** (Titus 3:6)
- **Jesus Christ** (Matthew 1:1; John 1:17; John 17:3; Acts 2:38; Acts 4:10; Acts 9:34; Acts 10:36; Acts 16:18; Romans 1:1, 3, 6; 2:16; 5:15, 17; 6:3; 1 Corinthians 1:1, 4; 2:2; 2 Corinthians 1:19; 4:6; 13:5; Galatians 2:16; Philippians 1:8; 2:11; 1 Timothy 1:15; Hebrews 13:8; 1 John 1:7; 2:1)
- **Jesus, the King of the Jews** (Matthew 27:37)
- **Jesus, the Son of God** (Hebrews 4:14)

Son of Joseph and Mary

Beyond his given name, Jesus is known by his parentage and his family. Though both Matthew and Luke tell us that Jesus was conceived by the Holy Spirit, not by Joseph (Luke 1:35; Matthew 1:21), those who weren't privy to the inside story, saw Jesus as the Son of Joseph. Thus he is called, **"Jesus, the son of Joseph"** (Luke 3:23; John 1:45; 6:42) and **"the carpenter's son"** (Matthew 13:55). He is called **"the child[11] Jesus"** (Luke 2:27) and **"the boy[12] Jesus"** (Luke 2:43). **Child** is not overtly divine in those cases, but is used in an important messianic prophecy: "For to us **a child** is born, to us **a son** is given" (Isaiah 9:6).

---

[11] The noun translated "child" is *paidion*, here, *"very young child, infant,"* used of boys and girls. *Paidion* is used of a very young child up to about seven years (BDAG 74).

[12] The noun translated "boy" is *pais*, "child," a young person normally below the age of puberty, with focus on age rather than social status, "boy, youth" (BDAG 75, 1).

Genealogies

Two genealogies of Jesus are provided, one in Matthew 1:1-17 and the other in Luke 3:23-38. In Matthew, Jesus' descent from David is traced through David's son Solomon, with Jacob given as the name of Joseph's father. In Luke, Jesus' descent is traced through David's son Nathan, with Heli given as the name of Joseph's father. Though there are several theories to explain the differences in these genealogies, we just don't know the reason.[13] Clearly, however, they are given to demonstrate that Jesus is a **Son of David** and a **Son of Abraham** (Matthew 1:1). We'll consider Jesus' title as "Son of David" in Lesson 4.

Carpenter

When Jesus taught in his hometown of Nazareth, he is referred to (in disbelief) as "the carpenter."

> "Isn't this **the carpenter**? Isn't this **Mary's son** and **the brother of James, Joseph, Judas and Simon**? Aren't his sisters here with us?" (Mark 6:3)

We know from later in Matthew's gospel that Joseph was a carpenter by trade (Matthew 13:55). But the town of Nazareth was small enough that carpentry and building wouldn't have been all he did. Carpenters and other tradesmen would also keep a garden and a couple of animals for food and perhaps do some subsistence farming to eke out a living in this agrarian society of rural Galilee. But when townspeople needed some carpentry done that was beyond their own skills and tools, Joseph was the one they came to.

As a rule the common man built his own house, probably with the help of family and neighbors. A family might have a knife and hammer of some kind. But a carpenter would possess both specialized tools, some fairly expensive, *and* the skills to use them – saws, axes, awls, drills, plumb lines, chisels, and planes, some of which have been recovered by archeologists.[14]

With these tools, a skilled carpenter might fashion doors, beams, and perhaps gates. He would make plows and yokes and other wood implements. There was no local Nazareth Furniture Store; all furniture would be made by hand. Each town had a rich

---

[13] Theories include: (1) Matthew gives the genealogy of Joseph, Luke of Mary (Annius of Viterbo, AD 1490). (2) Adoptive vs. physical descent (Afrianus, in Eusebius, *Church History*, 1:7). (3) Matthew gives legal line of descent from David, Luke gives the actual (Lord A. Hervey, 1853). These are discussed in Marshall, *Luke*, pp. 157-161.

[14] R.K. Harrison, "Tools," ISBE 4:874-876.

family or two. They would want some nice things made and their money would help the economy of the carpenter's family.

But carpentry doesn't make Joseph wealthy – not by any means. The offering Mary and Joseph bring to the temple on the occasion of Mary's purification from childbirth is the offering of a poor man, a pair of doves or pigeons (Luke 2:24; Leviticus 12:8).

Carpentry is Joseph's world, and the world in which Jesus grows up. He plays in the wood shavings on the floor of his father's shop. Carpentry is Joseph's trade and the trade he teaches his son. Jesus learns from Joseph to saw and plane, drill and smooth. He watches his father – the local contractor – make business contracts and deal with customers. Jesus sees it all.

Nazarene

According to Luke 2:1-7, Mary and Joseph are originally from Nazareth, but go to Bethlehem to enroll in a government-mandated census. While there, Jesus is born. They remain in Bethlehem for a couple of years, perhaps because their marriage after Mary's pregnancy is a kind of scandal. In Bethlehem, they find and worship Jesus. And because King Herod knows that the wise men had gone to Bethlehem, he orders the death of all the infants two years and under (Matthew 2:16). But Jesus avoids death, because Joseph heeds the warning given him in a dream and flees to Egypt, just before Herod's soldiers arrive for the slaughter.

Herod dies about 4 BC. When Joseph hears that he is dead, he returns, but not to Bethlehem, where Herod's brutal son Archelaus reigns, but to Nazareth in Galilee, where another of Herod's sons, Herod Antipas, reigns.

Jesus is raised in Nazareth, his parents' customary residence, and considers it his hometown (Luke 4:16). Thus, Jesus is sometimes called:

- **Jesus of Nazareth** (Mark 1:24; Luke 24:19).
- **Jesus of Nazareth, King of the Jews** (John 19:19).
- **The Nazarene** (Matthew 2:23).
- **The Nazarene, Jesus** (Mark 14:67).
- **Jesus the Nazarene** (Mark 16:6).

"Nazarene," however, is not a flattering title. Nazareth isn't mentioned at all in the Old Testament – nor by Jewish historian Josephus. Apparently, it was seen by Jews a kind of cultural backwater – and with a lot of Gentiles living in the area, making it suspect. You can catch a bit of Nazarene's reputation by Nathanael's comment when

Philip tells him of Jesus' hometown. Nathanael replies, "Can anything good come out of Nazareth?" Philip answers wisely, "Come and see" (John 1:46).

You may wonder about following One who came from such a humble hometown. One who made enemies of his religion's leaders. One who was publicly executed. One whose followers were persecuted. But part of following Jesus is being willing to humble ourselves as he is humble. And to take on ourselves whatever shame and persecution people dump on him and his followers in our day. Jesus said,

> "If anyone is ashamed of me and my words in this adulterous and sinful generation, the Son of Man will be ashamed of him when he comes in his Father's glory with the holy angels." (Mark 8:38)

They called him "Nazarene"! What will they call you?

Q2. In what ways does taking Jesus' name on ourselves, or identifying ourselves with him, open us to shame and persecution? Have you seen examples of this in your own experience? What actions might show that a Christian is ashamed of Jesus? What actions might show that a Christian is *unashamed* of Jesus? http://www.joyfulheart.com/forums/topic/1598-q2-unashamed/

Messianic Prophecy Concerning Galilee

It was important that Jesus be born in Bethlehem and raised in Galilee to fulfill important messianic prophecies. Micah prophesies about 700 BC,

> "But you, Bethlehem Ephrathah,
> though you are small among the clans of Judah,
> out of you will come for me one
> who will be ruler over Israel,
> whose origins are from of old,
> from ancient times." (Micah 5:2)

Isaiah prophesies the location of Messiah's ministry in the 7th century BC.

"There will be no more gloom for those who were in distress. In the past he humbled the land of Zebulun and the land of Naphtali, but in the future he will honor Galilee of the Gentiles, by the way of the sea, along the Jordan –
The people walking in darkness have seen a great light;
on those living in the land of the shadow of death a light has dawned." (Isaiah 9:1-2, quoted in Matthew 4:15)

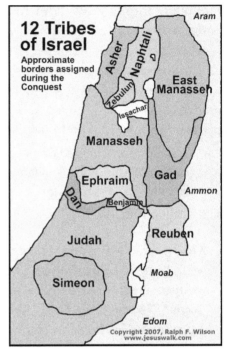

The Israelite tribes of Naphtali and Zebulun populated the area west of the Sea of Galilee where Jesus lived and ministered.

The Power of the Name of Jesus

We've considered Jesus' given name. Now let's consider how "name" is used in Hebrew language and thought (which underlies the Greek uses of the word in the New Testament). "Name" can simply be a person's proper name. But in Hebrew thought, a person's name can represent the person himself, his presence, or existence. Sometimes a person's name and existence are nearly one and the same thing. To believe in Jesus' name means to believe in Jesus' himself. "Name" can also indicate one's reputation.

There are three particular Hebraic uses of "name" in the New Testament that we especially need to understand.

1. Ownership. To speak one's name over something or someone, or to name it, was to exercise power and ownership over it. Thus to be baptized in Jesus' name was to place oneself under his authority and ownership (James 2:7).

2. Prayer in Jesus' name. Jesus' name is not just a formula for prayer. It is a privilege given to Jesus' disciples by their Master. Unbelievers may try to act in Jesus' name, but the power of his name is given only to those who believe in him (Acts 19:13-16). According to US law, a power of attorney can be used against the grantor's will. Not so with Jesus' name. Prayer in Jesus' name is similar to prayer that must be in accordance with God's will (John 15:7; 1 John 5:14-15).

Prayer is never intended to cajole God into giving in to our desires. Rather, prayer is about seeking him and his will with the intent of seeing his will come to pass in our lives. That doesn't mean that we have to always pray tentatively. Seek him, find the will of God, and then pray it boldly before the Father, in the name of Jesus.

3. Healing and exorcism in Jesus' name. To act in one's name, means that disciples spoke and acted like Jesus, in his place and with his authority.

In law we have this concept of "power of attorney," a written authorization to represent or act on another's behalf in private affairs, business, or some other legal matter. When my mother was in her nineties, she gave me power of attorney to act for her in financial affairs and make health decisions on her behalf. Later, when she suffered from dementia, I made decisions concerning her care without even consulting her. However, I felt bound as her son to act in what I felt was her best interest. I was her advocate with her caregivers to make sure she got the very best care. When I needed to make a financial transaction, I could present the power of attorney and act as if I were she.

Praying in Jesus' name is something like that. Jesus has given us his name to act on behalf of his kingdom. When people hear us, they are hearing Jesus through us, and are responsible to act on the information, as if it were given directly to them by Jesus itself. This is an awesome responsibility. As we act in the Spirit, Jesus even gives the church power to forgive sins in his name (John 20:23). Jesus gives his servants power to heal and cast out demons in his name (Mark 9:37, 39; 16:17).

The Gospels and Acts give examples of the power of Jesus' name in ministry and prayer as exercised by the apostles and the early church. We see:

- Baptism in Jesus' name.[15]
- Healing or exorcism commands in Jesus' name.[16] However, exorcism in Jesus' name backfired in the case of unbelievers (Acts 19:13). The ability to perform exorcism is no guarantee that the healer knows and loves Jesus (Matthew 7:21-23).
- Faith in Jesus' person and divinity.[17]
- Preaching in Jesus' name.[18]

---

[15] Acts 2:38; 8:12; 10:38; cf. 1 Corinthians 1:15.
[16] Mark 9:38-40; Mark 16:17; Luke 10:17; Acts 3:6, 16; 4:10; 16:18.
[17] 1 Corinthians 1:2; Acts 3:16; John 1:12; 2:23; 3:18.
[18] Acts 4:18; 5:40; 9:27; Luke 24:45-47.

- The person of or doctrine about Jesus,[19] as well as false claims to be the Christ.[20]
- Worship and prayer in Jesus' name.[21]
- The majesty of Jesus' name (Philippians 2:10).
- Welcoming a child on Jesus' behalf (Matthew 18:5).
- Sending the Holy Spirit in Jesus' name (John 14:26).

Q3. What does it mean when you pray "in Jesus' name"? Do you use the phrase "in Jesus' name" as you pray? Why or why not? How does praying "in Jesus' name" limit what we will pray for?
http://www.joyfulheart.com/forums/topic/1599-q3-prayer-in-jesus-name/

Q4. How did Jesus' disciples use his name when they healed and cast out demons? Do we have this kind of authority, or was it only for the apostles themselves? In what way does speaking or acting in Jesus' name demonstrate the concept of power of attorney? Why are we sometimes afraid to speak or act in Jesus' name? How might hearing his voice about a particular matter alleviate that fear?
http://www.joyfulheart.com/forums/topic/1600-q4-power-in-jesus-name/

Prayer

Father, thank you for the name of Jesus – the one who came to save his people from their sins. Save us, O God. Help us to trust Jesus with all our hearts. To come to know him and love him. And help us to pray and act with power in Jesus' name in the way you intend us to. Increase our faith. In Jesus' name, we ask this. Amen.

Names and Titles of Jesus

In this chapter we've begun to explore the various names and titles of Jesus. Here are the names, titles, and descriptors we've considered in this chapter, in the order of our studying them.

---

[19] Acts 8:12; 26:9.
[20] Matthew 24:5; Mark 13:6.
[21] Matthew 18:20; John 14:13-14; 15:15-16; 16:23-24, 26-27.

Jesus (often)

Jesus Christ our Lord (Romans 1:3; Romans 6:11; Romans 6:23; 1 Corinthians 1:9; 7:25)

Jesus Christ our Savior (Titus 3:6)

Jesus Christ (Matthew 1:1; John 1:17; John 17:3; Acts 2:38; Acts 4:10; Acts 9:34; Acts 10:36; Acts 16:18; Romans 1:1, 3, 6; 2:16; 5:15, 17; 6:3; 1 Corinthians 1:1, 4; 2:2; 2 Corinthians 1:19; 4:6; 13:5; Galatians 2:16; Philippians 1:8; 2:11; 1 Timothy 1:15; Hebrews 13:8; 1 John 1:7; 2:1)

Jesus, the King of the Jews (Matthew 27:37)

Jesus, the Son of God (Hebrews 4:14)

Son of Abraham (Matthew 1:1)

Son of David (Matthew 1:1)

Son of Joseph (Luke 3:23; John 1:45; 6:42)

Mary's Son (NIV, Mark 6:3)

Son of Mary (NRSV, ESV, KJV, Mark 6:3)

Brother of James, Joseph, Judas and Simon (Mark 6:3)

The Child Jesus (Luke 2:27)

The Boy Jesus (Luke 2:43)

Child, Son (Isaiah 9:6)

Carpenter's Son (Matthew 13:55)

Carpenter (Mark 6:3)

Jesus of Nazareth (Mark 1:24; Luke 24:19)

Jesus of Nazareth, King of the Jews (John 19:19)

Nazarene (Matthew 2:23)

Nazarene, Jesus (Mark 14:67)

Jesus the Nazarene (Mark 16:6)

Songs and Hymns

One of the reasons for this study of the names and titles of Jesus is to know him more fully, in ways that we hadn't explored before. To enter into this takes time in meditation and worship.

Songs and hymns are ways that we use the names and character of Jesus in our worship. To help those designing worship services around the names and titles of Jesus, and to facilitate personal worship, I have tried to include some of the most popular hymns and songs that I could find among the tens of thousands in the CCLI Song Select and Cyber Hymnal databases. I've looked for songs that actually include names and titles somewhat prominently, though that is a judgment call. These are included at the end of every lesson, and for all lessons in Appendix 3 available online. Special thanks in compiling these lists to: Brittney Land, David Pabalate, Darrel Fink, and Jonathan Fink.

If you'd like to learn some of these songs, you'll probably find one or more of them by searching on YouTube.com. It's a great sing-along resource for your personal devotions and will help you learn the songs.

Many songs relate more to the names and titles of God, rather than of Jesus. Here, we're focusing on the songs that relate more to Jesus. Songs that focus on God the Father can be found in my companion volume, *Names and Titles of God* (JesusWalk, 2010).

Key titles in Lesson 1 include: Jesus, son of Mary, Child, Carpenter, Jesus of Nazareth, and Nazarene. In this lesson's list, are also some more general songs that contain a number of names and titles. Others songs in this group focus on the power of the name of Jesus, such as "Break Every Chain."

"All Hail the Power of Jesus' Name" ("And crown him Lord of all"), words: Edward Perronet (1779), music: Coronation, Oliver Holden (1793)

"Blessed Be the Name" ("Redeemer, Savior, friend of man ... Counselor ... Prince of Peace"), words: William H. Clark, music: Ralph E. Hudson (1888)

"Break Every Chain" ("there is power in the name of Jesus"), by Will Reagan, © 2009 United Pursuit Music (Admin. by Capitol CMG Publishing)

"Celebrate the Child" ("the Child who is the Light ... Godhead and manhood became one ... First born of creation ... Lamb and Lion, God and Man ... Author of Salvation ... Almighty wrapped in swaddling bands"), by Michael Card (© 1989 Birdwing Music)

"Come, O Come, Emmanuel" ("Day-spring, Key of David, Root of Jesse, ensign of thy people, Desire of nations, King of Peace, Rod of Jesse, Wisdom from on high"), words: 12th century; music: 15th century

"Come, Thou Long Expected Jesus" ("Israel's strength and consolation, Hope of all the earth thou art, dear desire of every nation"), words: Charles Wesley (1745), music: Hyfrydol, Rowland H. Prich-ard (1830)

"Crown Him with Many Crowns" (the Lamb upon his throne ... the virgin's son, the God incarnate born .... the Babe of Bethlehem ... the Son of God ... the Son of Man ... the Lord of Life, who tri-umphed o'er the grave ... the Lord of Peace ... Lord of Love ... the Lord of Heav'n ... Lord of lords ... the Incarnate Word ... their God, Redeemer, King ... the Lord of years, the Potentate of time, Creator ... All hail, Redeemer hail! For Thou has died for me"), words: Matthew Bridges (1952), Godfrey Thring (1874); Music: Diademata, George J. Elvey (1868)

"He Shall Reign Forevermore," by Chris Tomlin and Matt Maher (© 2015 S. D. G. Publishing)

"His Name Is Jesus" (sad hearts weep no more), by G.M. Bills (public domain)

"His Name Is Master/Life," by William Gaither (1983 Gaither Music Company)

"His Name Is Wonderful," by Audrey Mieir (1959 Audrey Mieir. Renewed 1987 Manna Music, Inc.)

"How Majestic," by Kari Jobe, Chris Tomlin, Jason Ingram, Matt Redman (© 2014 KAJE Songs)

"How Sweet the Name of Jesus Sounds" ("Jesus! my shepherd, husband, friend, O prophet, priest and king, My Lord, my life, my way, my end, Accept the praise I bring"), words: John Newton (1779), music: St. Peter (Reinagle), Alexander R. Reingale (1836)

"I Am" ("Maker of the heavens, Bright and Morning Star ... Fount of Living Water, the Risen Son of Man, the Healer of the Broken .. Savior and Redeemer ... Author and Perfecter, Beginning and the End"), by Mark Schultz (© 2005 Crazy Romaine Music)

"I Know of a Name" ("a beautiful name"), words: Jean Perry (1916); music: Mabel J. Camp

"I Stand Amazed in the Presence" ("of Jesus the Nazarene"), words: Charles H. Gabriel (1905)

"In the Name of Jesus" (we have the victory)

"Jesus Is the Sweetest Name I Know," words and music: Lela B. Long (1924)

"Jesus, Name Above All Names," by Naida Hearn (1974, 1978 Scripture In Song)

"Jesus, Only Jesus," by Matt Redman (2003, sixsteps)

"Jesus, What a Wonder (How Lovely) You Are," words and music by Dave Bolton (1975 Thankyou Music ; Morning Star)

"Name of Jesus," by Chris Tomlin, Daniel Carson, Ed Cash, Jesse Reeves, Kristian Stanfill, Matt Redman

"O How I Love Jesus" ("There is a name I love to hear"), words: Frederick Whitfield (1855), music: 19th century American melody

"Sing, Sing, Sing" ("Lift high the name of Jesus ... Song of God, You are the One"), by Chris Tomlin, Daniel Carson, Jesse Reeves, Matt Gilder, Travis Nunn (© 2008, sixsteps Music)

"Son of the Carpenter, Receive," words: Charles Wesley (1739), music: Beatitudo, John B. Dykes (1875)

"There Is Something about that Name," by Gloria and Bill Gaither (1970 William J. Gaither, Inc.)

"These are the Names of God," by Tommy Walker (© 2014 McKinney Music, Inc.)

"What Child Is This," words: William Chatterton Dix (1865), music: Greensleeves (16th century English melody)

"You Are Holy" ("Prince of Peace"), by Marc Imboden and Tammy Rhoton (© 1994 Imboden Music)

"You Are" (Holy ... Faithful ... Savior ... Friend ... Lord on high ... the Way, the Truth, the Life ... the Word made flesh ... the Bright Morning Star ... Alpha and Omega ... Comfort ... Refuge ... Love Personified ... My God and my King"), by Mark Roach (© 2005 Dayspring Music)

Exercises to Help You Internalize the Names of Jesus (Appendix 6)

It would be sad if studying the names of Jesus were merely an intellectual or academic exercise for you. Beyond your study, here are some exercises that will help internalize what you're learning and let it begin to change you.

Over the several days you are studying a particular lesson, I recommend that you incorporate into your daily life some of the following exercises that will help implant the names in your heart and mind. Try one or more of the exercises listed in Appendix 6, or invent your own.

1. Pray to Jesus using one or more of the names in this lesson. As you pray, call on him in a way that relates to his name.

2. Meditate on one or more of the names in this lesson. Visualize Jesus in the ways suggested by the names in this lesson. Picture him in your mind's eye. See how he is strong for you in these ways.

3. Write down your own answers to the discussion questions in this lesson. Post them to the online forum or read what others have written.

4. Worship him by singing one of the songs suggested above.

5. Consider how you need to change to become like Jesus as reflected by one or more of the names in this lesson, and ask for his help to change you.

6. Draw or paint a scene, figure, or calligraphy related to one of the names.

7. Compose a song related to one of the names and then teach it to someone.

8. Community. Find a way to influence your community or church in a way inspired by one of these names, titles, descriptor, or metaphor of Jesus. What project could you help with or initiate that could make a positive difference in the lives of people. For example, if Jesus is the Good Shepherd, what people in your community are "like sheep without a shepherd"? Who are without their basic needs, for example? What project could give feet to being a shepherd to those in need?

9. Picture how a friend or relative of yours could benefit from Jesus' ministry as reflected by one of the names in a particular week's lesson. Pray for that person accordingly and minister to that person yourself when an opportunity presents itself.

2. Jesus our Rabbi, Teacher, Prophet, and Word

As people begin to encounter Jesus and his ministry, they try to put him in the various categories they have to describe people like him who are workers with words – teacher, prophet. Of course, Jesus is more than any of these titles and categories. But he very much fits each of them – and in a greater way than anyone could imagine at the time. In this lesson we'll consider Jesus titles and descriptors as they relate to his ministry of the Word of God.

Carl Heinrich Bloch (Danish painter, 1834-1890), detail from 'Sermon on the Mount'

Jesus the Rabbi

Jesus often attracts crowds through his miracles, and then teaches the multitudes who gather. He is widely seen as a teacher and even given the respected title of "rabbi," even by some of Jerusalem's elite, such as Nicodemus – a member of the ruling Jerusalem Sanhedrin and considered a "teacher of Israel" in his own right (John 3:10).

> "He came to Jesus at night and said, '**Rabbi**, we know you are a **teacher** who has come from God. For no one could perform the miraculous signs you are doing if God were not with him.'" (John 3:2)

"Rabbi," "teacher," and "master" are used synonymously in the New Testament.

"**Rabbi**" isn't really a word for the Jewish clergy of Jesus' time. *Rhabbi* (literally in Hebrew "my great one")[22] is used as a form of address: "lord, master." In Jesus' day it

---

[22] Hebrew *rābab* means "to be(come) many, much." A *rab* was a "captain, chief (*Rābab*, TWOT #2099). "The term *rab* denotes one who holds a respected position, e.g., an official. It is used by an inferior to a superior.... The use for teachers goes back to the second century BC. Students follow their teachers with respectful obedience. When qualified to teach, they themselves are given the title, which the people as a whole also uses. It occurs on many inscriptions from Palestine, Syria, Cyprus, and Italy." (E. Lohse, *rhábbi, rhabbouní*, TDNT 961–65).

was particularly used as an honorary title for outstanding teachers of the law.[23] Jesus castigates the scribes and Pharisees for desiring to be called by such an exalted title: "They love ... being called rabbi by others" (Matthew 23:5-7). This title was extended to John the Baptist (John 3:26), but is mainly used in the New Testament to refer to Jesus. Twice Jesus is called "**Rabboni**," an alternate form of Rabbi, which means, "my lord, my master" (Mark 10:51; John 20:16).[24]

If "rabbi" is a form of address, "**teacher**" is more of a descriptor or functional title. "Teacher" (*didaskalos*), from the verb *didaskō*, "to teach," is used many times as a form of address in the Gospels. When *didaskalos* is used in addressing Jesus, it probably corresponds to the title "rabbi" (John 1:38b).[25] Once Jesus refers to himself as the *kathēgētēs* of his disciples, "teacher, guide" (Matthew 23:10; "teacher," NIV; "**instructor**," NRSV, ESV; "**master**," KJV).[26]

The term "**master**" is commonly used by the KJV to translate *didaskalos*.[27] This is more a British usage than American English. In the British educational system, scholars are sometimes referred to as "master" (for example, "headmaster" or "master of arts"). Only rarely do modern translations use "master" with a teaching context (Matthew 23:8, NIV). Rather, they reserve the term "master" (*kyrios*, "lord, owner") for a master-servant relationship, which we'll consider in Lesson 5. Several times in Luke's Gospel, Jesus is called "**master**," *epistatēs*, an administrative technical term used for various officials (Luke 5:5; 8:24, 45; 9:33, 49; 17;13).[28]

All these words were used synonymously in the Gospels to reflect the kind of teaching conducted by a rabbi with his students or disciples.

A Rabbi and His Disciples

In Jesus' day there were no seminaries, institutions where students could prepare to be teachers themselves. Rather, a leading rabbi would gather around him disciples or students, who would literally follow him wherever he went, listening to him, follow his teaching, imitate him, and help him with his work. We see this pattern reflected in the Gospels. For example, Jesus said,

---

[23] *Rhabbi*, BDAG 90.
[24] *Rhabboni*, BDAG 90.
[25] *Didaskalos*, BDAG 24.
[26] *Kathēgētēs* (BDAG 49; Thayer 31) is from *kathēgeomai*, "to go before, lead").
[27] For example, Matthew 8:19; 9:11; 12:38; 19:16; 17:24; 19:16; 22:16, 24, 36; 23:8; 26:18; etc.
[28] *Epistatēs*, BDAG 38.

"A disciple is not above his teacher.... It is enough for the disciple to be like his teacher...." (Matthew 10:24-25, ESV)

The word "disciple" (*mathētēs*) means literally, "learner, pupil." In the Gospels it usually refers to "one who is rather constantly associated with someone who has a pedagogical reputation or a particular set of views, disciple, adherent."[29] It is not by accident that Jesus carefully chose twelve men to train to be apostles or "sent ones." Many people followed him, but these twelve were appointed "that they might *be with him*" (Mark 3:14). Jesus and his band of twelve, of course, were joined by other close associates, some of whom provided for his mission financially (Luke 8:1-3). But when Jesus moved, he travelled with an entourage that included these twelve.

I recently read the autobiography of a famous old country music star. The singer talks about believing in Jesus, loving the old hymns, and being raised by a godly grandmother. The last chapter finds him meditating in the quiet of the old Methodist Church in his hometown. The big disconnect, however, is that the singer never acknowledges trying to conform his *behavior* to Jesus' teaching. While he admits the damage done by his hard drinking and womanizing, he never express repentance or sees his behavior in the category of sin. By his own claim, this singer is a believer. But I wonder if a person could find evidence that would qualify him as a disciple?

And that's the question for each of us. Are *you* a disciple of Jesus? Am I? What are the marks of a disciple in the twenty-first century? I suppose disciples today would serve Jesus by participating in his mission, constantly seeking to spend time with him, attempting to resist temptation, asking forgiveness when they sin, and listening carefully to Jesus' teaching so they might internalize it.

I think of the familiar scene of Jesus in Mary and Martha's home in Bethany.

"[Martha] had a sister called Mary, who sat at the Lord's feet listening to what he said."

When Martha criticizes her sister for not helping with the preparations for the meal, Jesus gives Martha a mild rebuke.

"Only one thing is needed. Mary has chosen what is better, and it will not be taken away from her" (Luke 10:39, 42).

---

[29] *Mathētēs*, BDAG 60, 2b.

So often we are busy rather than devoted; engaged in good works rather than basking in Jesus' presence. He is our Rabbi, our Teacher, our Master, our Guide, and as such, he deserves our full and constant attention.

Jesus calls us to obey him as disciples. In the Upper Room, Jesus exhorts the Twelve as Teacher/Rabbi and Lord (*kyrios*), the one who has a right to command (which we'll consider further in Lesson 5):

> "You call me '**Teacher**' and 'Lord,' and rightly so, for that is what I am. Now that I, your Lord and **Teacher**, have washed your feet, you also should wash one another's feet. I have set you an example that you should do as I have done for you." (John 13:13-15)

Q1. What is your relationship to Jesus as your Rabbi? How often do you come to him to teach you? How do you receive his teaching? How teachable do you think you are?
http://www.joyfulheart.com/forums/topic/1601-q1-jesus-your-rabbi/

Jesus the Prophet

Another term that people used to describe Jesus was "prophet."

> "When Jesus entered Jerusalem, the whole city was stirred and asked, 'Who is this?' The crowds answered, 'This is Jesus, **the prophet** from Nazareth in Galilee.'"(Matthew 21:10-11)

Prophētēs refers to "a person inspired to proclaim or reveal divine will or purpose, prophet."[30] True prophets even had the power to rebuke kings, as Nathan did to King David (1 Samuel 12:1-15).

The nation of Israel had a long history of prophets (beginning with Moses) who serve as leaders, as spokesmen for God, and occasionally predictors of the future. Some of the more famous are Isaiah, Jeremiah, Ezekiel, and Daniel. There are also twelve "minor prophets" in the Old Testament canon, which meant that their writings were relatively short, not that they were of lesser importance.

Jesus had been preceded by his cousin John the Baptist, who was widely seen by the people (if not the Jerusalem leaders) as a true prophet of God (Matthew 21:26; Luke

---

[30] *Prophētēs*, BDAG 890, 1c; G. Friedrich, TDNT 6:828–861.

7:28). After John had been imprisoned and beheaded, people see Jesus as following in John's tradition (which he surely does). Exactly which prophet Jesus represented isn't as clear:

> "Some say John the Baptist; others say Elijah; and still others, Jeremiah or one of the prophets." (Matthew 16:14)

The Prophets Elijah and Elisha are famous for their miracles. People probably see Jesus as a prophet because he speaks authoritatively from God, performs miracles, and calls people to repentance and to righteousness.

> "They were all filled with awe and praised God. 'A **great prophet** has appeared among us,' they said. 'God has come to help his people.'" (Luke 7:16)

> "He was a **prophet**, powerful in word and deed before God and all the people." (Luke 24:19)

Jesus is widely perceived throughout Israel to be a prophet (John 4:19; 9:17).

But not just any prophet. Many see Jesus as the prophet whom Moses had foretold hundreds of years before.

> "The LORD your God will raise up for you a prophet like me from among your own brothers. You must listen to him…. I will put my words in his mouth, and he will tell them everything I command him." (Deuteronomy 18:15, 18)

Many people wonder if Jesus is indeed just this prophet:

> "After the people saw the miraculous sign that Jesus did, they began to say, 'Surely this is the **Prophet** who is to come into the world.'" (John 6:14; cf. 1:21)

> "On hearing his words, some of the people said, 'Surely this man is **the Prophet**.'" (John 7:40)

Sometimes people distinguish between prophets as "foretellers" and "forthtellers." Old Testament prophets were "forthtellers," that is, proclaiming God's Word and calling to account the corruption of Israel's kings, priests, and people. It is fair to say that Jesus was such a truth-teller to his generation. He is a greater prophet than Jonah – "**one greater than Jonah**" – who brought Nineveh to repentance (Matthew 12:41; Luke 11:32). But he was also a "foreteller," one who told his disciples what the future held. For example, he proclaimed the coming of the Kingdom of God, told in advance of his own death and resurrection, and gave a rather detailed account of the Last Days. It would be fair to say that Jesus was God's Prophet par excellence. But there is a reason for this.

Jesus Is the Word, the Logos

So far we've examined Jesus' use of words such as rabbi, teacher, and prophet. This shouldn't surprise us, because at the very outset of his Gospel, the Apostle John reveals him as **the Word, the Logos of God.**

> "In the beginning was **the Word**, and **the Word** was with God, and **the Word** was God. He was with God in the beginning.... **The Word** became flesh and made his dwelling among us. We have seen his glory, the glory of the One and Only, who came from the Father, full of grace and truth." (John 1:1-2, 14)

"Word" is the extremely common Greek noun *logos*, "word," a communication by which the mind finds utterance. It can have a wide range of meanings, depending on the context, such as "statement, assertion, message, declaration." Another use is as "computation, reckoning." But the use in John 1:1 is unique. Here *logos* is "the independent personified expression of God."[31] You see hints of this in other Johannine books as well (1 John 1:1; Revelation 19:3).

Jehovah Witnesses, who deny the concept of the Trinity,[32] have mistranslated John 1:1 to conform to their doctrine that Jesus is not Jehovah or God himself, but a created being – divine, yes, but lesser than Jehovah.

> "In the beginning was the Word, and the Word was with God, and the Word was **a god**." (John 1:1, *New World Translation*, 1950)

The Jehovah's Witness translators added the indefinite article "a" to indicate that Jesus was a divine being, one among other divine beings. The problem with their translation is that there is no indefinite article in the Greek text or suggested by Greek grammar – they've added it![33]

It is quite clear, however, that the Apostle John sees Jesus as fully divine – on the same level of divinity as the Father!

---

[31] *Logos*, BDAG 601, 3.

[32] For more on the doctrine of the Trinity, see my article, "Four Reasons Why I Believe in the Trinity," http://www.joyfulheart.com/scholar/trinity.htm

[33] The Greek grammar here gets very technical. For more information, consult a critical commentary. See, for example, Bruce M. Metzger, "On the Translation of John 1:1," *Expository Times*, LXIII (1951-52), 125 f., But suffice it to say, the Jehovah's Witness translation breaks the well-established rules of Greek grammar, because, when properly translated, John 1:1 indicates something that their doctrine denies – that Jesus is God at the same level as the Father.

Logos

John's usage of *logos* most likely draws on a Jewish background, in particular, as the prophetic word of God that came to prophets in the Old Testament – the Word that accomplishes God's work (Genesis 1:1; Isaiah 55:11).[34] Up to this time, the Word was abstract. Now, in Jesus, it is concrete.

Jesus is the exact expression of God's word and will, thus he is God's Word personified. In Jesus, God expresses himself with complete clarity:

[He] "speaks the *words* of God...." (John 3:34)

"My *teaching* is not my own. It comes from him who sent me." (John 7:16)

"The *words* I say to you are not just my own. Rather, it is the Father...." (John 14:10)

"These *words* you hear are not my own; they belong to the Father who sent me." (John 14:24)

"I have given them *your word* and the world has hated them...." (John 17:14)

John 1:1 is saying that Jesus in the flesh is the very Expression of God Himself, and that this Jesus *IS* God himself – a very bold statement indeed, with which to begin John's Gospel.

Two similar titles are found in John's writings.

"That which was from the beginning, which we have heard, which we have seen with our eyes, which we have looked at and our hands have touched – this we proclaim concerning the **Word of life**." (1 John 1:1)

"He is dressed in a robe dipped in blood, and his name is the **Word of God**." (Revelation 19:13)

When Jesus speaks, they are not just his words. They are the Father's words. Jesus is God in the flesh, the Word. This explains his communication as Teacher, Rabbi, Master, and Prophet.

Q2. (John 1:1-3, 14) In what sense is Jesus the Word of God? Why do you think he is called this? Why does John call him the Word of Life (1 John 1:1)? What does this

---

[34] In Platonic and neo-Platonic philosophy *logos* is the all-pervading Reason that gives form to and governs the universe. The term was also used in Hellenistic circles, in particular by Philo, a first-century Jewish philosopher. Philo uses *logos* as the word by which God created the world and as a mediator between the ideal and real worlds. There is much written on this subject summarized in general articles: Paul A. Rainbow, "Logos Christianity," DLNT, pp. 665-667; D.H. Johnson, "Logos," DJG, pp. 481-484; Raymond E. Brown, "Appendix II: The 'Word,'" *The Gospel According to John* (Doubleday, 1966), vol. 1, pp. 519-524; George Eldon Ladd, *A Theology of the New Testament* (Eerdmans, 1974), pp. 237-242.

say to us about the importance of hearing, meditating on, and internalizing Jesus' words?

http://www.joyfulheart.com/forums/topic/1602-q2-jesus-the-word/

Jesus Is the Faithful and True Witness

Because Jesus is a faithful teacher, Jesus is also the Faithful Witness to the Father and the Father's words. John introduces him as:

"Jesus Christ the **faithful witness**...." (Revelation 1:5a)

Then John attests that what he has written is not his own, but the words of Jesus.

"These are the words of **the Amen**, the **faithful and true witness**...." (Revelation 3:14b)

"Amen" is a transliteration of the Hebrew word *'āmēn*, "verily, truly, amen." The Hebrew word expresses a certain affirmation in response to what has been said. It is used after the pronouncement of solemn curses and after prayers and hymns of praise. It comes from the root *'āman*, "to confirm, support, uphold; to be established, be faithful; to be certain."[35] Thus in our text *amēn* indicates a strong affirmation of what is stated. Thus Christ is the ultimate affirmation, **the Amen**.[36]

"**Faithful**" is a very similar concept. The word is *pistos*, "pertaining to being worthy of belief or trust, trustworthy, faithful, dependable, inspiring trust/faith."[37] Jesus is the Faithful One because he always keeps his word and can be trusted.

"**True**" also points to trustworthiness. *Alēthinos* means "pertaining to being in accord with what is true, true, trustworthy" as well as "pertaining to being real, genuine, authentic."[38]

Finally, "**witness**" *martys*, basically means, "one who testifies in legal matters, witness." Then, in a transferred sense, "one who affirms or attests, testifier, witness." Finally, the word refers to someone, like our "martyr," who testifies at the cost of his life.[39] Certainly, Jesus' witness to the Father cost him his life. In bearing the Father's

---

[35] Jack B. Scott, *'āman*, TWOT #116c.

[36] *Amēn*, BDAG 53.

[37] *Pistos*, BDAG 820, 1.

[38] *Alēthinos*, BDAG 43, 1 and 3.

[39] *Martys*, BDAG 620.

words, Jesus is faithful, that is dependable and trustworthy to communicate the Father's words accurately. After all, he is the Word (John 1:1). He is also true, the genuine article, the Son of God himself. And he is the ultimate witness.

In Isaiah's messianic prophecy we see Messiah as a **Witness to the Peoples**.

> "I will make an everlasting covenant with you,
> my faithful love promised to David.
> See, I have made him **a witness**[40] **to the peoples**,
> a leader and commander of the peoples." (Isaiah 55:3-4)

The final instance of the title in Revelation is where the Warrior Christ appears astride a battle steed to defeat evil in a final battle.

> "Then I saw heaven opened, and behold, a white horse! The one sitting on it is called **Faithful and True**, and in righteousness he judges and makes war." (Revelation 19:11)

Q3. (Revelation 3:14) Why is Jesus called the "true and faithful witness"? What did he witness to? How was he faithful in his witness? As a disciple, to what degree are you a "true and faithful witness" to the Word that your Rabbi has taught and has done in your life? What would it look like if you improved as a witness?
http://www.joyfulheart.com/forums/topic/1603-q3-faithful-witness/

Jesus is the Truth

Jesus is the Word of God, the very Expression of God himself. He is also the Truth. Jesus gave to his disciples a saying that includes three titles.

> "I am the way and **the truth** and the life. No one comes to the Father except through me." (John 14:6)

(We'll look at Jesus the Truth here, Jesus the Way in Lesson 8, and Jesus the Life in Lesson 9.)

Especially in John's Gospel, *alētheia*, "truth," carries the idea of "authenticity, divine reality, revelation."[41] When the so-called "reality" of this dark world system is

---

[40] "Witness" is *'ēd*, derived from the root *'ûd* meaning return or "repeat, do again." The semantic development apparently is that a witness is one, who by reiteration, emphatically affirms his testimony (Carl Schultz, *'ûd*, TWOT #1576b).

[41] Rudolf Bultmann, *alētheia*, TDNT 1:245.

confronted with the intense Light of truth and revelation, God's reality, there is dissonance. And it is God's reality that prevails and gives freedom. Jesus, who is "full of grace and truth" (John 1:14, 18), is the embodiment of what is true in this world and the next. His words are true, and therefore must be believed and obeyed. Jesus says,

> "If you hold to my teaching, you are really my disciples. Then you will know the truth, and the truth will set you free." (John 8:31-32)

When we embrace distortions and outright lies about the meaning of life, we lose freedom. Only when we conform our lives to Jesus' true reality, can we be truly free. When Jesus says, "I am ... the truth," it is a powerful, exclusive statement.

In our day, we have largely displaced Jesus' teachings with political correctness, the wisdom of our commercialized world, street smarts, and lessons from the "school of hard knocks." But Jesus is the Truth; his Word is Truth; he speaks to us the words of the Father. His truth, his reality, gives us freedom from slavery to the Lie.

Jesus Is the Wisdom of God

This is probably a good place to include another title related to Truth – Wisdom.

> "To those whom God has called, both Jews and Greeks, Christ **the power of God** and **the wisdom of God**." (1 Corinthians 1:24)

Some see Christianity as weak, but Paul sees Christ as the power (*dynamis*) of God. Certainly this was demonstrated by his miracles, as well as by his resurrection from the dead. In the context of this passage, Paul is contrasting the wisdom of the Greek philosophers and the world's way of life with the message of the cross. In Paul's world – as ours – the cross was and is seen as foolishness. What is this? – Jesus dying for our sins as a sacrifice before God? Paul reminds us:

> "The foolishness of God is wiser than man's wisdom, and the weakness of God is stronger than man's strength." (1 Corinthians 1:25)

Do we want true wisdom? Wisdom that will stand the test of time and eternity? Then we must find it in Jesus and his way, in contrast to man's so-called wisdom that is "earthly, unspiritual, demonic" (James 3:15).

> "But the wisdom that comes from heaven is first of all pure; then peace-loving, considerate, submissive, full of mercy and good fruit, impartial and sincere." (James 3:17)

Jesus and Lady Wisdom of Proverbs 8

In John 1, the Word, the Logos creates the world:

"He was with God in the beginning.
Through him all things were made;
without him nothing was made that has been made." (John 1:2-3)

Some see hints of this in the personified Lady Wisdom of Proverbs 8, though no solid connection can be established between the two.

"The LORD brought me forth as the first of his works,
before his deeds of old;
I was appointed from eternity,
from the beginning,
before the world began....

I was there when he set the heavens in place,
when he marked out the horizon on the face of the deep,
when he established the clouds above
and fixed securely the fountains of the deep....
Then I was the craftsman at his side.
I was filled with delight day after day,
rejoicing always in his presence." (Proverbs 8:22-23, 27-28, 30)

Though Jesus is not the same person as Lady Wisdom of Proverbs 8, Jesus *does* connect with the wisdom literature of the Old Testament, as well as its prophetic tradition. To a "wicked and adulterous generation" people who will not heed his words, Jesus compares his teaching to the Queen of Sheba's reverence for the wisdom of Solomon.

"The Queen of the South ... came from the ends of the earth to listen to Solomon's wisdom, and now **one greater than Solomon** is here." (Matthew 12:42; Luke 11:31)

(We can probably see "One Greater than Solomon" as a descriptor.)

> **Q4. (John 4:16; 1 Corinthians 1:24) How does Jesus' truth contrast with your culture's dearly held "truths"? How does Jesus' wisdom differ from the worldly wisdom that your culture teaches you? What would help you hold on to Jesus' truth and wisdom more effectively?**
> **http://www.joyfulheart.com/forums/topic/1604-q4-jesus-wisdom-and-truth/**

Wonderful Counselor

We've seen Jesus in the roles of Teacher, Prophet, Word, and Witness. Here is another title related to the spoken word.

In one of Isaiah's messianic prophecies, Jesus is called "**Wonderful Counselor**" (Isaiah 9:6). "Counselor" is *yā'as,* "advise, counsel, purpose, devise, plan." In Isaiah 11:2 it says that the "Spirit of counsel" will rest upon the Messiah. Thus, "the child who is to come, on whose shoulders the government of the world shall rest, is one whose plans, purposes, designs and decrees for his people are marvelous."[42] Do you lack wisdom? Jesus, through his Holy Spirit, is the Counselor, the one who will guide you – if you let him. John implies that Jesus is the disciples' **Counselor**, because he refers to the Holy Spirit as "another counselor" (John 14:16).

"Counselor" is used in John's Gospel as a title of the Holy Spirit four times (John 14:16, 26; 15:26; 16:7). The word, sometimes translated "Comforter" (KJV), "Advocate" (NRSV), and "Helper" (ESV), is *paraklētos,* generally, "one who is called to someone's aid" from *para-,* "alongside or motion to the side of" + *kaleō,* "to call." ... one who appears in another's behalf, mediator, intercessor, helper."[43] As we'll see in Lesson 3, Jesus is also our Advocate (*paraklētos*) with the Father (1 John 2:1, ESV), and the Consolation (*paraklēsis*) of Israel (Luke 2:25), based on similar Greek words.

Prayer

Father, thank you for Jesus' faithfulness to You and to your Words. He was and is your Word, though they killed him for it. Help us to hold to your Word, to your Wisdom, and to your Truth with the same tenacity as Jesus our Lord. In his holy name, we pray. Amen.

Names and Titles of Jesus

Rabbi (John 3:2)
Rabonni (Mark 10:51; John 20:16)
Teacher (often)
Instructor (Matthew 23:10)
Master (*epistatēs*, Luke 5:5; 8:24, 45; 9:33, 49; 17;13)
Master (KJV, often, in the sense of honored teacher)
Prophet (Matthew 21:11; Luke 7:16; 24:19; John 6:14; 7:40; cf. John 4:19; 9:17)

---

[42] Paul R. Gilchrist, *yā'as,* TWOT #887.
[43] *Paraklētos,* BDAG 76.

One Greater than Jonah (Matthew 12:41; Luke 11:32)
Word, Logos (John 1:1-2, 14)
Word of Life (1 John 1:1)
Word of God (Revelation 19:13)
Faithful Witness (Revelation 1:5a)
Amen (Revelation 3:14b)
Faithful and True Witness (Revelation 3:14b)
Witness to the Peoples (Isaiah 55:4)
Faithful and True (Revelation 19:11)
Truth (John 14:6)
Wisdom of God (1 Corinthians 1:24)
Power of God (1 Corinthians 1:24)
One Greater than Solomon (Matthew 12:42; Luke 11:31)
Wonderful Counselor (Isaiah 9:6)
Counselor (John 14:16, by implication)

Songs and Hymns

Songs for this lesson include key titles that center around Jesus' oral ministry, such as: Rabbi, Teacher, Master, Prophet, Word, and Wonderful Counselor.

"Be Thou My Vision" ("and Thou my true Word"), words attributed to Dallan Forgaill, translated from Gallic to English by Mary E. Byrne (1905), versed by Eleanor H. Hull (1912); music: Slane, Irish folk origin.

"Blessed Be the Name" ("Redeemer, Savior, friend of man ... Counselor ... Prince of Peace"), words: William H. Clark, music: Ralph E. Hudson (1888)

"Breathe" ("Your very Word spoken to me"), by Marie Barnett (© 1995, Mercy/Vineyard Publishing)

"Come, O Come, Emmanuel" (Wisdom from on high"), words: 12th century; music: 15th century

"He Leadeth Me, O Blessed Thought," by Joseph Henry Gilmore and William Batchelder Bradbury

"I Have Decided to Follow Jesus" ("no turning back")

"I Will Follow," by Chris Tomlin, Jason Ingram, and Reuben Morgan (© 2010 SHOUT! Music Publishing)

"I'll Go Where You Want Me to Go" by Carrie E. Rounsefell, Charles Edward Prior, and Mary Brown.

"Jesus, Name Above All Names" ("Beautiful Savior, Glorious Lord, Emmanuel, God with Us, Blessed Redeemer, Living Word" by Naida Hearn (1974, 1978 Scripture In Song)

"O Master, Let Me Walk with Thee," words: Washington Gladden (1789), Music: Maryton, H. Percy Smith (1874)

"O Word of God Incarnate," words: William W. Howe (1867), music: Felix Mendelssohn (1847)

"The Word," by Michael Card (© 1988 Birdwing Music)

"Thy Word Is a Lamp unto My Feet," by Amy Grant and Michael W. Smith (© 1984, Word Music)

"Trust and Obey," words: John H. Sammis (1887), music: Daniel B. Towner

"What Child Is This" ("The silent Word is pleading"), words: William Chatterton Dix (1865), music: Greensleeves (16th century English melody)

"Wonderful Counselor," by Brandon Seibert, James Mark Gulley, Stephen Gulley, Thomas Wilson (© 2013 Clear Day Praise)

"Wonderful Counselor," by John Michael Talbot (© 1980 Universal Music - Brentwood Benson Publishing)

"Wonderful Words of Life," words and music: Philip P. Bliss (1874)

"Your Name," by Paul Baloche and Glenn Packiam (© 2006 Integrity Worship Music)

Exercises

From Appendix 6. Exercises to Help You Internalize the Names of Jesus, select some activities that will help you internalize the truths of this lesson's names, titles, descriptors, and metaphors. This week, how can you creatively pray, meditate, write, worship, consider, draw or paint, compose, picture, and live out these truths in your community?

Actively participating in these ways will help you grow to be like Christ.

3. Jesus the Son of Man

We've looked at what Jesus' parents called him, and the names and titles that others used for him. But what did Jesus call himself?

Most of the time, he probably introduced himself simply as Jesus, his given name. But on special teaching occasions he would refer to himself with the peculiar designation – in the third person – "the Son of Man." It was the only title that Jesus himself freely used. No one else ever used that title to designate Jesus. Nor does the phrase occur in the New Testament outside of the Gospels, except in the words of Stephen (Acts 7:56). But the title occurs on Jesus' lips at least 65 times in the Gospels. What did he mean by it?

In this lesson we'll consider the important title "Son of Man," as well as several other titles that relate to Jesus' human journey. I'll spend quite a bit of time on

Heinrich Hofmann, detail of 'Christ at Thirty-three' (about 1889)

Son of Man. It isn't widely understood by the average Christian, but it is of vital importance to who Jesus believed himself to be.

I've heard people say that Jesus was the "Son of Man" and "Son of God," as if Son of Man referred to Jesus' human nature, while Son of God referred to his divine nature. As we'll see, that kind of analysis is both simplistic and wrong.

The Hebrew Idiom

To understand the title Son of Man, we first need to look at the Hebrew idioms "son of" and "daughter of." Of course, the phrases are used literally many times in genealogies and at the introduction of a new person in the story. For example, the book of Jeremiah begins: "The words of Jeremiah son of Hilkiah, one of the priests at Anathoth in the territory of Benjamin."

But we often see a peculiar idiom, both in the Old Testament (written in Hebrew and Aramaic) and in the Gospels (translated from Aramaic, the language that Jesus spoke).

"Son of" often denotes "one who shares in something or who is worthy of it, or who stands in some other close relation to it."[44]

Here are a few examples – sometimes smoothed out in modern translations, but given explicitly in the NASB and KJV:

- "sons of disobedience" (Ephesians 2:2, those who are disobedient);
- "son of perdition" (John 17:12; 2 Thessalonians 2:3, the one destined to perish);
- "son of peace" (Luke 10:6, a man inclined toward peace);
- "sons of the kingdom" (Matthew 8:12; 13:38a; those destined to inherit the kingdom);
- "sons of thunder" (Mark 3:17; loud people);
- "son of encouragement" ("Barnabas," Acts 4:36, one who encourages).

Often in the Old Testament, the designation "son of man" means just that – a human being, man, such as in Numbers 23:19 and Psalm 144:3. In the Book of Ezekiel, "son of man" is the peculiar form of address by which God speaks to the prophet some 90 times.

Daniel's Heavenly Son of Man

But as Jesus' self-title in the Gospels, Son of Man means more than "man." It is rather clear, as we shall see, that Jesus is referring to a specific figure who occurs in Daniel's prophecy:

> "In my vision at night I looked, and there before me was **one like a son of man, coming with the clouds of heaven**. He approached the Ancient of Days and was led into his presence. He was given authority, glory and sovereign power; all peoples, nations and men of every language worshiped him. His dominion is an everlasting dominion that will not pass away, and his kingdom is one that will never be destroyed." (Daniel 7:13-14)

Later in the prophecy, the Son of Man is not mentioned. In his place "the saints of the Most High" receive the kingdom and possess it forever (Daniel 7:18, 22, 27).

In Daniel the idiom "son of man" at this point doesn't seem to be the messianic title that it became later. Rather the prophet speaks of a man contrasted with the four beasts seen previously. Here's what we know about this son of man figure or can infer from these verses. He:

- Resembles a **man**.
- Comes on the clouds of heaven, perhaps denoting his **heavenly origin**.

---

[44] *Huios,* BDAG 1025, 2cβ.

- Approaches the Ancient of Days, a figure obviously representing **God**.
- Receives **authority**, glory, and sovereign power.
- Is **worshipped** by people of all nations and languages.
- Possesses an **everlasting kingdom**.

Ladd concludes that Daniel's son of man is "a heavenly messianic eschatological figure who brings the kingdom to the afflicted saints on earth."[45]

It is clear from the Gospels, however, that the title Son of Man was not widely recognized in Jesus' time as a messianic title. That is probably why Jesus was able to use it as a title to refer to himself. He less often uses the title Son of God – and that only in the third person. In the same way, Jesus never uses Messiah or Christ to refer to himself, though he acknowledges its use by others (John 4:25-26; Matthew 16:16-17). Even so, he warns his disciples not to tell anyone that he is the Messiah (Matthew 16:20), probably to avoid the political implications of the title and the attention such a title would bring him (Mark 1:45).

But Son of Man, though veiled in its meaning to nearly all Jews of his time, had a clear and explicit meaning for Jesus. Use of this title indicates that Jesus claimed to be "a pre-existent heavenly kind of messiah who has appeared unexpectedly as a man among men."[46] And it is clear from Jesus exchange with the high priest at his trial, that he saw himself as Daniel's "one like a son of man":

> "The high priest said to him, 'I charge you under oath by the living God: Tell us if you are the Christ, the Son of God.'
>
> 'Yes, it is as you say,' Jesus replied. 'But I say to all of you: In the future you will see the **Son of Man** sitting at the right hand of the Mighty One and coming on the clouds of heaven.'" (Matthew 26:63-64)

Q1. (Daniel 7:13-14) What attributes does the "one like a son of man" have in Daniel's prophecy? In what ways does this personage possess divine elements? What authority does he have? How do we know that Jesus identified himself with this Son of Man in Daniel?
http://www.joyfulheart.com/forums/topic/1605-q1-one-like-a-son-of-man/

---

[45] Ladd, *Theology*, p. 148. This Son of Man figure also appears in the *Similitudes of Enoch*, a Jewish writing somewhat later than the rest of Enoch. Though there is no evidence that Jesus knew of the *Similitudes*, for some Jewish circles in Jesus' time, at least, "the Son of Man has become a messianic title for a pre-existent heavenly being who comes to earth with the glorious Kingdom of God" (Ladd, *Theology*, p. 149).

[46] Ladd, Theology, p. 152.

Q2. (Daniel 7:13-14) Since Jesus is the Son of Man in Daniel's prophecy, what implications does that have for your obedience, your worship, your estimation of Jesus' power and glory?
http://www.joyfulheart.com/forums/topic/1606-q2-authority-of-son-of-man/

Jesus' Use of Son of Man in the Gospels

In the Synoptic Gospels, Jesus uses the title of Son of Man in three ways:

1. Earthly Son of Man
2. Suffering Son of Man
3. Apocalyptic or Eschatological Son of Man

He begins his ministry by using Son of Man in a variety of ways. But only after Peter recognizes him as "the Christ, the Son of the living God" at Caesarea Philippi does he begin to share the other aspects of his title, that the Son of Man will suffer and then return in glory. In John's Gospel, Jesus uses the title 12 times in three major themes related to the Son of Man.

1. Heavenly Son of Man
2. Life-Giving Son of Man
3. Glorified Son of Man.

For more detail on this see Appendix 4. The Title Son of Man in the Gospels.

From the Gospels we learn that for Jesus, his role as Son of Man was all encompassing. It included his divinity, his suffering, his authority, his glory, and his return at the end of time.

The remainder of the New Testament contains only two additional references to the Son of Man: Stephen's vision of "heaven open and the **Son of Man** standing at the right hand of God" at his martyrdom (Acts 7:56) and John's vision of Christ in Revelation, **"someone like a Son of Man"** walking among the golden lampstands (Revelation 1:13).

The Man Christ Jesus

Now that we've examined Son of Man, we'll consider a few other titles that include the word "man." While Son of Man is a messianic title, the phrase "son of man" in Daniel hints of the human aspect of this figure. We see Jesus' humanness emphasized several times in Scripture:

Pilate declares Jesus: "Behold, **the Man**" (ESV, KJV, John 19:5).

Paul writes:

> "For there is one God and one mediator between God and men, **the man Christ Jesus**, who gave himself as a ransom for all men." (1 Timothy 2:5-6)

Elsewhere Paul has written eloquently of Jesus' divine nature. But here he is speaking about his role as mediator, and so emphasizes his humanness, the "man" who gave himself as a ransom for all "men." We'll consider this role as Mediator in just a moment.

In Paul's comparison between Adam and Christ (which we'll discuss below) Jesus is twice referred to as "**the one man Jesus Christ**" (Romans 5:15, 17).

Two Natures in One Person

One question that has puzzled Christians from earliest times is Jesus' nature. Is he really a human being, or only a divine figure pretending to be human, like the second century Docetist heretics claimed. Or is he a human being who is exalted at his baptism to be divine, like the Arian heretics (and present-day Jehovah Witnesses) believe? Or is he just a human being, whose followers believed and proclaimed to be divine (as many liberals today believe)?

There was considerable debate in the first couple centuries of the Church about this. But as they studied the Scriptures, the resolution began in the Nicene Creed as formulated at the Council of Constantinople in 381 AD.

> "We believe ... in one Lord Jesus Christ,
> the only-begotten Son of God
> Begotten of his Father before all worlds,
> God of God, Light of Light,
> Very God of very God,
> Begotten, not made,
> Being of one substance with the Father,
> By whom all things were made;
> Who for us men, and for our salvation came down from heaven,
> And was **incarnate** by the Holy Ghost of the Virgin Mary,
> And was **made man**."[47]

At the First Council of Ephesus in 431 AD, the term "hypostatic union" emerged to clarify the union of Christ's humanity and divinity in one hypostasis, or individual

---

[47] From the *Book of Common Prayer*, Church of England, 1662.

existence. Jesus is *both* God and man, not one or the other. That is what the Bible teaches – that Jesus is both God and man.

Man of Sorrows

In the Suffering Servant passage, Jesus is described as a Man of Sorrows, that is, a sorrowful man.

> "He was despised and rejected by men;
> **a man of sorrows**, and acquainted with grief;
> and as one from whom men hide their faces he was despised,
> and we esteemed him not." (Isaiah 53:3)

In his humanity he suffered for us and bore our sins, but in the end, "he shall see the fruit of the travail of his soul and be satisfied" (Isaiah 53:11).

You can sense sorrow in Jesus when he sees gross unbelief in his followers, even his disciples. There is deep sorrow in Jesus on the cross, where he as Sin-Bearer is carrying the weight of all our sins, and cries, "My God, my God, why have you forsaken me?" (Matthew 27:46).

Yet the earthly Jesus also experienced joy and prayed that this joy might be shared by his disciples (Luke 10:21; John 15:11; 17:13; Hebrews 12:2; cf. Jude 24).

> **Q3. (Isaiah 53:3) How can Jesus be the Man of Sorrows as well as the one who finds joy in his Father? How can we experience sorrow without it coming to dominate our lives?**
> **http://www.joyfulheart.com/forums/topic/1607-q3-man-of-sorrows/**

Seed of the Woman, Seed of Abraham

We also see an identification between Jesus and his archetypical parents, Adam and Eve. In the curse upon the serpent in the Garden of Eden, God says to the serpent, an embodiment of Satan:

> "And I will put enmity
> Between you and the woman,
> And between your seed and **her seed**[48];

---

[48] "Offspring" (NIV, NRSV, ESV), "seed" (KJV) is *zera'*, "sowing, seed, offspring" from *zāra'*, "to scatter seed, sow." "Seed" can be used both as semen and offspring (Walter C. Kaiser, TWOT #582a).

> He shall bruise you on the head,
> And you shall bruise him on the heel." (Genesis 3:15, NASB)

"Seed" (KJV) tends to be rendered "offspring" in newer translations (NIV, NRSV). This prophecy is sometimes called by theologians "the *protoevangelium*," literally, the first gospel. In one sense, "her seed" refers to all of Eve's descendents, all humankind. But the ultimate Offspring of Eve will be bruised (wounded) on the heel by Satan, resulting in physical death, but the Offspring of Eve will bruise Satan on the head, that is, utterly destroy him (1 John 3:8). Jesus passes on this authority to his disciples too:

> "Behold, I have given you authority to tread upon serpents and scorpions, and over all the power of the enemy; and nothing shall hurt you." (Luke 10:19)

> "Then the God of peace will soon crush Satan under your feet." (Romans 16:20a)

Christ is also referred to as **the Seed** (Galatians 3:16, 19) and **seed of Abraham** (Hebrews 2:16), indicating that he is the ultimate Jew, the ultimate descendent of Abraham, a **Son of Abraham** (Matthew 1:1). Since we are "in Christ," we are included in Abraham's seed.

> "If you belong to Christ, then you are Abraham's seed,
> and heirs according to the promise." (Galatians 3:29)

The Last Adam

To help his readers understand the significance of Jesus to redeem mankind, in two passages Paul contrasts Adam with Jesus. In his Letter to the Roman Church, Paul explains Adam as "a type of the one who was to come" (Romans 5:14), that is Jesus. Through Adam, sin and death entered the world; through Jesus, grace and life (Romans 5:12-15). In the same way that Adam as the prototype man sinned and brought down his descendants after him, so **"the one man, Jesus Christ"** (Romans 5:15, 17) is the bringer of life to all who are "in him."

When Paul teaches on physical resurrection in his first letter to the Corinthians, he develops this same analogy, in which four new descriptors of Christ are born:

Adam	Christ
First Adam	Last Adam
Living being	Life-Giving Spirit
First man	Second Man
Man of dust	Man of Heaven

Here is Paul's teaching:

"Thus it is written, 'The first man Adam became a living being'; the **last Adam** became **a life-giving spirit**. But it is not the spiritual which is first but the physical, and then the spiritual. The first man was from the earth, a man of dust; **the second man** is from heaven. As was the man of dust, so are those who are of the dust; and as is **the man of heaven**, so are those who are of heaven. Just as we have borne the image of the man of dust, we shall also bear the image of **the man of heaven**." (1 Corinthians 15:45-49)

While our solidarity with the First Adam brought death, our union with the Second Adam brings life and the promise of heaven. This "Man of Heaven" circles back to the heavenly Son of Man, which began this lesson.

This concept of "corporate personality" can be difficult for those of us in cultures which overemphasize individualism. However, the whole idea of being "in Christ," is the same idea.

Mediator of a New Covenant

Jesus is the heavenly Son of Man, a divine figure. He is also Man, the Last Adam. And as such he alone is qualified to stand between God and man to intercede for our salvation. Paul writes:

"For there is one God and **one mediator between God and men**, the man Christ Jesus, who gave himself as a ransom for all men." (1 Timothy 2:5-6)

"**Mediator**" is *mesitēs*, "one who mediates between two parties to remove a disagreement or reach a common goal, mediator, arbitrator."[49] The analogy or picture here is two parties that are separated by some issue.

I think that this role of Mediator relates to his role as High Priest that we discuss in Lesson 6. He continually intercedes for us (Hebrews 7:25; Isaiah 53:12; Romans 8:34). And, as we'll see shortly, he is our Advocate before the Father (1 John 2:1).

Incidentally, observe that Paul calls Jesus the "one mediator between God and men." "One" is *heis*, "a single person or thing, with focus on quantitative aspect, one."[50] Our dear Roman Catholic brothers and sisters have long referred to Mary as the Mediatrix, that is, a mediator of the graces of her Son. Sadly, many of the devout spend more time praying to Mary (a major focus of the rosary prayer), than praying to Jesus. Dear friends,

---

[49] *Mesitēs*, BDAG 634.
[50] *Heis*, BDAG 29, 1aα.

we must honor Mary for her unique role as the mother of Jesus, but we must not look to her to intercede for us or mediate between us and God. Jesus is our One Mediator.

Jesus is also **"the Mediator of a New Covenant"** (Hebrews 11:24). He is also the our personal mediator with God, the one who negotiates the covenant between the Covenant maker and those he came to save.

Jesus the Advocate and Reconciler

Another title from the world of law and covenants is advocate. As we saw in Lesson 2, Jesus is our Counselor as well as **Advocate** (*paraklētos*) with the Father. In secular Greek *paraklētos* is sometimes used in a the sense of a legal assistant advocate in a court setting.[51] The Apostle John tells us:

> "My little children, I am writing these things to you so that you may not sin. But if anyone does sin, we have **an advocate** (*paraklētos*) **with the Father**, Jesus Christ the righteous." (1 John 2:1, ESV)

The word is translated functionally in the NIV as "one who speaks to the Father on our behalf." From heaven, we read of "the accuser of our brothers, who accuses them before our God day and night, has been hurled down" (Revelation 12:10). Now Jesus is at our side to intercede for us. We are not worthy in our own right, but he, "the Righteous One" is worthy, and we are "in him." Hallelujah!

In our world, an emissary or negotiator, perhaps a Secretary of State or Prime Minister, is sent to resolve the problem and bring the parties together. Jesus is our representative, our Advocate.

The words used in the New Testament for this task are "reconciliation" and "peacemakers."

> "When we were God's enemies, **we were reconciled** to him through the death of his Son...." (Romans 5:10)

> "God was **reconciling the world** to himself in Christ, not counting men's sins against them." (2 Corinthians 5:19)

> "But now he has **reconciled you** by Christ's physical body through death to present you holy in his sight." (Colossians 1:22)

Though the New Testament doesn't use the title Reconciler for Jesus, this role is described as him being our Advocate with the Father.

---

[51] Liddell-Scott, *Greek-English Lexicon.*

Jesus is called the "**Prince of Peace**" (Isaiah 9:6) and "**the Lord of Peace**" (2 Thessalonians 3:16). He said, "Blessed are the peacemakers, for they will be called sons of God" (Matthew 5:9).

Q4. (1 Timothy 2:5-6; 1 John 2:1) In what sense is Jesus our "one Mediator between God and man"? What happens to this personal relationship with Jesus when we ask a minister or a saint to intercede for us? How is Jesus our Advocate before the Father? In what ways are you an advocate for the powerless in your community? How do you function as a reconciler, a mediator, a peacemaker as you serve Christ? http://www.joyfulheart.com/forums/topic/1608-q4-jesus-our-mediator/

Consolation of Israel

Paraklētos can mean "advocate" from *parakaleō*, "to come alongside" to assist. Another word from this root is *paraklēsis*, to come alongside to provide comfort.

"Now there was a man in Jerusalem called Simeon, who was righteous and devout. He was waiting for **the consolation of Israel**, and the Holy Spirit was upon him." (Luke 2:25)

"Consolation" is *paraklēsis*, "lifting of another's spirits, comfort, consolation."[52] Here it is in an eschatological sense, where consolation refers to Messianic salvation. We read prophecies of this coming consolation of Israel.

"**Comfort, comfort** my people, says your God.
Speak tenderly to Jerusalem,
and proclaim to her that her hard service has been completed,
that her sin has been paid for,
that she has received from the LORD's hand double for all her sins." (Isaiah 40:1-2)

"The Spirit of the Sovereign LORD is on me,
because the LORD has anointed me to preach good news to the poor.
He has sent me to **bind up the brokenhearted**,
to proclaim freedom for the captives
and release from darkness for the prisoners,
to proclaim the year of the LORD's favor

---

[52] *Paraklēsis*, BDAG 776, 3.

> and the day of vengeance of our God,
> **to comfort all who mourn**,
> and provide for those who grieve in Zion–
> to bestow on them a crown of beauty instead of ashes,
> the oil of gladness instead of mourning,
> and a garment of praise instead of a spirit of despair." (Isaiah 61:1-3a)

Jesus taught,

> "Blessed are those who mourn,
> for they will be **comforted**." (Matthew 5:4)

Our Hope

Comfort comes when we have hope. Paul begins his first letter to Timothy with this descriptor of Christ: "Christ Jesus **our hope**" (1 Timothy 1:1). Jesus is the Son of "the God of hope" (Romans 15:13), he is the hope of the Gentiles (Romans 15:12), he is in us, our "hope of glory" (Colossians 1:27), and his resurrection has given us "a living hope" (1 Peter 1:3).

Jesus, the Apostle of God

Two titles are related in that they have to do with God's sending of Jesus to us as gift and apostle. The writer of Hebrews exhorts us,

> "Fix your thoughts on Jesus, the **apostle** and high priest whom we confess." (Hebrews 3:1)

We will look at Jesus as High Priest in Lesson 6. Here we consider him as Apostle. The Greek word is *apostolos*, from the verb *apostellō*, "to send." Sometimes in secular Greek it refers to persons who are dispatched for a specific purpose, and the context determines the status or function expressed in such English terms as "ambassador, delegate, messenger."[53] Jesus used the title for the Twelve Disciples whom he especially chose to lead the early church, who were "sent" with a special mission. But Jesus is the ultimate "Sent One." The apostles' mission was a derivative of his own mission to bring salvation to the world. Jesus talks to his Father.

> "As you sent me into the world, I have sent them into the world." (John 17:18)

After his resurrection, he commissions his disciples with the same commission as he had received.

---

[53] *Apostolos*, BDAG 12, 2b.

"As the Father has sent me, I am sending you." (John 20:21)

We serve because Jesus the Great Apostle of our profession was willing to be sent by the Father and was faithful.

Jesus, the Indescribable Gift

Finally, God sent Jesus to us as a gift, an indescribable gift. Jesus told the Samaritan woman at the well:

"If you knew the gift of God and who it is that asks you for a drink, you would have asked him and he would have given you living water." (John 4:10)

In 2 Corinthians 9:15, Paul calls Jesus God's **"indescribable gift"** (NIV, NRSV), **"inexpressible gift"** (ESV), **"unspeakable gift"** (KJV).[54] This is underscored in the famous verse, John 3:16 – "For God so loved the world that he gave his only begotten Son...." Jesus is God's gift to us.

Jesus is the glorious Son of Man prophesied in Daniel, who will set up an everlasting Kingdom. He is also a Man of Sorrows, the Seed of Woman who will crush Satan, the Seed of Abraham, and the Last Adam, the Man from Heaven who brings to us Eternal Life. He is our Mediator between God and Man, our Advocate with the Father, our Reconciler and Prince of Peace, our Hope, our Consolation, and our Indescribable Gift. We are so thankful!

Prayer

Father, as we consider the titles of Jesus, we see him possessing great glory and power, and yet humbling himself to die for us, to take our sins and give us life; for bridging the gulf between God and man on our behalf. Thank you for sending him. In Jesus' name, we pray. Amen.

Names and Titles of Jesus
One Like a Son of Man (Daniel 7:13-14)
Son of Man (often in the Gospels)
The Man (John 19:5)
The Man Christ Jesus (1 Timothy 2:5-6)
Man of Sorrows (Isaiah 53:3)

---

[54] The word is *anekdiēgētos*, "indescribably" in a good sense (BDAG 76). It is a compound word formed from *a-*, a negative particle, + *ekeiegeomai*, "to provide detailed information when telling something, tell (in detail) something (BDAG 300).

Seed of Woman (Genesis 3:15)

Seed (Galatians 3:16, 19)

Seed of Abraham (Hebrews 2:16)

Last Adam (1 Corinthians 15:45)

Life-Giving Spirit (NIV, NRSV, ESV; 1 Corinthians 15:45)

Quickening Spirit (KJV, 1 Corinthians 15:45)

Second Man (1 Corinthians 15:47)

Man from/of Heaven (1 Corinthians 15:47, 49)

Mediator of a New Covenant (Hebrews 11:24)

One Mediator between God and Men (1 Timothy 2:5)

Advocate with the Father (ESV, NRSV, KJV, 1 John 2:1)

Prince of Peace (Isaiah 9:6)

Lord of Peace (2 Thessalonians 3:16)

Consolation of Israel (Luke 2:25)

Our Hope (1 Timothy 1:1)

Apostle (Hebrews 3:1)

Indescribable Gift (NIV, NRSV, 2 Corinthians 9:15)

Inexpressible Gift (ESV, 2 Corinthians 9:15)

Unspeakable Gift (KJV, 2 Corinthians 9:15)

Songs and Hymns

Songs in this lesson focus around key titles such as Son of Man, the Man, Man of Sorrows, Seed of Woman, Last Adam, Mediator, Advocate, Prince of Peace, and Hope.

"Celebrate the Child" ("the Child who is the Light ... Godhead and manhood became one ... First born of creation ... Lamb and Lion, God and Man ... Author of Salvation ... Almighty wrapped in swaddling bands"), by Michael Card (© 1989 Birdwing Music)

"Come, Thou Long Expected Jesus" ("Israel's strength and consolation, Hope of all the earth thou art, dear desire of every nation"), words: Charles Wesley (1745), music: Hyfrydol, Rowland H. Prichard (1830)

"Everlasting God" ("Our Hope, our Strong Deliverer"), by Brenton Brown, Ken Riley (© 2005 Thankyou Music)

"Fairest Lord Jesus" ("O Thou of God and man the Son"), words: 17th century, translated from German Joseph A. Seiss (1873); music: Crusader's Hymn, Silesian folk tune

"Forever Reign" ("You are Hope, You are Hope"), by Scott Ingram, Reuben Morgan (© 2009 Hillsong Music Publishing)

"Hallelujah! What a Savior" ("Man of Sorrows! What a name"), words and music: Philip P. Bliss (1875)

"Hark, the Herald Angels Sing" ("Hail the heav'nly Prince of Peace ... Second Adam from above, Reinstate us in Thy love ... Rise, the woman's conqu'ring Seed, Bruise in us the serpent's head"), words: Charles Wesley (1739), music: Felix Mendelssohn (1740)

"I Extol You," by Jennifer Randolph (© 1985 Integrity's Hosanna! Music)

"I Will Look Up" ("Jesus, Lord of All ... Prince of Peace, Perfect Healer, King of Kings, Mighty Savior"), Chris Brown, Jason Ingram, Mack Brock, Matt Redman, Wade Joye (© 2013 Said And Done Music)

"Jesus Messiah," by Chris Tomlin, Daniel Carson, Ed Cash, Jesse Reeves (2008 sixsteps Music)

"Man of Sorrows," by Brooke Ligertwood, Matt Crocker (© 2012 Hillsong Music Publishing)

"Shout to the Lord" ("My comfort, my shelter"), by Darlene Zschech (© 1993, Darlene Zschech and Hillsong Publishing)

"You Are Holy" ("Prince of Peace"), by Marc Imboden, Tammi Rhoton (© 1994 Imboden Music)

Exercises

From Appendix 6. Exercises to Help You Internalize the Names of Jesus, select some activities that will help you internalize the truths of this lesson's names, titles, descriptors, and metaphors. This week, how can you creatively pray, meditate, write, worship, consider, draw or paint, compose, picture, and live out these truths in your community?

Actively participating in these ways will help you grow to be like Christ.

4. Jesus the Messiah, Christ, and Son of David

What if I were to ask you: What is Jesus' last name? You might say: Christ. Jesus Christ. But you'd be wrong. His last name in Bible days would have been "ben Joseph" (son of Joseph). Christ is his title, his most common title in the New Testament. In the Old Testament, he is known as Messiah, the king that the Jews looked forward to who would save them from their enemies and set up the Kingdom of God on earth.

Richard Hook (1914-1975), "Head of Christ," © Concordia Publishing House.

Anointing

To understand this title, we need to look at the original languages. Christ (*christos*) is Greek for "anointed one." The basic verb is *chrio*, "to rub, stroke," with oils, "to smear, to anoint." But the word didn't originate in the Greek culture but in the Hebrew world. In the Greek Septuagint translation of the Old Testament, *christos* was the word used to translate the Hebrew word *māshîah*, "anointed one," which we transliterate as "Messiah."

In the Pentateuch, objects and people were set apart to God as his own sacred property when they were anointed with specially-formulated olive-oil-based anointing oil (Exodus 30:22-25). For example, the tabernacle was ritually anointed to set it apart to God (Exodus 40:9). Aaron, the first high priest, and his sons, were anointed by Moses to set them apart to God (Exodus 28:41; 29:7; 30:30; 40:13), as were subsequent priests, by pouring oil over the priest's head (Exodus 29:7; Psalm 133:2).

When God granted Israel a king, Saul was anointed by the prophet Samuel (1 Samuel 10:1). But when Saul showed himself unworthy, God told Samuel to call together the sons of Jesse of Bethlehem so that he might anoint one of them to replace Saul as king (1 Samuel 16:1). When young David was brought before the prophet, the Lord spoke to him:

"Arise, anoint him, for this is he."
Then Samuel took the horn of oil and anointed him in the midst of his brothers. And the Spirit of the LORD rushed upon David from that day forward." (1 Samuel 16:12-13)

The oil is a symbol of the Holy Spirit coming upon a person for service. As we'll see, there is a close relationship between anointing and the Holy Spirit.

The Davidic Covenant

Later in his reign, David sought to build a house for God, a temple. God replied that David's son Solomon would build the temple, but that God wanted to build a "house" for David. The Hebrew word for "house" can refer not only to one's physical dwelling, but also to one's family and dynasty.

"The LORD declares to you that the LORD himself will establish a house for you: When your days are over and you rest with your fathers, I will raise up your off-spring to succeed you, who will come from your own body, and I will establish his kingdom.... Your house and your kingdom will endure forever before me; your throne will be established forever." (2 Samuel 7:11b-12, 16)

This is an amazing promise, known as the Davidic Covenant, that David's dynasty will last forever. David's descendants, the kings of Judah, did continue to reign, father to son, son to grandson for nearly 500 years, until Jerusalem fell to Nebuchadnezzar, king of Babylon in 587 BC.

The destruction of Jerusalem, exile, and end of the Davidic line of kings was a huge shock to the people. In a psalm written during the exile, you read a recital of the Davidic Covenant, followed by the cry:

"How long, O Lord? Will you hide yourself forever?
How long will your wrath burn like fire?" (Psalm 89:46)

In the years that followed the exile, a hope rose within God's people that David's descendant, the Messiah, would restore glory to the Kingdom. There are hints of this throughout the prophets, encouragements to see God's people through difficult days. In the last century or two before Christ was born, there was intense expectation among the Jews that a descendent of David would come as Messiah to deliver the people from their bondage.

Q1. What is the meaning of the words "Christ" and "Messiah? How does the Davidic Covenant influence messianic expectation in Jesus' day?
http://www.joyfulheart.com/forums/topic/1609-q1-christ-and-messiah/

Messianic Prophecy

If this were a study of messianic prophecy, we'd spend a lot more time with these powerful promises. But since our purpose is to understand Jesus' title as Messiah, I'll give you just a sampling of some important messianic prophecies, putting in bold some of the titles and metaphors that appear.

In the Pentateuch, we find two passages that were interpreted by the Jews – and later, by the Christians – as referring to the Messiah. The first is a prophecy by Balaam:

> "I see him, but not now;
> I behold him, but not near.
> **A star** will come out of Jacob;
> **a scepter** will rise out of Israel...." (Numbers 24:17)

A second passage is Jacob's prophecy over his son Judah, progenitor of the tribe from which Jesus arose:

> "The scepter will not depart from Judah,
> nor the ruler's staff from between his feet,
> until he comes to whom it belongs
> and the obedience of the nations is his." (Genesis 49:10)

Though David's line had been cut off, there was still a stump, and there was hope.

> "A **shoot** will come up from the stump of Jesse;
> from his roots a **Branch** will bear fruit.
> The Spirit of the Lord will rest on him –
> the Spirit of wisdom and of understanding,
> the Spirit of counsel and of power,
> the Spirit of knowledge and of the fear of the LORD...." (Isaiah 11:1-2)

(The KJV has "a **rod** out of the stem of Jesse" in verse 1.) This passage, especially, was interpreted messianically in the Isaiah Targum (that is, an Aramaic translation or paraphrase of the Old Testament) and by the early rabbis.[55] Isaiah foresees the Messiah bringing in a time of peace and rest for God's people.

> "The wolf will live with the lamb,
> the leopard will lie down with the goat,
> the calf and the lion and the yearling together;
> and a little child will lead them.
> The cow will feed with the bear,
> their young will lie down together,
> and the lion will eat straw like the ox.
> The infant will play near the hole of the cobra,
> and the young child put his hand into the viper's nest.
> They will neither harm nor destroy on all my holy mountain,
> for the earth will be full of the knowledge of the LORD
> as the waters cover the sea." (Isaiah 11:6-9)

This Messiah is called "the Prince of Peace" (Isaiah 9:6), that is, the one who brings peace.

Isaiah indicates that Messiah's reign will be a time of righteous rule, conquering of enemies, of the regathering of the Jews that have been scattered through exile (Isaiah 11:10-12). Later, Isaiah prophesies that God will restore the Davidic king to the throne once again.

> "Give ear and come to me;
> hear me, that your soul may live.
> I will make an everlasting covenant with you,
> my faithful love promised to David." (Isaiah 55:3)

Messianic psalms give witness to this coming King.

> "The kings of the earth set themselves,
> and the rulers take counsel together,
> against the LORD and against his **Anointed** (*māshîah*)...." (Psalm 2:2, ESV)

The prophet Micah foresees this restoration of David's throne, referred to by Jewish scholars when the wise men came to find Jesus (Luke 2:4).

---

[55] Craig A. Evans, "Messianism," in *Dictionary of New Testament Background* (Inter-Varsity Press, 2000), p. 700. Evans' article provides excellent background into the development of the messianic movement in Israel leading up to Jesus' day.

"But you, Bethlehem Ephrathah,

though you are small among the clans of Judah,

out of you will come for me one who will be **ruler over Israel**,

whose origins are from of old, from ancient times.

Therefore Israel will be abandoned

until the time when she who is in labor gives birth

and the rest of his brothers return to join the Israelites.

He will stand and shepherd his flock in the strength of the Lord,

in the majesty of the name of the Lord his God.

And they will live securely,

for then his greatness will reach to the ends of the earth." (Micah 5:2-4)

Jeremiah saw this also:

"David will never fail to have a man to sit on the throne of the house of Israel...."
(Jeremiah 33:17)

Ezekiel, too, saw this.

"My servant David will be king over them,

and they will all have **one shepherd**.

They will follow my laws and be careful to keep my decrees." (Ezekiel 37:24)

(We'll consider the title Shepherd in Lesson 7.)

Daniel's prophecy speaks of an "**Anointed One**" (NIV, ESV, Daniel 9:25, 26), "**Anointed Prince**" (NRSV), "**Messiah**" (KJV), who is also called a "prince" or "ruler."

In the third and second centuries BC, in reaction to the oppression of Greek and Roman rule over the land of Israel, there began to grow an eschatological expectation that Messiah would come to set things right and bring in the Kingdom of God.

Three passages in particular played an important role: Genesis 49:10 ("the scepter will not depart from Judah"); Numbers 24:17 ("a star will come out of Jacob"[56]); and Isaiah 11:1-6 ("a shoot from the stump of Jesse"). They are discussed messianically in scrolls from the Qumran community. They are interpreted messianically in the Targums, that is, Aramaic translations or paraphrases of the Old Testament. And they appear in the intertestamental Jewish literature of the time.[57]

---

[56] Simon Bar-Kokhba ("son of the star," based on Numbers 24:17), who some claimed to be the expected Messiah, rebelled against the Roman empire in 132 AD.

[57] There are many mentions in intertestamental of the Messiah. For a sampling see: 1 Enoch 90:37f; 2 Baruch 72:1-5; Psalms of Solomon 18:7-9.

Q2. Which are your favorite messianic prophecies? Which titles from those are dearest to you? Why?
http://www.joyfulheart.com/forums/topic/1610-q2-messianic-prophecies/

Jesus the Messiah

By the time of John the Baptist and Jesus, messianic expectation is rampant. John the Baptist is asked if he is the Messiah – and denies it (John 1:19). People openly wonder if Jesus is this expected Messiah (John 4:25, 29; 7:41).

Andrew, one of Jesus' new followers, tells his brother Simon:

> "'We have found **the Messiah** [Greek *Messias*]' (that is, **the Christ** [Greek *Christos*])." (John 1:41b)

One of the high points of the disciples' spiritual understanding occurs when Jesus takes them away from Jewish regions to Caesarea Philippi so that he can teach them privately.

> "When Jesus came to the region of Caesarea Philippi, he asked his disciples, 'Who do people say the Son of Man is?'
> They replied, 'Some say John the Baptist; others say Elijah; and still others, Jeremiah or one of the prophets.'
> 'But what about you?' he asked. 'Who do you say I am?'
> Simon Peter answered, 'You are **the Christ**, the **Son of the living God**.'" (Matthew 16:13-16)

(We'll consider Son of the Living God in Lesson 5.) Jesus strongly affirms Peter for this statement and declares that it was revealed to Peter by "my Father in heaven" (verse 17). But then we read something curious:

> "Then he warned his disciples not to tell anyone that he was **the Christ**." (Matthew 16:20; cf. Luke 4:41)

Why would Jesus hide his title as Messiah from the masses? Probably to avoid the political implications of the title and the attention such a title would bring him (Mark 1:45). For the same reason, he forbad the demons from speaking and telling who he was (Mark 1:34; 3:12; Luke 4:41). Jesus did acknowledge that he was the Messiah to the women at the well of Samaria (John 4:25-26) and to Peter after his great confession

(Matthew 16:17), but to others he did not. As I explained in Lesson 3, the more ambiguous "Son of Man" was Jesus' preferred title.

Finally, at Jesus' trial, the high priest asks him to declare who he is under oath before a court of law:

> "'I charge you under oath by the living God: Tell us if you are the **Christ**, the **Son of God**.'
>
> 'Yes, it is as you say,' Jesus replied. 'But I say to all of you: In the future you will see the **Son of Man** sitting at the right hand of the Mighty One and coming on the clouds of heaven.'" (Matthew 26:63-64)

Now there is no reason to hide his Messiahship. Jesus openly acknowledges that he is the Messiah, but then points to his true title: the Son of Man whom Daniel had referred to in his prophecy, to whom all authority and worship will be given. (We'll consider Son of God in Lesson 5.)

Titles as Christ

The usual form of Jesus' title in the New Testament is "**Jesus Christ**" – the given name and then the title. But occasionally the order is reversed: the title and then the given name: "**Christ Jesus**."[58] There isn't much difference between the two, though having the title before the given name might emphasize the title a bit more – and vice versa. In Acts and the Epistles we often see "Lord" appended to this, the "**Lord Jesus Christ**," emphasizing Jesus' divinity. (We'll discuss "Lord" in Lesson 5.)

The term "Christ" is also used in several less common combinations in the New Testament:

- **Christ Jesus our Lord** (Romans 8:39; 1 Timothy 1:12)
- **Christ of God** (Luke 9:20)
- **Christ the Lord** (Luke 2:11)
- **Christ, the power of God** (1 Corinthians 1:24)
- **Christ, the wisdom of God** (1 Corinthians 1:24)
- **Christ, a King** (Luke 23:2)
- **Christ, Son of the Blessed** (Mark 14:61)
- **Christ, the Son of God** (Acts 9:20)

[58] Acts 19:4; Romans 3:24; Romans 8:1; 1 Cor. 1:2; 1 Cor. 1:30; Hebrews 3:1; 1 Peter 5:10; 1 Peter 5:14.

- **The Christ**, used absolutely (Matthew 1:16; 16:20; Mark 14:61)[59]
- **The Lord's Christ** (Luke 2:26)

Q3. (Matthew 16:13-16) Whom did Peter believe Jesus to be? How did Peter come to believe this? Why does Jesus command his disciples not to tell others that he is the Messiah? (Matthew 16:20).
http://www.joyfulheart.com/forums/topic/1611-q3-peters-confession/

Son of David

In Israel, there were many people who could trace their lineage to King David. But when people called Jesus "Son of David," they clearly were indicating their belief in him to be the Messiah, the long-expected king of David's line who would come and restore the Kingdom. Though Jesus didn't use the title Son of David concerning himself, others did.

Blind Bartimaeus: "Jesus, **Son of David**, have mercy on me!" (Mark 10:47-48; Luke 18:38-39; cf. Matthew 9:27; 20:30-31)

"And all the people were amazed, and said, 'Can this be the **Son of David**?'" (Matthew 12:23)

Syro-Phoenician Woman: "O Lord, **Son of David**; my daughter is severely oppressed by a demon." (Matthew 15:22)

Especially, during Jesus' triumphal entry, this was part of the outcry of the multitudes.

"And the crowds that went before him and that followed him were shouting, 'Hosanna to the **Son of David**! Blessed is he who comes in the name of the Lord! Hosanna in the highest!'" (Matthew 21:9, 15)

Seed or Offspring of David

Sometimes, instead of son, Jesus is called the seed or offspring of David.

"Remember Jesus Christ, raised from the dead, **descended from David**." (2 Timothy 2:8)

---

[59] In Acts 9:22 the KJV uses the title "the very Christ," but the word "very" is not in the text – the word *houtos* is better rendered, "this one" rather than the archaic "very."

The KJV translates it literally: "**the seed of David**" (KJV), from the Greek noun *sperma*, "seed." Revelation 22:16 uses another Greek noun, *genos*, "descendant," to describe this relationship of "**Offspring of David**" (NIV, KJV) or "**Descendant of David**" (NRSV, ESV, NASB). We'll consider this verse in the next section for its other titles.

Finally, in several Old Testament passages, this future descendant of David is simply referred to in shorthand as "**David**" (Jeremiah 30:9; Ezekiel 34:23; 37:24-25; Hosea 3:5).

Q4. (Matthew 21:9, 15) Why were the chief priests and scribes so angry when little children referred to Jesus as "Son of David"? What does the title "Son of David" signify?
http://www.joyfulheart.com/forums/topic/1612-q4-son-of-david/

Root, Branch, and Shoot

Now to some agricultural metaphors. A root, of course, is the source of a tree's life. A branch is a stem or extension from the axis of a tree. Both of these metaphors are based on the idea of a "family tree," with sometimes Jesse (David's father) and sometimes David himself designated as the Root, Branch, or Shoot.

> "In that day **the Branch of the LORD** will be beautiful and glorious,
> and the fruit of the land will be the pride and glory of the survivors in Israel." (Isaiah 4:2)

> "A **shoot** will come up from the stump of Jesse;
> from his roots a **Branch** will bear fruit." (Isaiah 11:1)

Isaiah uses a related simile to describe the Suffering Servant in Isaiah 53 who will die on behalf of the nation.

> "He grew up before him like **a tender shoot**,
> and like **a root out of dry ground**." (Isaiah 53:2a)

Isaiah also sees David's descendant as the rallying point for all peoples.

> "In that day **the Root of Jesse** will stand as **a banner for the peoples**;
> the nations will rally to him,
> and his place of rest will be glorious." (Isaiah 11:10)

(See more on the title "Banner" in Lesson 8.) Citing this passage along with Isaiah 11:1, Paul paraphrases:

> "The **Root of Jesse** will spring up,
> one who will arise to rule over the nations;
> the Gentiles will hope in him." (Romans 15:12)

Jeremiah also declares the coming Messiah with the image of the Branch.

> "'The days are coming," declares the LORD,
> 'when I will raise up to David a **righteous Branch**,
> a King who will reign wisely
> and do what is just and right in the land.'" (Jeremiah 23:5)

> "In those days and at that time
> I will make a **righteous Branch** sprout from David's line;
> he will do what is just and right in the land." (Jeremiah 33:15)

This expression is also used in Zechariah 3:8 and 6:12, where it seems that the "Branch" represents Jesus in his role as High Priest.[60] (See more on this in Lesson 6.)

The Lion of Judah

The book of Revelation carries on this image.

> "I am **the Root and the Offspring of David**,
> and the bright Morning Star." (Revelation 22:16)

> "See, **the Lion of the tribe of Judah**,
> the **Root of David**, has triumphed." (Revelation 5:5)

According to Jacob's ancient prophecy, the lion was the symbol of the tribe of Judah, and Jesus, as the principle descendant of that tribe is seen as the Lion himself. What is ironic is the contrast within two verses in the passage between the Lion, an aggressive animal who is at the top of the food chain, and the Lamb, who is a passive animal, often a victim. Jesus is both the willing sacrifice for our sins and the conquering king. (More on the Bright Morning Star in Lesson 9.)

Q5. Where did the title "Branch" come from? How does the imagery differ from the title "Root"?
http://www.joyfulheart.com/forums/topic/1613-q5-the-branch-and-root/

---

[60] The high priest and his associates are called "men symbolic of things to come" (Zechariah 3:8).

The Chosen One

Isaiah proclaims a Suffering Servant who would come and bring justice. This Servant (as we'll see in Lesson 6) is Jesus.

> "Here is **my servant**, whom I uphold,
> **my chosen one** in whom I delight;
> I will put my Spirit on him
> and he will bring justice to the nations." (Isaiah 42:1)

Notice the title: "my chosen one." This passage is quoted in Matthew 12:18 as pointing directly to Jesus.

> "Behold, **my servant** whom I have chosen,
> **my beloved** with whom my soul is well pleased." (Matthew 12:18, ESV, RSV, KJV)

"Chosen One" is also used as a messianic title in the mouths of Jesus' enemies at the cross:

> "Let him save himself if he is the Christ of God, the **Chosen One**." (Luke 23:35b)

But Jesus is indeed the Chosen One of God! At Jesus' transfiguration, we read:

> "And a voice came out of the cloud, saying,
> 'This is my Son, **my Chosen One**;
> listen to him!'" (Luke 9:35)

This designation is echoed elsewhere.

> "As you come to him, the living Stone –
> rejected by men but chosen by God and precious to him....
> For in Scripture it says:
> 'See, I lay a stone in Zion,
> a **chosen** and precious cornerstone,
> and the one who trusts in him will never be put to shame.'" (1 Peter 2:4, 6)

(We'll discuss the titles Stone and Cornerstone in Lesson 8).

Q6. (Luke 9:35) Since Jesus is God's Chosen One, what does it mean to "listen to him"? In what ways does your life reflect listening to him? In what ways do you need to heed him more explicitly?

http://www.joyfulheart.com/forums/topic/1614-q6-chosen-one/

In this lesson we've examined Jesus' titles of Anointed One, Messiah, Christ, Ruler, Seed, and Son of David. He is the Branch, the Root, and the Chosen One. As we review the wonderful promises made three millennia ago to David, we see how wonderfully they have been fulfilled in David's ultimate descendent – Messiah Jesus.

Prayer

Father, thank you for fulfilling the prophecies declaring that a descendant of David would be our Messiah and Deliverer. Help me to listen to him daily and heed his words. In Jesus' name, I pray. Amen.

Names and Titles of Jesus

Star (Numbers 24:17b)
Scepter (Numbers 24:17b)
Anointed (Psalm 2:2)
Anointed One (NIV, ESV, Daniel 9:25, 26)
Anointed Prince (NRSV, Daniel 9:25, 26)
Messiah (KJV, Daniel 9:25, 26)
Ruler over Israel (Micah 5:2)
Messiah (John 1:41b)
Christ (often, especially John 1:41b; Matthew 16:16, 20; 26:63-64; Luke 4:41; etc.)
Jesus Christ (often)
Christ Jesus (often)
Lord Jesus (Acts 7:59)
Lord Jesus Christ (often)
Christ Jesus our Lord (Romans 8:39; 1 Timothy 1:12)
Christ of God (Luke 9:20)
Christ the Lord (Luke 2:11)
Christ, the Power of God (1 Corinthians 1:24)
Christ, the Wisdom of God (1 Corinthians 1:24)
Christ, a King (Luke 23:2)
Christ, Son of the Blessed (Mark 14:61)
Christ, the Son of God (Acts 9:20)
The Christ (used absolutely, Matthew 1:16; 16:20; Mark 14:61)
Son of David (Mark 10:47-48; Luke 18:38-39; Matthew 9:27; 12:23; 15:22; 20:30-31; 21:9, 15)

Seed of David (KJV, 2 Timothy 2:8)
Offspring of David (NIV, KJV, Revelation 22:16; ESV, 2 Timothy 2:8)
Descendant of David (NRSV, ESV, Revelation 22:16; NRSV, 2 Timothy 2:8)
David (Jeremiah 30:9; Ezekiel 34:23; 37:24-25; Hosea 3:5)
Branch of the Lord (Isaiah 4:2)
Shoot (NIV, NRSV, ESV, Isaiah 11:1a)
Rod (KJV, Isaiah 11:1a)
Branch (Isaiah 11:1b; Zechariah 3:8; 6:12)
Tender Shoot (Isaiah 53:2a)
Root out of Dry Ground (Isaiah 53:2a)
Root of Jesse (Isaiah 11:10; Romans 15:12)
Banner for the Peoples (Isaiah 11:10)
Righteous Branch (Jeremiah 23:5; 33:15)
Root and Offspring of David (Revelation 22:16)
Lion of the Tribe of Judah (Revelation 5:5)
Root of David (Revelation 5:5)
Chosen One (Isaiah 42:1; Luke 23:35b; 9:35)
My Beloved (Matthew 12:18, ESV, RSV, KJV)
Chosen and Precious Cornerstone (1 Peter 2:6)

Songs and Hymns

Songs in this lesson focus on Jesus' messianic ministry, with titles such as, Anointed, Messiah, Christ, Son of David, Branch, Shoot, Root of Jesse, Banner, Lion of the Tribe of Judah, Root of David, Chosen One, and Beloved.

"All Glory, Laud and Honor" ("to thee, Redeemer, King ... king of Israel ... David's royal Son ... the King and Blessed One"), words: Theodulph of Orleans (c. 820 AD; translated by John M. Neale (1851), music: St. Theodulph, Melchior Teschner (1615)
"Come, O Come, Emmanuel" ("Root of Jesse ... Rod of Jesse"), words: 12th century; music: 15th century
"Cornerstone" ("Christ Alone"), by Edward Mote, Eric Liljero, Jonas Myrin, Reuben Morgan, William Batchelder Bradbury (© 2011 Hillsong Music Publishing)
"Holy and Anointed One," by John Barnett (© 1988 Mercy / Vineyard Publishing)
"How Great Is Our God" ("The splendor of the King ... Beginning and the End ... Lion and the Lamb"), by Chris Tomlin, Ed Cash, Jesse Reeves (© 2004 sixsteps Music)
"I Will Exalt You" (My Friend and King Anointed One") by Brooke Ligertwood (© 2009 Hillsong Music Publishing)

"In Christ Alone" ("This Cornerstone, this solid Ground") by Keith Getty, Stuart Townend (© 2001 Thankyou Music)

"Jesus Messiah," by Chris Tomlin, Daniel Carson, Ed Cash, Jesse Reeves (2008 sixsteps Music)

"Like a Lion" ("God's Not Dead"; "He's living on the inside roaring like a lion"), by Daniel Bashta (© 2009 Go Forth Sounds)

"Lion of Judah," by Mark McCoy (© 1997, Mercy / Vineyard Publishing)

"Messiah," by Andy Park (© 1989 Mercy / Vineyard Publishing). Many names of Jesus.

"Messiah," by Phil Wickham (© 2006 Phil Wickham Music)

"Messiah," by Twila Paris (© 2005 Integrity's Hosanna! Music)

"Shout for Joy" ("Like a banner high, lift up your grateful heart to the Morning Star ... He's the Saving One"), by Jason Ingram, Lincoln Brewster, Paul Baloche (© 2010 Integrity Worship Music)

"The Conquering Lion," by Tommy Cowan? (Embassy Music Corp.)

"The Lion of Judah," words: Fanny Crosby (1878), music: W. Howard Doane

"There is a Redeemer" ("Precious Lamb of God, Messiah") by Melody Green (© 1982 Universal Music - Brentwood Benson)

"Victory Chant" ("Hail Jesus! You're my King ... Hail, hail, Lion of Judah"), by Joseph Vogels (© 1985, Universal Music – Brentwood Benson Publishing)

Exercises

From Appendix 6. Exercises to Help You Internalize the Names of Jesus, select some activities that will help you internalize the truths of this lesson's names, titles, descriptors, and metaphors. This week, how can you creatively pray, meditate, write, worship, consider, draw or paint, compose, picture, and live out these truths in your community?

Actively participating in these ways will help you grow to be like Christ.

5. Jesus our Lord, the Divine Son of God

Perhaps the central understanding of Jesus in the New Testament is as "Son of God." For Christians this title has always been a mark of Jesus' divine nature.

While Messiah and Son of David were not considered titles of divinity, Son of God is often an overtly divine title. So is Lord. In this lesson we'll explore some of Jesus' clearly divine titles.

Christ Pantocrator (1148 AD), mosaic, dome of Cathedral of Cefalu, Palermo, Italy

Uses of Son of God

When we survey the Old and New Testaments, we find at least four different ways in which "Son of God" is used.

1. Creation Usage. One of God's creatures can be termed a "son of God" because he owes his existence to God's creative activity. Malachi observes: "Have we not all one Father? Did not one God create us?" (Malachi 2:10a). Paul says to the Athenians, "As some of your own poets have said, 'We are his offspring'" (Acts 17:28). The idea of "the Fatherhood of God and the brotherhood of man" is built on this concept, but as Ladd observes, "This is a theology of creation, not of redemption."[61]

2. Family Usage. "Son of God" can describe the relationship of men to God as the objects of his loving care, spiritual sonship. Israel as God's elect people is sometimes referred to in this way. For example, God declares, "Israel is my firstborn son" (Exodus 4:22). Or, "You are the sons of the LORD your God. You shall not cut yourselves..." (Deuteronomy 14:1). In the New Testament, we Christians are described in terms of sonship to God, by both spiritual birth (John 3:3; 1:12) and by adoption (Romans 8:14, 19; Galatians 3:26; 4:5).

3. Messianic Usage. "Son of God" is used in a messianic way, where the king whom God has set in place is referred to as the "son of God," especially in the promise made to David. In the Old Testament, Son of God is used three times in clear messianic passages:

[61] Ladd, *Theology*, p. 160.

"I will be his **father**, and he will be **my son**." (2 Samuel 7:14a)

"He will call out to me, 'You are my **Father**,
my God, the Rock my Savior.'
I will also **appoint him my firstborn**,
the most exalted of the kings of the earth.
I will maintain my love to him forever,
and my covenant with him will never fail.
I will establish his line forever,
his throne as long as the heavens endure." (Psalms 89:26-29)

"As for me, I have set **my King** on Zion, my holy hill.
I will tell of the decree: The LORD said to me,
'You are **my Son**;
today I have **begotten** you.'" (Psalm 2:6-7, ESV)

Note especially the final phrase of Psalm 2:7, translated in the NRSV, ESV, and KJV with the verb "begotten," which we'll explore later in this chapter.[62] It seems that the Judaism of Jesus' time recognized the term Son of God as a messianic title.[63] We see a hint of this in the high priest's question at Jesus' trial: "Are you the Christ, the Son of the Blessed?" (Mark 14:61b = Matthew 26:63b = Luke 22:67, 70).

4. Divine Son Usage. Finally, and most important, Son of God is used in a theological way. Both in the New Testament and later in Christian theology, Jesus is said to be the Son of God because he *is* God and shares the divine nature.

As we study the names and titles of Jesus Christ, we recognize that Jesus is both Messiah and Son of God. My question, as I explore Son of God, is: What did Son of God mean when applied to Jesus during his lifetime? And in what sense did he begin to think of himself as Son of God?

---

[62] NIV translates it, "Today I have become your Father." The verb is *yālad*. "In its narrowest sense *yālad* describes the act of a woman in giving birth to a child, but it is sometimes used of the father's part in becoming a parent" (TWOT #867). The "begats" of the Old Testament use this word.

[63] Son of God appears in a messianic context in Enoch 105:2; IV Ezra and the Apocalypse of Baruch 70:9; and in several Dead Sea scrolls: 4Q174 (*Florilegium*), 4Q246 (*Aramaic Apocalypse*), and 1QSa 28a. Ladd, *Theology*, pp. 161-162, denies that Son of God was a common messianic designation in New Testament times, but he wrote prior to careful examination of several Dead Sea scroll texts.

The Son in the Synoptic Gospels

In the Synoptic Gospels, Son of God is a title that others sometimes use to refer to Jesus; it is not a title by which Jesus designated himself. Nevertheless, to portray Jesus as the Son of God was the purpose of Mark's Gospel:[64]

"The beginning of the gospel about Jesus Christ, the Son of God." (Mark 1:1)

Let's examine the various incidents in the first three (or Synoptic) Gospels where this title is used to see the development and meaning of this title.

When Jesus was twelve at the Temple: "Didn't you know I had to be in my Father's house?" (Luke 2:50).

As we'll see later in this lesson, at Jesus' baptism and transfiguration, the Father calls him "**my Beloved Son.**"

At Jesus' temptation: "If you are the **Son of God**..." (Matthew 4:3, 6). Satan takes the Father's words and twists them. His temptation to Jesus is two-pronged. First, Satan seeks to cast doubt on Jesus' title of Son of God. Second, he tempts Jesus to prove his title by performing miracles. Satan tempts Jesus to act like the Hellenistic miracle worker "son of God." Jesus steadfastly refuses, citing the Scriptures: "It is written...."[65]

When Jesus' encounters demons in people, they cry out: "I know who you are – **the Holy One of God!**" (Luke 4:34). Again: "You are **the Son of God!**" (Luke 4:41). Jesus didn't allow the demons to speak, not because what they said wasn't true, but precisely because it was true. Jesus did not want to be publicly characterized as Son of God, especially out of the mouths of evil spirits.[66] In one of the great confessions of the Bible, Peter declares:

"You are the Christ, the **Son of the living God.**" (Matthew 16:16)

In one of Jesus' prayers found in the Synoptic Gospels, we see Jesus' understanding of his Sonship:

---

[64] It is also the purpose of John's Gospel: "But these are written that you may believe that Jesus is the Christ, the Son of God, and that by believing you may have life in his name" (John 20:31).

[65] Is the idea of the messianic Son of God present in the temptation? Is Satan saying, "If you are the Messiah...."? I don't think so. The temptations have little to do with messianic expectations. Rather, they seek to turn the Father's Beloved into a puppet of Satan. As Ladd puts it, "Sonship is antecedent to messiahship, and not synonymous with it" (Ladd, *Theology,* p. 164).

[66] In Acts 16:17, an evil spirit in a slave girl has a similar understanding of who Paul is, "servants of the Most High God," but he also sought to prevent her from speaking this.

"All things have been committed to me by **my Father**. No one knows **the Son** except the Father, and no one knows the Father except **the Son** and those to whom **the Son** chooses to reveal him." (Matthew 11:27 = Luke 10:22)

This prayer sounds a good deal like the Father-Son vocabulary that we see in John.

Son of God in John's Gospel

Though Son of God is often used as a term of divinity in the Synoptic Gospels, in John's Gospel, that is the predominant use of the term. In John, Jesus talks openly of his relation to the Father as Son, which the Jews recognized was tantamount to "making himself equal with God" (John 5:18; cf. 10:33). You can see examples in John 5:17-27; 6:40; 10:25-37; 14:12-14; chapter 17; etc. John the Baptist is one of the first to recognize Jesus as divine:

"I have seen and I testify that this is **the Son of God**." (John 1:34)

Alternate Divine Titles

There are several titles that are similar to Son of God.

- **Son of the Blessed** (Mark 14:61). This title reflects the reticence of the high priest to utter the name of God.
- **Son of the Father** (KJV), **the Father's Son** (NIV, NRSV, ESV, 2 John 3).
- **Son of the Highest** (KJV), **Son of the Most High** (NIV, NRSV, ESV, Luke 1:32). "Most High" (Luke 1:35) reflects on of the early names of God in the Old Testament (Genesis 14:18-22).
- **Son of the Most High God** (Mark 5:7).

Q1. In what way does the title Son of God make Jesus equal with the Father? When you deal with the Son, is that the same as dealing with the Father? Do you know Jesus the Son of God? Do you love him?
http://www.joyfulheart.com/forums/topic/1615-q1-son-of-god/

My Beloved Son

Jesus is the one the Father loves. We see this idea in messianic prophecy: "my chosen, in whom my soul delights" (Isaiah 42:1). It is also in God's voice from heaven at both

Jesus' baptism and transfiguration: "This is **my beloved Son**, with whom I am well pleased (Matthew 3:17; 17:5), or "**my Son, the Beloved**" (NRSV).

At Jesus' baptism, we hear the Father's voice: "**You are my Son, the Beloved; with you I am well pleased.**" (NRSV, Mark 1:10-11 = Matthew 3:17 = Luke 3:22). Quoting Isaiah, Matthew says:

> "Behold, **my servant** whom I have chosen,
>   **my beloved** with whom my soul is well pleased." (Matthew 12:18, ESV, RSV, KJV)

The word "beloved" or "whom I love" is *agapētos*, "pertaining to one who is in a very special relationship with another, only, only beloved."[67] For example, *agapētos* is used in reference to an only son in the story of Abraham: "Take your son, your only son, Isaac, whom you love" (Genesis 22:2; Septuagint).

The words seem to echo, though not quote directly, the messianic psalm we mentioned earlier: "**You are my son**; today I have begotten you." (Psalms 2:7, NRSV). We also see an echo of another passage concerning the Servant of Yahweh: "**My chosen one in whom I delight**; I will put my Spirit on him..." (Isaiah 42:1). The idea is also in Paul's writings: **His Beloved Son** (NRSV, ESV), **His Dear Son** (KJV, Colossians 1:13) and **The Beloved** (Ephesians 1:6).

In the Parable of the Tenants (Mark 12:1-12 = Matthew 21:33-46 = Luke 20:9-19), Jesus is, in the allegory, "**a beloved son.**"

> **Q2. (Mark 1:10-11; Ephesians 1:6) If Jesus is the Father's Beloved, how can the Father send him to die? How does that make sense, given what we know of parental love? What does that say about God's love for us?**
> **http://www.joyfulheart.com/forums/topic/1616-q2-the-beloved/**

Jesus the "Only-Begotten"

One of the characteristic titles in John's Gospel is Jesus as God's "**only begotten**" (KJV, NASB), though modern translations tend to translate it as "One and Only" (NIV) or "only" (NRSV, ESV). The word in question is the adjective *monogenēs*, which means, "pertaining to being the only one of its kind within a specific relationship, one and only,

---

[67] *Agapētos*, BDAG 7, 1.

only."[68] Here, "pertaining to being the only one of its kind or class, unique (in kind)," of something that is the only example of its category.[69,70] Jesus is utterly unique. He is not just another created human being. He is unique from the Father.

Some scholars tell us that we shouldn't overly stress the idea of begetting, since technically the word derives from the verb *ginomai*, "be born, become," rather than *gennaō*, "beget."[71] However, since all nine uses in the New Testament are found in connection with a parent and child, begetting is clearly implied. I know some may disagree, but I think "only begotten" is a good and clear translation – *and* the sense in which the early Church Fathers understood the word. John uses *monogenēs* to describe Jesus five times in his writings:

> "The Word became flesh and made his dwelling among us. We have seen his glory, the glory of the **One and Only**, who came from the Father, full of grace and truth." (John 1:14)

> "No one has ever seen God, but **God the One and Only**, who is at the Father's side, has made him known." (John 1:18)

> "For God so loved the world that he gave **his one and only Son**, that whoever believes in him shall not perish but have eternal life." (John 3:16)

> "Whoever does not believe stands condemned already because he has not believed in the name of God's **one and only Son**." (John 3:18)

> "This is how God showed his love among us: He sent **his one and only Son** into the world that we might live through him." (1 John 4:9)

The prologue of John's Gospel and the word *monogenēs* had a very strong influence on orthodox Christology, as evidenced in the Nicene Creed (325, 381 AD). Note that the Church Fathers (for whom Greek was their native language) understood *monogenēs* in the sense of "begotten" rather than merely "unique."

---

[68] It is used in the New Testament as "only son" (of Abraham, Hebrews 11:17; of the widow of Nain, Luke 7:12; of the man with the demon-possessed son, Luke 9:38) and "only daughter" (of Jairus, Luke 8:42). In the Septuagint you see it with Jephthah's daughter, an only child (Judges 11:34).

[69] *Monogenēs*, BDAG 658, 2.

[70] Morris, *John*, p. 105, fn. 93.

[71] Morris, *John*, p. 105, fn. 93. This compound adjective is formed from *monos*, "sole, single" + *genos*, "kind." Brown (*John* 1:13) says, "*Monogenēs* describes a quality of Jesus, his uniqueness, not what is called in Trinitarian theology his 'procession.'"

"We believe ... in one Lord Jesus Christ, the **only-begotten**[72] Son of God, **begotten**[73] of the Father before all worlds, Light of Light, very God of very God, **begotten, not made**, being of one substance with the Father; by whom all things were made...."

John's use of the word *monogenēs* indicate that Jesus is utterly unique in his Sonship. We become sons and daughters of God by spiritual birth or adoption (depending upon which analogy you choose). Praise God! What a privilege this is! However, though we resemble Jesus, he is unique in his relationship to God, since he is the Son from eternity, the Second Person of the Trinity. He is not just another created human being who is a "son" or "child" by creation, or by new birth. Jesus is unique from the Father. He is the Only Begotten – in a class by himself, one of a kind.

The Only-Begotten God

One of the most remarkable sentences in the New Testament uses the word *monogenēs*.

"No one has ever seen God, but **God the One and Only**, who is at the Father's side, has made him known." (John 1:18)

What makes this so remarkable is that John seems to refer to Jesus as fully God "at the Father's side." He distinguishes between Jesus and the Father, but calls Jesus, "the Only Begotten God." Wow!

However, not all translations render this bold statement thus. While the earliest Greek manuscripts read "only-begotten God," the KJV, NKJV, and the New Jerusalem Bible (in the tradition of the Latin Vulgate), followed by the NRSV use the word "Son" instead of "God," following the majority of Greek manuscripts (though not the earliest).[74] Whatever the original text in this particular verse, John clearly places Jesus right next to God as fully divine (John 1:1-3, etc.).

---

[72] *Monogenēs.*

[73] *Gennaō.* The very Father-Son relationship supports the idea of "begetting" vs. "making."

[74] "Only begotten God" is found in a substantial number of the earliest texts (P66,75 Aleph[1,*], B C*, L, etc.), as well as in quotations from early Fathers such as Irenaeus, Origin, Didymus of Alexandria. "Only begotten Son" is found in A, C3, Θ, Ψ, f1,13, and the Byzantine texts, and Latin and Syriac translations. Clearly, the majority of Greek manuscripts support "only-begotten Son," but it seems that among the earliest Greek manuscripts more support "only-begotten God." You would expect it to read "only-begotten Son," because the phrase is used elsewhere (John 3:16, 18; 4:9; Hebrews 11:17). You wouldn't expect "only-begotten God." The field of Textual Criticism seeks to determine the original text from several principles. The original text is likely to have the strongest "external support" from the early Greek manuscripts. The original text is likely to be the "hardest reading," since you'd expect scribes to change a less-expected text to a more-expected text. For these reasons most modern translations agree with the majority of Editorial

Q3. (John 1:18) How does the title "Only Begotten God" signify Jesus' divinity? How does the Only Begotten Son differ from you and me as sons and daughters of God? What does "only-begotten" say about Jesus' status with the Father? About the costliness of the cross?
http://www.joyfulheart.com/forums/topic/1617-q3-only-begotten/

Lord (and Master)

Though it isn't clear unless you understand the background, Jesus title as Lord is a title of divinity. Let me explain.

The generic Hebrew word for God is *'El* or *'Elohim*. But God revealed himself to Moses with his own name: Yahweh. Moses is at the burning bush receiving a commission from God to deliver the Israelites from Egypt. During the conversation, Moses asks, "What is your name?"

> "God (*elohim*) said to Moses, 'I AM WHO I AM. This is what you are to say to the Israelites: "I AM has sent me to you."'" (Exodus 3:14)

God reveals to Moses his name in a new way: "I AM WHO I AM." What does it mean? The phrase consists of three words in Hebrew: the verb "to be" (*hāyā*)[75] occurs twice, and sandwiched between them is *'ashar*, a "particle of relation," that can be translated "that," "who," etc., depending on the context.[76] Since both verbs are in the Hebrew imperfect tense they can be translated either:

I AM WHO I AM	"He who is," the "Self-Existent One," OR
I WILL BE WHO I WILL BE	"He who will continue to be (present with his people)."

Committee of the United Bible Societies' Greek New Testament, which gives "only-begotten God" a {B} or "some degree of doubt" rating, on a scale of A to D (Metzger, *Textual Commentary*, p. 198).

[75] Albright and others suggest a slight emendation of the Hebrew text from the Qal stem, "to be," to the Hiphil stem, which carries the causative idea, "to cause to be." If you were to accept this theory, God would be saying, "I cause to be whom I cause to be," that is, a revelation of the Creator. However, since there is no known example of this verb in the Hiphil and the context of the passage doesn't talk about God as Creator, but God's role as the redeeming, covenant God, the Qal stem is preferred. (So Christopher J. H. Wright, "God, Names of," ISBE 2:507 and Victor P. Hamilton, *hāyā*, TWOT #491. On the other view David W. Baker, DOTP 362).

[76] *'Ashar*, BDB 81-84.

(This title extends into the New Testament in the title "Alpha and Omega," which we'll consider in Lesson 10.)

In English these four Hebrew letters (YHWH, called the Tetragrammaton) were formerly rendered "Jehovah" (KJV), but are better pronounced "Yahweh". However, in modern Bibles you rarely see the Divine Name given. As the pre-Christian era drew to a close, there was a strong movement among devout Jews to avoid pronouncing the Divine Name at all, lest they misuse it and break the commandment: "You shall not misuse the name of the Lord [Yahweh] your God, for the Lord will not hold anyone guiltless who misuses his name" (Exodus 20:7; Deuteronomy 6:11). Their avoidance even extended to reading the divine name from Scripture in the synagogue. It became the custom in the synagogue that when the reader came to YHWH, he would read it as *Adonai*, the Hebrew word for "Lord."

So most of our English Bibles follow this same tradition. In the Old Testament, when you see "Lord" in small caps, that indicates God's given name Yahweh. When you see "Lord" in upper and lower case that indicates the Hebrew word *Adonai*, "Lord."

All this linguistic history is confusing – but important. When the Bible was translated from Hebrew into the Greek Septuagint, YHWH (which the Jews pronounced as *Adonai*), was consistently rendered with the Greek word *kyrios*, "owner, one who is in charge by virtue of possession," then anyone in a position of authority, "lord, master." So in Judaism, the Greek *kyrios* was often used to refer to God himself.

Thus, to extend the title of "Lord" to Jesus means, at the very least, "master, superior," but is usually intended to refer to Jesus as divine. The characteristic Christian statement of faith is, "**Jesus is Lord**" (1 Corinthians 12:3).

Thus, the title, "Lord Jesus Christ" contains a powerful and comprehensive statement about who Jesus is! He is God himself! Let's consider some of the combinations used with "Lord."

- **Lord** (often)
- **Lord and Savior Jesus Christ** (2 Peter 1:11; 3:18)
- **Lord Christ** (Colossians 3:24)
- **Lord from heaven** (KJV, 1 Corinthians 15:47) seems to be a gloss added to explain the nature of the "man from heaven," and does not occur in the earliest Greek manuscripts.[77]
- **Lord Jesus Christ**, is used extensively, especially in Paul's epistles.[78]

---

[77] Metzger, *Textual Commentary*, p. 568.

- **Lord Jesus** is also used extensively, especially in Acts and in Paul's epistles.[79]
- **One Lord** (Ephesians 4:5)
- **Lord both of the dead and living** (Romans 14:9). This title, the text explains, was won by Christ's resurrection.
- **The Lord, the God of the spirits of the prophets** (Revelation 22:6)

Lord of glory (1 Corinthians 2:8) seems to echo Psalm 24 which speaks of the "King of glory." The phrase "our glorious Lord Jesus Christ" (James 2:1) also contains this idea.

Lord of lords (Revelation 17:14; 19:16; 1 Timothy 6:15) is used in the context of "king of kings." It is an emperor's title, one who is the ultimate king, with other kings and lords subservient to him. A similar title is given to God in Deuteronomy 10:17 and Psalm 136:3.

Lord of the Sabbath (Matthew 12:8; Mark 2:28; Luke 6:5). By Jesus' masterful explanation of the true purpose and meaning of the Sabbath, he demonstrates that he as the heavenly Son of Man is also Lord of the Sabbath, that is, the One who knows and created Sabbath's true meaning.

The Lord Our Righteousness (Jeremiah 23:6). Jeremiah has prophesied that God will raise up among David's descendents "a righteous Branch, a King who will reign wisely, and do what is just and right in the land." This King will be called: "The LORD (that is, Yahweh) Our Righteousness." Because this prophecy is about the coming Messiah, it is a powerful statement of Jesus' divinity, that he will both demonstrate *and* bring righteousness. In the New Testament we see the corollaries:

> "It is because of him that you are in Christ Jesus, who has become for us wisdom from God – that is, **our righteousness,** holiness and redemption." (1 Corinthians 1:30)

> "God made him who had no sin to be sin for us, so that in him we might become **the righteousness of God**." (2 Corinthians 5:21)

---

[78] "Lord Jesus Christ": Acts 11:17; 15:26; 28:31; Romans 1:7; 5:1, 11; 13:14; 15:6, 30; 1 Corinthians 1:2, 3, 7, 8, 10; 6:11; 8:6; 15:57; 2 Corinthians 1:2, 3; 8:9; 13:14; Galatians 1:3; 6:14, 18; Ephesians 1:2, 3, 17; 5:20; 6:23, 24; Philippians 1:2; 3:20; 4:23; Colossians 1:3; 1 Thessalonians 1:1, 3; 5:9, 23, 28; 2 Thessalonians 1:1, 2, 12; 2:1, 14, 16; 3:6, 12, 18; 1 Timothy 6:3, 14; Philemon 3, 25; James 1:1; 2:1; 1 Peter 1:3; 2 Peter 1:8, 14, 16; Jude 17, 21.

[79] "Lord Jesus": Matthew 16:19; Luke 24:3; Acts 1:21; 4:33; 7:59; 8:16; 9:17; 11:20; 15:11; 16:31; 19:5, 13, 17; 20:21, 24, 35; 21:13; Romans 14:4; 16:20; 1 Corinthians 5:4 (twice); 11:23; 16:23; 2 Corinthians 1:14; 4:14; 11:31; Ephesians 1:15; Philippians 2:19; Colossians 3:17; 1 Thessalonians 2:15, 19; 3:11; 3:13; 4:1, 2; 2 Thessalonians 1:7, 8; 2:8; Philemon 1:5; Hebrews 13:20; Revelation 22:20.

"... Jesus Christ, **the Righteous One**. He is the atoning sacrifice for our sins...." (1 John 2:1-2).

See more above in Lesson 6 on Jesus as the holy and righteous one.

Lord of all. "For there is no difference between Jew and Gentile – the same Lord is **Lord of all** and richly blesses all who call on him" (Romans 10:12). "Lord over all" (KJV). Also Acts 10:36.

Finally, Simeon is promised that he will not die before seeing "**the Lord's Christ**" (Luke 2:26). Here "Lord" refers to Yahweh, not Jesus.

Q4. Why is the title "Lord Jesus" such an exalted one. What does it tell us about Jesus' divinity?
http://www.joyfulheart.com/forums/topic/1618-q4-lord-jesus/

Lord and Rabbi

As we saw in Lesson 2, the KJV uses "master" to translate *didaskalos*, a common form of address for a rabbi, though most modern versions translate this as "teacher." Several times in Luke's Gospel, Jesus is called "**master**," *epistatēs*, an administrative technical term used for various officials.[80]

But it is also true that sometimes in the Gospels, when Jesus is addressed as "**lord**" (*kyrios*), the speaker is using the sense of someone in a position of authority, "lord, master."[81] This title was sometimes used as a term of respect by a disciple for a rabbi, an acknowledgement that the rabbi had the power to command the disciple.

This is particularly evident in two passages from Luke's Gospel.

"[Jesus] said, 'Follow me.' But he said, '**Lord** (*kyrios*), let me first go and bury my father.' And Jesus said to him, 'Leave the dead to bury their own dead. But as for you, go and proclaim the kingdom of God.' Yet another said, "I will follow you, **Lord** (*kyrios*), but let me first say farewell to those at my home." Jesus said to him, 'No one who puts his hand to the plow and looks back is fit for the kingdom of God.'" (Luke 9:59-62)

"Why do you call me, '**Lord, Lord**,' and do not do what I say?" (Luke 6:46)

---

[80] *Epistatēs*, BDAG 38. Luke 5:5; 8:24, 45; 9:33, 49; 17:13.
[81] For example, Matthew 15:22, 25, 27; 17:15; 20:30, 31, 33; Luke 5:8, 12; 7:6; 9:54, 59, 61; 10:40; 11:1; 12:41.

We use the title "Lord" so lightly. If Jesus is our Lord, then we shouldn't hesitate to obey immediately. Rather than just mouth the word, we must do what he says. He is Lord God of all. He is also the Lord who has absolute authority over us, his disciples.

> **Q5. (Luke 9:59-62; 6:46) Is Jesus our Lord if we don't obey him immediately? Is he our Lord if we don't follow his teachings? What areas of your life do you need to surrender to his Lordship?**
> http://www.joyfulheart.com/forums/topic/1619-q5-jesus-lordship/

The "I Am" Sayings in John's Gospel

John's Gospel includes a number of passages that emphasize Jesus' deity by placing two Greek words together, *egō eimi*, "**I am.**"[82] When these words are used emphatically, "I am" is a rather unveiled reference to the name by which God revealed himself to Moses as Yahweh – "I AM THAT I AM" (Exodus 3:14). In saying "I am" in this way, Jesus is declaring his divinity and oneness with the Father.

Here are the "I AM" passages found in John that include a predicate:

"I am the bread of life" (John 6:35, 48, 51).

"I am the light of the world" (John 8:12, cf. 9:5).

"I am the gate for the sheep" (John 10:7, 9).

"I am the good shepherd" (John 10:11, 14).

"I am the resurrection and the life" (John 11:25).

"I am the way, the truth, and the life" (John 14:6).

"I am the vine" (John 15:1, 5).

It is no coincidence that John emphasizes Jesus' "I AM" statements. He wants his readers to believe in Jesus as the Son of God and have eternal life (John 20:31).

> **Q6. Since Yahweh seems to be formed from "I AM" as God's own name, what is the significance of Jesus' "I am" statements? Which of these "I am" statements means the most to you personally?**
> http://www.joyfulheart.com/forums/topic/1620-q6-i-am/

---

[82] There are more verses in John translated, "I am," but in most cases they don't include the pronoun *egō*, which can be implied by the verb *eimi* itself, since in Greek the distinctive inflection of the verb tells us gender, tense, and voice. When the pronoun appears with the verb, it is emphatic – there to make a point.

Jesus as God

In this lesson we've examined "Son of God, "Only Begotten," and "Lord" as divine titles. It is clear that during Jesus' ministry, his enemies saw the implications of his words, and the titles his followers used as blasphemy (John 19:4), that he was "making himself equal with God" (John 5:18). Now we come to a series of references that place Jesus on the same level as God the Father.

In a clear messianic passage from Isaiah we see the Messiah with explicitly divine titles.

> "For to us a child is born,
> to us a son is given,
> and the government will be on his shoulders.
> And he will be called Wonderful Counselor,
> **Mighty God**,
> **Everlasting Father**,
> Prince of Peace." (Isaiah 9:6)

Paul also declares Jesus, without qualification, as God over all.

> "To [the Jewish people] belong the patriarchs, and from their race, according to the flesh, is **the Christ, who is God over all**, blessed forever. Amen." (Romans 9:5, ESV)

Thomas's confession when Christ appears to him after the resurrection is one of the most profound of any disciple.

> "Then he said to Thomas, 'Put your finger here, and see my hands; and put out your hand, and place it in my side. Do not disbelieve, but believe.' Thomas answered him, '**My Lord and my God!**'" (John 20:27-28)

In Revelation 1:8 it appears that Jesus is speaking and has the title "**the Lord God**" and "**the Almighty**" (*pantokratōr*), though the speaker could be God the Father.[83] But often in Revelation and elsewhere, titles used of God are then used of Christ as well. As the early church developed, *Pantokratōr*, which means, "Almighty, All-Powerful, Omnipotent (One)," became a title of Christ, especially in the Eastern Orthodox Church. The icon of Christ Pantocrator is one of the most widely used religious images of Orthodox Christianity.

As we saw in Lesson 2, at the beginning of John's Gospel, Jesus, the Logos, is declared to be God.

---

[83] In Revelation 15:3, Lord God Almighty (*pantokratōr*)" seems to be addressed to God.

> "In the beginning was the Word,
> and the Word was with God,
> and **the Word was God**." (John 1:1)

John's first epistle concludes with a similar declaration.

> "And we are in him who is true – even in his Son Jesus Christ. **He is the true God** and eternal life." (1 John 5:20)

Some writers would add here titles in the Old Testament that might refer to the Christ, but probably refer to Yahweh. We'll show restraint.

Image of Invisible God

Finally, Paul and the writer of Hebrews see in the visible Jesus, the incarnation of the Invisible God.

> "Who is **the image of the invisible God**...." (Colossians 1:15)

> "The Son is the radiance of God's glory and **the exact representation of his being**, sustaining all things by his powerful word...." (Hebrews 1:3a)

We see this explained in John's Gospel in a somewhat different way.

> "Philip said to him, 'Lord, show us the Father, and it is enough for us.'
> Jesus said to him, 'Have I been with you so long, and you still do not know me, Philip? Whoever has seen me has seen the Father. How can you say, 'Show us the Father'?'" (John 14:8-9)

Jesus is God in the flesh! Incidentally, the title "God manifest in the flesh" (KJV) relies on less reliable manuscripts. Modern translations render this verse as, "He was manifested in the flesh...." (1 Timothy 3:16).[84]

Emmanuel, God with Us

"**Emmanuel**" or "**Immanuel**" (depending upon how one spells it) is a transliteration of the Hebrew name in Isaiah 7:14, literally meaning, "with us is God."[85] The name originally symbolized the presence of God (*'el*) to deliver his people from the Assyrian army that threatened their very existence in Isaiah's day. However, Matthew 1:23 takes Isaiah 7:14 messianically, and applies the name of the child of the virgin as prophecy of

---

[84] Metzger (*Textual Commentary*, p. 641) sees "He" as supported by "external evidence and transcriptional probability," which best explains the other readings. It is supported by "the earliest and best uncials (Aleph*, A*, C* G^gr. D* is similar).

[85] BDB 769.

Jesus. The title Immanuel certainly applied to Jesus, since "God with us" is a perfect way to describe the birth of the God-Man, Jesus Christ, who is fully man and fully God.

The Bible is rather clear. Jesus is not a mere man, a good and great man. He is God himself, God in the flesh. Thus how we believe his words, how we obey his teachings, how we serve him, how we love Jesus, reflect how much we really love God. My prayer for you is that you may fulfill the first great commandment, to love God with all your heart, soul, mind, and strength in your devotion to his Son Jesus.

Prayer

Father, thank you for sending to us your Only Son, your Beloved Son. Help us to love him as you do. Thank you for your sacrifice of the one closest to you that we might be saved. It's hard to understand how this can be, but we profoundly thank you. In Jesus' name, we pray. Amen.

Names and Titles of Jesus

My Son (often)
Son of God (many times)
The Son (many times in John; also Matthew 11:27; Luke 10:22)
Son of the Blessed (Mark 14:61)
Son of the Father (KJV, 2 John 1:3)
Son of the Highest (KJV, Luke 1:32)
Son of the Living God (Matthew 16:16)
Son of the Most High (NIV, NRSV, ESV, Luke 1:32)
Son of the Most High God (Mark 5:7)
The Father's Son (NIV, NRSV, ESV, 2 John 1:3)
Only Begotten of the Father (KJV, John 1:14)
Only Begotten Son (KJV, John 1:18; 3:16, 18; 1 John 4:9)
One and Only (NIV, John 1:14)
One and Only Son (NIV, John 3:16, 18; 1 John 4:9)
God the One and Only (NIV, John 1:18)
Only Son (ESV, NRSV; John 3:16, 18; 1 John 4:9)
I Am (several times in John)
Beloved Son (Matthew 3:17; 17:5; Colossians 1:13; Mark 12:6)
Dear Son (KJV, Colossians 1:13)
The Beloved (Ephesians 1:6)

My Beloved (Matthew 12:18, ESV, RSV, KJV)

Mighty God (Isaiah 9:6)

The Almighty (Revelation 1:8)

Everlasting Father (Isaiah 9:6)

Lord (often)

Lord and Savior Jesus Christ (2 Peter 1:11; 3:18)

Lord Christ (Colossians 3:24).

Lord from heaven (KJV, 1 Corinthians 15:47)

Lord Jesus Christ (often)

Lord Jesus (often)

Lord of all (Acts 10:36)

One Lord (Ephesians 4:5)

Lord of glory (1 Corinthians 2:8; Psalm 24)

Lord of lords (Revelation 17:14; 19:16; 1 Timothy 6:15)

Lord of the Sabbath (Matthew 12:8; Mark 2:28; Luke 6:5)

The Lord Our Righteousness (Jeremiah 23:6)

Our Righteousness (1 Corinthians 1:30)

The Righteousness of God (2 Corinthians 5:21)

Righteous One (1 John 2:1-2)

Lord of all (Romans 10:12)

Lord both of the dead and living (Romans 14:9)

The Lord, the God of the spirits of the prophets (Revelation 22:6)

Lord God (Revelation 1:8)

God over All (Romans 9:5)

My Lord and My God (John 20:28)

God (John 1:1)

The True God (1 John 5:20)

The Image of the Invisible God (Colossians 1:15)

The Exact Representation of His Being (Hebrews 1:3a)

Emmanuel, Immanuel (Isaiah 7:14; Matthew 1:23)

Songs and Hymns

The titles in this lesson center around Jesus revealed as divine, with key titles, such as I Am, Son of god, Only Begotten, One and Only, Beloved Son, Mighty God, Everlasting Father, Lord, Righteous One, My Lord and My God, Emmanuel, etc.

"Come, O Come, Emmanuel," words: 12th century; music: 15th century

"Cornerstone" ("My hope is built on nothing less than Jesus' blood and righteousness"), by Edward Mote, Eric Liljero, Jonas Myrin, Reuben Morgan, William Batchelder Bradbury (© 2011 Hillsong Music Publishing)

"Emmanuel" ("His name is called Emmanuel"), by Bob McGee (© 1976, C.A. Music)

"Emmanuel" ("My Shepherd King, you're watching over me"), by Reuben Morgan (© 2005 Hillsong Music Publishing)

"God With Us" ("Oh Emmanuel God with us"), by Jason Ingram and Leslie Jordan (© 2012, Integrity's Praise Music)

"Hark, the Herald Angels Sing" ("Veiled in flesh the Godhead see; Hail th'incarnate Deity, Pleased with us in flesh to dwell, Jesus our Emmanuel"), words: Charles Wesley (1739), music: Felix Mendelssohn (1840)

"He Is Lord," author unknown

"He's the Lord of Glory" ("He is the great I am ... the everlasting Father"), by Phyllis C. Spiers (© 1950, 1962, Gospel Publishing House)

"His Banner Over Me is Love" ("I am my Beloved's and he is mine"), unknown author.

"His Banner Over Me," by Kevin Prosch (© 1991 Mercy / Vineyard Publishing)

"Holy" ("Jesus You Are"; "You're the Great I Am ... You will come again in glory to judge the living and the dead"), by Jason Ingram, Jonas Myrin, Matt Redman (© 2011 Atlas Mountain Songs)

"How Majestic Is Your Name" ("Prince of Peace, Mighty God"), by Michael W. Smith (© 1981, Meadowgreen Music Co.)

"I Am," by Michael W. Smith and Wayne Hillard (© 1980 Designer Music Group, Inc.)

"I Am" ("Maker of the heavens, Bright and Morning Star ... Fount of Living Water, the Risen Son of Man, the Healer of the Broken .. Savior and Redeemer ... Author and Perfecter, Beginning and the End"), by Mark Schultz (© 2005 Crazy Romaine Music)

"I Will Look Up" ("Jesus, Lord of All ... Prince of Peace, Perfect Healer, King of Kings, Mighty Savior"), Chris Brown, Jason Ingram, Mack Brock, Matt Redman, Wade Joye (© 2013 Said And Done Music)

"Jesus Messiah" ("Blessed Redeemer, Emmanuel") by Chris Tomlin, Daniel Carson, Ed Cash, Jesse Reeves (2008 sixsteps Music)

"Jesus Son of God," Chris Tomlin, Jason Ingram, Matt Maher (© 2012 S. D. G. Publishing, sixsteps)

"Jesus the Son of God," words and music: Garfield T. Haywood (c. 1914)

"Jesus, Name Above All Names" ("Beautiful Savior, Glorious Lord, Emmanuel, God with Us, Blessed Redeemer, Living Word" by Naida Hearn (1974, 1978 Scripture In Song)

"Jesus, Only Jesus" (He is our hope, our righteousness ... Holy, King Almighty Lord"), by Christ Tomlin, Matt Redman, et al. (© 2013 S. D. G. Publishing)

"Joy to the World" ("the Lord is come ... the Savior reigns"), words: Isaac Watts, music: Antioch, arranged by Lowell Mason (1836)

"Lord I Need You" ("my one defense, my righteousness"), by Christy Nockels, Daniel Carson, Jesse Reeves, Kristian Stanfill, Matt Maher (© 2011, sixsteps Music)

"My Hope is Built on Nothing Less" ("than Jesus' blood and righteousness ... on Christ the solid rock I stand"), words: Edward Mote (1834), music: Solid Rock: William B. Bradbury (1863)

"Sing, Sing, Sing" ("Lift high the name of Jesus ... Song of God, You are the One"), by Chris Tomlin, Daniel Carson, Jesse Reeves, Matt Gilder, Travis Nunn (© 2008, sixsteps Music)

"This Is Amazing Grace" ("Worthy is the Lamb who was slain"), by Jeremy Riddle, Josh Farro, Phil Wickham (© 2012 Phil Wickham Music)

"We Will Glorify" (We will glorify the King of kings ... "who is the great I Am"), by Twila Paris (1982 New Spring)

"When I Survey the Wondrous Cross" ("Save in the death of Christ my God"), words: Isaac Watts (1707), music: Hamburg, Lowell Mason (1824)

"Worthy Is the Lamb" ("High and lifted up Jesus Son of God") by Darlene Zschech (© 2002, Hillsong Publishing)

"Your Great Name" ("Son of God and man") by Krissy Nordhoff and Michael Neele (2008, Integrity's Praise! Music)

Exercises

From Appendix 6. Exercises to Help You Internalize the Names of Jesus, select some activities that will help you internalize the truths of this lesson's names, titles, descriptors, and metaphors. This week, how can you creatively pray, meditate, write, worship, consider, draw or paint, compose, picture, and live out these truths in your community?

Actively participating in these ways will help you grow to be like Christ.

6. Jesus the Lamb of God, Holy and Righteous One

The Apostle Peter wrote:

> "You were redeemed ... with the precious blood of Christ, a lamb without blemish or defect." (1 Peter 1:18-19)

This passage capsulizes two themes we'll explore in this lesson: (1) Jesus' righteousness and holiness – that he was without blemish or defect – and (2) Jesus' sacrificial death for our sins, "the righteous for the unrighteous" to bring us to God (1 Peter 3:18).

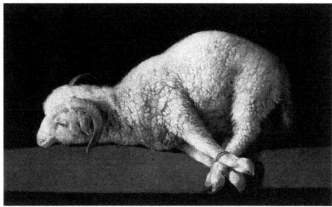

"Agnus Dei" (1635-40), Francisco de Zurburan (1598-1664), oil on canvas 38 x 62 cm., Museo Nacional del Prado, Madrid

Holiness and Righteousness

We'll begin by exploring Jesus' titles that relate to his holiness and righteousness. At the outset, it will help to differentiate between these two related concepts.

1. "Righteous" is the adjective *dikaios*, "pertaining to being in accordance with high standards of rectitude, upright, just, fair."[86] This is how a person might describe an upstanding man or woman who lived according to the laws of God and man.

2. "Holy," on the other hand, is a more theological descriptor, used sparingly. The adjective is *hagios*, "dedicated or consecrated to the service of God," or when used as a substantive, the word means simply "the holy (thing or person)." This word is used to describe the temple, angels, Christ, and God himself. God's people are called "saints" or "holy ones."[87]

---

[86] *Dikaios*, BDAG 24, 1bβ.
[87] *Hagios*, BDAG 11.

Absolute Goodness

We'll start with the concept of righteousness. The rich young ruler meets Jesus desiring eternal life.

> "'**Good teacher**,' he asked, 'what must I do to inherit eternal life?' 'Why do you call me good?' Jesus answered. 'No one is good – except God alone.'" (Mark 10:17-18; cf. Luke 18:18)[88]

The young man was using "good" loosely, with mild flattery. But Jesus insisted that he see true goodness as residing in God alone. No mere man is "good" or "righteous" in an absolute sense. Jesus isn't denying his absolute "goodness" in this passage. Rather, he is forcing the rich young ruler to see him with clarity.

Jesus is affirmed as righteous at his trial before Pilate (John 19:46).

> "While [Pilate] was sitting on the judgment seat, his wife sent word to him, 'Have nothing to do with **that righteous man**, for I have suffered much because of him today in a dream.'" (Matthew 27:19, ESV)

The word is *dikaios*, "righteous," which is also translated "**that innocent man**" (NIV, NRSV) and "**that just man**" (KJV).[89] The term is used again at the cross by the centurion:

> "Surely this was a **righteous man**." (Luke 23:47, NIV)

The Righteous One

Pilate's wife and the centurion used "righteous" in the sense of innocent of charges, upstanding. However, following Christ's resurrection, the word is used by Jesus' followers with all its theological fullness – absolute righteousness. Jesus is not merely "relatively good." He is the only Righteous One by virtue of his divinity.

Just before Stephen was stoned, he proclaimed Jesus as "**the Righteous One**. And now you have betrayed and murdered him" (Acts 7:52, NIV, NRSV, ESV). The KJV calls him "**the Just One**." Ananias declared to the newly converted Paul:

---

[88] In Matthew 19:16, the KJV "good master" adds the adjective "good" to *didaskalos*, to conform it to parallel accounts in other gospels. "Good" is "absent from early and good representatives of the Alexandrian and the Western texts, was manifestly brought in by copyists from the parallel accounts" (Mark 10:17; Luke 18:18) (Metzger, *Textual Commentary*, p. 49).

[89] Some manuscripts record the term again in Pilate's mouth (Matthew 27:24, KJV). Metzger (*Textual Commentary*, p. 68) notes that the words *tou dikaiou* don't occur "in the best representatives of the Alexandrian, Western, and Caesarean texts." He give the reading a {B} "some degree of doubt" designation.

"The God of our fathers has chosen you to know his will and to see **the Righteous One** and to hear words from his mouth." (Acts 22:14)

KJV translates it "**that Just One**."After Peter and John healed the crippled beggar at the temple, Peter proclaimed to the assembled crowds:

"You disowned the **Holy and Righteous One**[90] and asked that a murderer be released to you." (Acts 3:14)

Jesus, the representative Man, is righteous. "He committed no sin, and no deceit was found in his mouth" (1 Peter 2:22; quoting Isaiah 53:9). He alone is worthy to die for the sins of all mankind (Revelation 5:12).

Righteous Branch

There is another theme in messianic prophecy the points to the righteousness and justice of the Messiah. We saw in Lesson 4 the "righteous branch" of David's family tree who is to come.

"'The days are coming,' declares the LORD,
'when I will raise up to David a **righteous Branch**,
a King who will reign wisely
and do what is just and right in the land.'" (Jeremiah 23:5)

"In those days and at that time
I will cause a **righteous Branch** to spring up for David,
and he shall execute justice and righteousness in the land." (Jeremiah 33:15)

Isaiah also proclaims that his Servant "will bring justice to the nations" (Isaiah 42:1).

In Israel, the king is the ultimate Chief Justice in the land. All the hardest cases are brought to him. If the king's justice is corrupt and for sale, then his example will be followed by all the judges under him. But if he is righteous, then his kingdom will be a righteous kingdom. As we'll see in a moment, Jesus will come as the Righteous Judge over all at the end of the Age.

In the great Suffering Servant passage we'll consider later in this lesson, Jesus is called "**the righteous one**."

"**The righteous one**, **my servant**, shall make many righteous,
and he shall bear their iniquities." (Isaiah 53:11b)

---

[90] KJV: "the Holy One and the Just."

Ironically, the Righteous One inserts himself on our behalf. He is the righteous sacrifice who takes our place to atone for our sins. He bears our sins on himself.

"For Christ died for sins once for all,
the righteous for the unrighteous,
to bring you to God." (1 Peter 3:18a)

The Apostle John urges his disciples not to sin. But then he reminds them:

"But if anyone does sin, we have **an Advocate** with the Father, **Jesus Christ the Righteous**." (1 John 2:1)

Our Righteousness

Jesus is in himself the Righteous and Holy One. When he lives in us and we in him, he infuses his own righteousness into our lives.

"He is the source of your life in Christ Jesus, who became for us wisdom from God, and **righteousnes**s and sanctification and redemption." (1 Corinthians 1:30)

Through Jesus, as the New Israel, we will fulfill the New Covenant proclaimed by Jeremiah. And he will be given a grand title:

"In his days Judah will be saved and Israel will live in safety.
This is the name by which he will be called:
The LORD Our Righteousness." (Jeremiah 23:6)

Righteous Judge

Because Jesus is the Righteous One, he alone is fit to be our Judge on the Last Day. Israel viewed Yahweh as the Righteous Judge, Lawgiver, and King (Isaiah 33:22). Before he appointed kings to govern his people, the loose confederation of Israelite tribes were governed by judges, as described in the Books of Judges and 1 Samuel. Some of these were military leaders. But all had the role of settling the cases brought to them, a role later taken over by the king (e.g., 2 Samuel 15:1-4), as seen in King Solomon's famous decision to divide a disputed baby in half, thus revealing the true mother (1 Kings 3:16-28).

Paul calls Jesus, "**the Lord, the righteous Judge**" (2 Timothy 4:8), pointing to the judgment at the Last Day. We'll wait to explore further Jesus as Judge until Lesson 10.

Jesus is righteous in judicial terms; it is he who justifies us, that is, declares us righteous. He thus calls us to be righteous in our dealings – honesty, truthfulness, fairness, etc. We must also treat the poor, the homeless, and immigrants with righteousness, because we serve a righteous Lord.

The Holy One

Now we turn to Jesus as the Holy One, the one who is sacred, who belongs to God and is set apart for his Father's purposes.

The idea of holiness draws on concepts of holiness by which God revealed himself and taught holiness to Israel. The primary lessons of God's holiness came in the wilderness after God had delivered the people out of Egypt. Yahweh appeared in fire and thunder on Mt. Sinai. When the people rebelled and turned to other gods, he disciplined them. Through the tabernacle and priesthood he taught them the importance of setting people and things apart for God's exclusive ownership and service, and thus taught the holiness of God and of his people. The wilderness was a training ground in holiness.

> "Consecrate yourselves and be holy, because I am the LORD your God. Keep my decrees and follow them. I am the LORD, who makes you holy." (Leviticus 20:7-8)

This is echoed in the New Testament.

> "As obedient children, do not conform to the evil desires you had when you lived in ignorance. But just as he who called you is holy, so be holy in all you do; for it is written: 'Be holy, because I am holy.'" (1 Peter 1:14-16, quoting Leviticus 11:44-45; 19:1; 20:7)

In our conduct, our words, and our thoughts, God calls us to live like his people, not like a bunch of pagans.

In the Old Testament, God is called "the Holy One of Israel" (Isaiah 41:14; 54:5). As God the Father is Holy, so is Jesus the Son. The use of "Holy One" with regard to Jesus is one indication of Jesus' deity. At the Annunciation, the angel Gabriel explains to Mary about the child she shall bear:

> "The Holy Spirit will come upon you, and the power of the Most High will over-shadow you. So the **holy one** to be born will be called the Son of God." (Luke 1:35)

Ironically, a demon recognizes its own uncleanness before this Holy Jesus, saying,

> "I know who you are – **the Holy One of God**!" (Mark 1:24b)

In the apostles' early preaching we see the phrase also, quoting Psalm 16:10, applying the passage to Jesus.

"You will not abandon me to the grave,
nor will you let your **Holy One** see decay." (Acts 2:27)

Later, Peter says of Jesus:

"You disowned the **Holy and Righteous One**
and asked that a murderer be released to you." (Acts 3:14)

The Apostle Paul, reflecting on Jesus' work of making us holy before God, says,

"It is because of him that you are in Christ Jesus, who has become for us wisdom from God – that is, our **righteousness, holiness** and redemption." (1 Corinthians 1:30)

The implications of serving a holy God for you and me is to seek to live holy lives. To do else is a mockery.

"God's solid foundation stands firm, sealed with this inscription: 'The Lord knows those who are his,' and, 'Everyone who confesses the name of the Lord must turn away from wickedness.'" (2 Timothy 2:19)

"Make every effort to live in peace with all men and to be holy; without holiness no one will see the Lord." (Hebrews 12:14)

Q1. What does Jesus' holiness and righteousness demand of our lives as his disciples? In the Parable of the Sheep and the Goats, what was the primary characteristic of the sheep vs. the goats?
http://www.joyfulheart.com/forums/topic/1621-q1-holiness-and-righteousness/

The Lamb of God

Closely related to the theme of Christ's righteousness and holiness is Jesus, the perfect Sacrifice, Jesus the Lamb of God, "a lamb without blemish or defect" (1 Peter 1:19).

John the Baptist is preaching a message of repentance and baptism for the forgiveness of sins. Thousands have come to him as he is baptizing along the Jordan River. One day, John speaks about the Messiah, for whom he has been sent to prepare.

"John saw Jesus coming toward him and said, 'Look, **the Lamb of God**, who takes away the sin of the world!'" (John 1:29)

John repeats this saying a little later (John 1:36). Let's look at this verse phrase by phrase.

- **"Lamb,"** the Greek noun *amnos*, refers to a young sheep, including at least up to one year old.[91] In the Book of Revelation we find the noun *arnion*, used to designate a sheep of any age.[92]
- **"Of God"** can mean either "sent from God" or perhaps "owned by God." John says that Jesus is in some way like a lamb sent from or provided by God himself.
- **"Sin"** is the common Greek noun *harmartia*. Originally it meant "to miss the mark, be mistaken." In the New Testament it occurs 173 times as a comprehensive expression of everything opposed to God.[93]
- **"Of the world"** employs the Greek noun *kosmos*, which refers here to "humanity in general."[94]
- **"Take away"** describes what the Lamb will do with sin, employing the Greek verb *airō*, which means generally "to lift up and move from one place to another." Here it means "to take away, remove, blot out."[95]

Animal Sacrifice

John the Baptist indicates that Jesus is the Lamb of God in some sacrificial sense, since lambs were commonly used by the Jews for sacrifices to obtain forgiveness for sin.

Nearly every culture throughout the world has employed sacrifice, usually animal sacrifice, to somehow appease the anger of the gods. Abraham, Isaac, and Jacob sacrificed to God as part of their worship. God provides animal sacrifice as a way that justice can be done, that men's and women's sins can be atoned for, and that they can approach God once more.

We moderns are often repulsed by the very idea of killing an animal. The Israelites were herdsmen. Our forebears were farmers who raised and slaughtered animals. But city folk don't routinely butcher animals, drain out their blood, and cut them up. The closest many people come is cold meat in a Styrofoam tray or butcher's wrap from the market. Most of us eat meat, but we are insulated from the killing that is required.

---

[91] *Amnos*, BDAG 54.

[92] *Arnion*, BDAG 133.

[93] Walther Günther, "Sin," NIDNTT 3:573-583.

[94] *Kosmos*, BDAG 562.

[95] *Airō*, BDAG 28. Joachim Jeremias (*airō*, TDNT 1:185-186) indicates that *airo* can refer here to either the substitutionary bearing of penalty (if the Suffering Servant of Isaiah 53 is in mind) or "the setting aside of sin by the expiatory power of the death of Jesus." Jeremias prefers the latter approach.

Nevertheless, taking of any life should affect us as it affected the Israelites. The Israelites were very well aware that blood required taking of life. And taking life, even to eat, is never a trivial thing. God tells Moses:

> "For the life of a creature is in the blood, and I have given it to you to make atonement for yourselves on the altar; it is the blood that makes atonement for one's life." (Leviticus 17:11)

The word translated "atonement" here is the Hebrew verb *kāpar, kipper*, "to make an atonement, make reconciliation, purge."[96] Our English word "atonement" comes from the Middle English "at-one-ment" or "reconciliation," which expresses the result of an atoning sacrifice. To sum up, "atonement" in Hebrew seems to mean, "to wipe clean, purge," a sacrifice that cleanses from sin.

Behold, the Lamb of God

That is the context from which John the Baptist speaks when he says, "Behold, the **Lamb of God** who takes away the sin of the world" (John 1:29). Jesus is greater than our analogies, of course. But there is a sense in which the metaphor of the sacrificial Lamb fits Jesus accurately, since he, as Holy and Righteous Son of God is the only one perfect and great enough to actually atone for sin and, at the same time, represent and substitute for all in this atonement – once and for all. Look! This is the Lamb of God, who takes away the sin of the world!

Throughout the New Testament we see this theme of Jesus the Lamb of God (John 1:29, 36), who is our sacrifice for sin. Some of these are used as metaphors, if not actual titles.

- **Lamb** occurs numerous times in the Book of Revelation (5:6, 8; 6:16; 7:9-10, 17; 12:11; 13:8, 11; 14:1, 4; 15:3; 17:14; 19:7, 9; 21:9, 14, 22-23, 27).
- **Our Passover lamb** (NIV, ESV), **our paschal lamb** (NRSV), **our Passover** (KJV, 1 Corinthians 5:7). The Greek word is *pascha*.[97]
- **Propitiation** (KJV, ESV) **Atoning Sacrifice** (NIV, NRSV).[98] As we saw earlier in this lesson, John writes:

---

[96] An equivalent Arabic root means "cover" or "conceal," but evidence that the Hebrew root means "to cover over sin" is weak. Rather, the root idea of *kipper* seems to be "to purge," related to an Akkadian cognate *kuppuru* meaning "to wipe clean." Richard E. Averbeck, "Sacrifices and Offerings," DOTP 706-732, especially p. 710. R. Laird Harris, *kāpar*, TWOT #1023.

[97] *Pascha*, "the Passover," then "the Passover Lamb" (BDAG 784, 1, 2).

[98] *Hilasmos*, "appeasement necessitated by sin, expiation" (BDAG 474, 1).

> "... If anybody does sin, we have one who speaks to the Father in our de-
> fense – Jesus Christ, the Righteous One. He is the **atoning sacrifice** for
> our sins, and not only for ours but also for the sins of the whole world."
> (1 John 2:1-2)

- **Fountain.** Jesus is also pictured prophetically as a fountain to wash away sin.

  > "On that day **a fountain**[99] will be opened to the house of David and the
  > inhabitants of Jerusalem, to cleanse them from sin and impurity." (Zecha-
  > riah 13:1)

Jesus as the Lamb of God is similar to Jesus as our Ransom (Mark 10:45; 1 Timothy
2:6), except that "atoning sacrifice" is from a sacrificial vocabulary, while "ransom" is
from a commercial vocabulary, especially related to the manumission of slaves. We
consider Jesus as Redeemer and Ransom in Lesson 7. We considered Jesus as Mediator
in Lesson 3.

**Q2. (John 1:29) Why is Jesus referred to as the Lamb of God? To what degree does
he take away our sins? How does he come to represent *you* – as *your* sacrifice for
sin?**
http://www.joyfulheart.com/forums/topic/1622-q2-lamb-of-god/

**Q3. (1 Corinthians 11:23-26) What is the purpose of the Lord's Supper? Why should
we partake often? Why is it so easy to forget what Jesus has done for us on the
cross?**
http://www.joyfulheart.com/forums/topic/1623-q3-the-lords-supper/

Jesus the Servant

Closely related to the theme of Jesus being the sacrifice for sin, is that of Jesus as
Servant of the Lord in Isaiah's so-called Servant Songs (Isaiah 42:1-4; 49:1-6; perhaps
49:7; 50:4-9; 52:13-53:12). Sometimes, the servant in these passages seems to be the nation
Israel (41:8; 44:1, 21; 45:4; 49:3, 6-7). But in other places it is clear that the Servant is an

---

[99] "Fountain" is *māqôr*, "well, spring, fountain," figuratively as a source of purification, life, and vigor (BDB
881). Because there are no actual descriptors in the scripture, we haven't listed Jesus in his other roles
using the image of water. But they might be: Source of Living Water (John 4:10; Revelation 22:17).

individual, perhaps one who represents Israel, and accomplishes God's purpose for his people.

> "Here is **my Servant**, whom I uphold,
> **my chosen one** in whom I delight;
> I will put my Spirit on him
> and he will bring justice to the nations." (Isaiah 42:1)

This is quoted in Matthew's Gospel:

> "Behold, **my servant** whom I have chosen,
> **my beloved** with whom my soul is well pleased." (Matthew 12:18, ESV, RSV, KJV)

This is especially clear in the Suffering Servant passage, Isaiah 52:13-53:12. For time's sake I'll quote only a portion of it. For more, see my book *Lamb of God: Jesus' Atonement for Sin* (JesusWalk, 2011). It is quite clear from the Gospels (especially Mark 10:45) that Jesus saw himself as the fulfillment of the Servant in Isaiah 53. Isaiah prophesies of one whom Yahweh speaks of as "**my Servant**" (52:13):

> "He was pierced for our transgressions,
> he was crushed for our iniquities;
> the punishment that brought us peace was upon him,
> and by his wounds we are healed.
> We all, like sheep, have gone astray,
> each of us has turned to his own way;
> and the LORD has laid on him the iniquity of us all." (Isaiah 53:4-6)

A Servant Mentality

In one place, Jesus calls his disciples "friends" (John 15:14-15). But in the Parable of the Unworthy Servants (Luke 17:7-10), he reminds us that were are "servants," who are undeserving of special favors. Jesus had a servant mentality, epitomized by him washing his disciples feet (John 13). In Romans 15:8 he is called "**a Servant of the Jews**" (NIV), "**Servant of/to the Circumcised**" (NRSV, ESV), "**Minister of the Circumcision**" (KJV).

In the Garden of Gethsemane, Jesus the Man struggled with his mission to die. But ultimately he prayed the servant's prayer: "Not my will, but yours be done" (Luke 22:42b). Paul wrote:

> "[He] made himself nothing,
> taking the very nature of a **servant**,

being made in human likeness.
And being found in appearance as a **man**,
he humbled himself and became obedient to death –
even death on a cross!" (Philippians 2:7-8)

Obedience is what is expected of a servant, and Jesus is the Servant par excellence. He is our example in this. In Philippians 2:7, Jesus is in the nature of a **Servant** (NIV, ESV, KJV), **Slave** (NRSV, Philippians 2:7).

Q4. (Philippians 2:7-8) How are we to follow Jesus' example as the Servant? Why is humility difficult? Why is obedience hard? Where are you struggling right now to be humble and obedient?
http://www.joyfulheart.com/forums/topic/1624-q4-servant/

Jesus our Priest

In the final verses of Isaiah 53, the Servant acts as a priest for his people. In addition to personally bearing their sins, he "will justify many" (Isaiah 53:11b) and "made intercession for the transgressors" (Isaiah 53:12c). He continually intercedes for us (Hebrews 7:25; Romans 8:34). And, as we saw in Lesson 3, he is our Advocate before the Father (1 John 2:1).

This theme is picked up in the New Testament Book of Hebrews, that sees Jesus as our Priest. Just as the Israelites had a high priest who presided over the sacrifices in the Tabernacle, and later, the Temple, so Jesus is our High Priest, who serves in the True Sanctuary in heaven.

"We do not have a **high priest** who is unable to sympathize with our weaknesses, but we have one who has been tempted in every way, just as we are – yet was without sin." (Hebrews 4:15)

"We do have such a **high priest**, who sat down at the right hand of the throne of the Majesty in heaven, and who serves in the sanctuary, the true tabernacle set up by the Lord, not by man." (Hebrews 8:1-2)

Some translations render "serves in the sanctuary" (NIV) in noun form, as "**a minister of the sanctuary**" (KJV, cf. NRSV, NASB), "**a minister in the holy places**" (ESV).

In Isaiah we see a messianic prophecy that seems to point to Jesus as "**a sanctuary**," though he is a stumbling stone to the rebellious Jews (Isaiah 8:14-15).

As **High Priest**, Jesus is also **the Forerunner**, who goes before us into heaven as our precursor or scout.[100]

> "We have this as a sure and steadfast anchor of the soul, a hope that enters into the inner place behind the curtain, where Jesus has gone as a **forerunner** on our behalf, having become a **high priest forever after the order of Melchizedek**." (Hebrews 6:19-20, ESV)

Jesus is seen as **a priest in the Order of Melchizedek** (Hebrews 5:6, 10; 7:17, quoting the messianic Psalm 110:4). Melchizedek was King of Salem and priest of the Most High who led Abraham in worship (Genesis 14:18). Because Melchizedek's ancestry is not given in Genesis, the author of Hebrews sees him as a type of the Son of God (Hebrews 7:1-3).

We've covered a lot of territory in this lesson, looking at titles of Jesus' righteousness and holiness and his sacrificial death for our sins as the Lamb of God and Atoning Sacrifice.

In ourselves, we are unrighteous. As Isaiah said:

> "We have all become like one who is unclean,
> and all our righteous deeds are like a polluted garment." (Isaiah 64:6a)

We are lost. We have no hope. We cannot earn our way into God's good graces. But Jesus has become **Our Righteousness**. He is not only the Righteous One; he is also our Atoning Sacrifice (1 John 2:1-2).

> "Christ died for sins once for all,
> **the Righteous** for the unrighteous,
> to bring you to God." (1 Peter 3:18a)

He is the one who makes us righteous at such great cost. In Lesson 7 we'll consider Jesus as our Savior and Redeemer, another way of understanding our great salvation.

Prayer

Father, none of us is righteous. We are totally dependent upon your grace. Thank you for sending Jesus, the Holy and Righteous One, the Lamb of God, who takes away our sin. Infuse us with his righteousness, so that our lives might reflect holiness and righteousness on earth as it is in heaven. Thank you. In Jesus' name, we pray. Amen.

---

[100] "Forerunner" is *prodromos*, "pertaining to being a precursor, going (lit. running) before, going ahead, a scout," from *pro-* "motion forward, before another who follows, in advance" (Thayer 537, dα) + *trecho*, "to run."

Names and Titles of Jesus

Good Teacher (Mark 10:17-18; Luke 18:18)

Righteous Man (Matthew 27:19, ESV; Luke 23:47)

Innocent Man (Matthew 27:19, NIV, NRSV)

Just Man (Matthew 27:19, KJV)

Righteous One (NIV, RSV, ESV, Acts 7:52; 22:14; Isaiah 53:11)

Just One (KJV, Acts 7:52, 22:14)

Righteous Branch (Jeremiah 23:5; 33:15)

The Righteous (1 Peter 3:18a; 1 John 2:1)

Our Righteousness (1 Corinthians 1:30)

The LORD Our Righteousness (Jeremiah 23:6)

Righteous Judge (2 Timothy 4:8)

Holy One (Luke 1:35)

Holy One of God (Mark 1:24b; Luke 4:34)

Your Holy One (Acts 2:27)

The Holy and Righteous One (Acts 3:14)

Lamb of God (John 1:29, 36)

Lamb without Blemish or Defect (1 Peter 1:19)

Lamb (often in Revelation)

Passover Lamb (NIV, ESV, 1 Corinthians 5:7)

Paschal Lamb (NRSV, 1 Corinthians 5:7)

Passover (KJV, 1 Corinthians 5:7)

Propitiation (KJV, ESV, 1 John 2:1-2)

Atoning Sacrifice (NIV, NRSV, 1 John 2:1-2)

Fountain (Zechariah 13:1)

Servant (Isaiah 42:1; 53:13; Matthew 12:18; NIV, ESV, KJV, Philippians 2:7)

Slave (NRSV, Philippians 2:7)

Servant of the Jews" (NIV, Romans 15:8)

Servant of/to the Circumcised" (NRSV, ESV, Romans 15:8)

Minister of the Circumcision" (KJV, Romans 15:8)

High Priest (Hebrews 4:15; 7:26; 8:1)

Minister of/in the Sanctuary (KJV, NRSV, Hebrews 8:2)

Minister in the Holy Places (ESV, Hebrews 8:2)

Sanctuary (Isaiah 8:14)

Priest in the Order of Melchizedek (Hebrews 5:6, 10; 6:19-20; 7:17; Psalm 110:4)

Forerunner (Hebrews 6:20)

Songs and Hymns

Songs in the lesson focus on titles of Jesus that relate to him as the holy and blameless sacrifice for our sins. Titles include: Righteous One, Our Righteousness, Holy One, Lamb of God, Atoning Sacrifice, Fountain, Servant, High Priest, and Forerunner.

"Agnus Dei" ("Worthy is the Lamb"), by Michael W. Smith (© 1990, Sony/ATV Milene Music)

"All Who Are Thirsty" ("Come to the Fountain"), Brenton Brown and Glenn Robertson (© 1998 Vineyard Songs (UK/Eire))

"Be Unto Your Name" ("Holy, Holy, Lord God Almighty, Worthy is the Lamb who was slain"), by Lynn DeShazo and Gary Sadler (© 1998 Integrity's Hosanna! Music)

"Before The Throne Of God Above" ("I have ... a great High Priest whose name is love"), by Charitie Lees Bancroft, Vikki Cook (© 1997 Sovereign Grace Worship)

"Enough" ("You're my sacrifice of greatest price ... You're my coming King"), by Chris Tomlin and Louie Giglio (© 2002 sixsteps Music)

"Forever" (We Sing Hallelujah ... the Lamb has overcome"), by Brian Johnson, Kari Jobe, et al. (© 2013 KAJE Songs)

"Give Thanks with a Grateful Heart" ("Give thanks to the Holy One"), by Henry Smith (© 1978, Integrity's Hosanna! Music)

"How Great Is Our God" ("The splendor of the King ... Beginning and the End ... Lion and the Lamb"), by Chris Tomlin, Ed Cash, Jesse Reeves (© 2004 sixsteps Music)

"I Stand in Awe" ("You are beautiful beyond description, Lamb of God who died for me"), by Mark Altrogge (© 1987 Sovereign Grace Praise)

"I Will Rise" ("worthy is the Lamb"), by Christ Tomlin, Jesse Reeves, Louie Giglio, Matt Maher (© 2008 sixsteps Music)

"Jesus, Only Jesus" (He is our hope, our righteousness ... Holy, King Almighty Lord"), by Christ Tomlin, Matt Redman, et al. (© 2013 S. D. G. Publishing)

"Knowing You" ("You're my joy, my Righteousness"), by Graham Kendrick (© 1994, Make Way Music)

"Lamb of God," by Twila Paris (© 1985, Straightway Music)

"Revelation Song" ("Worthy is the Lamb who was slain ... Lord God Almighty ... King of kings"), Jennie Lee Riddle (© 2004 Gateway Create Publishing)

"Righteous One," Bruce Muller (© 1991 Universal Music - Brentwood Benson)

"There is a Redeemer" ("Precious Lamb of God, Messiah") by Melody Green (© 1982 Universal Music - Brentwood Benson)

"We Fall Down" ("Holy, holy, holy is the Lamb"), by Chris Tomlin (© 1998, Worshiptogether.com Songs)

"We Will Glorify" (We will glorify the King of kings, we will glorify the Lamb"), by Twila Paris (1982 New Spring)

"Worthy Is the Lamb," by Darlene Zschech (© 2002, Hillsong Publishing)

"Worthy, You Are Worthy" ("Holy, You are Holy"), by Don Moen (© 1986, Integrity's Hosanna! Music)

"You Are My All in All" ("Jesus, Lamb of God, worthy is your name"), by Dennis Jernigan (© 1991, Shepherd's Heart Music, Inc.)

"Your Great Name" ("Worthy is the Lam that was slain for us") by Krissy Nordhoff and Michael Neele (2008, Integrity's Praise! Music)

Exercises

From Appendix 6. Exercises to Help You Internalize the Names of Jesus, select some activities that will help you internalize the truths of this lesson's names, titles, descriptors, and metaphors. This week, how can you creatively pray, meditate, write, worship, consider, draw or paint, compose, picture, and live out these truths in your community?

Actively participating in these ways will help you grow to be like Christ.

7. Jesus our Savior, Shepherd, and Redeemer

Perhaps the simplest form of the Wonderful Story is found in John 3:16.

> "For God so loved the world that he gave his one and only Son, that whoever believes in him shall not perish but have eternal life." (John 3:16)

You see, our problem is grave. Though we have been created in God's image with his goodness, yet creation is fallen. We are broken. Oh, we're pretty good most of the time, but each of us have fatal flaws that lead to sin and separation from God.

There was a time that a lot of people believed that mankind was getting better

Edward Burne-Jones, Good Shepherd stained glass window (1895), Harris Manchester College, Oxford

and better. Education led to their betterment and continual advance. Then came "the Great War" (World War I) to shake this belief. It was followed by the evil that spawned World War II. And we began to realize that within men and women are the seeds of our destruction. We fall short – far short – of God's goodness and glory (Romans 3:23). You look at the world today, with its wars and rumors of wars, and you realize that within the human heart lie deceit and pride, selfishness and violence. All we can look forward to is more separation, more heartache, more war, more hurt.

We need a Savior! The Good News, the Gospel, is that God has sent us a Savior and his name is Jesus!

The problem we couldn't solve, God came to solve for us. It cost him greatly, for he "gave his one and only Son," who was subjected to terrible torture and insult. Jesus died for our sins, and then released into us his Holy Spirit, who can change us from the inside.

Let's examine these titles of Savior, Redeemer, and Shepherd. Savior and Deliverer come from military vocabulary. Redeemer comes from the vocabulary of family law in the Old Testament, and the business of slavery in the New Testament. Shepherd is a metaphor of a Savior, reflective of the herding culture of Israel.

God My Savior

Like many other titles of Jesus, Savior is first used of God the Father.

"All mankind will know that I, the LORD, am your Savior,
your Redeemer, the Mighty One of Jacob." (Isaiah 49:26)

Many times in the Old Testament he is referred to as "God our Savior" (NIV) or, literally, "the God of our salvation" (ESV, KJV).[101] Indeed, in the New Testament we see "God our Savior" again and again, especially in 1 Timothy and Titus.[102] Thus it is another sign of Jesus' divinity that the title of Savior is bestowed upon Jesus. The Greek word for "Savior" is *sōtēr*, from *sōzō*, "to preserve or rescue from natural dangers and afflictions, save, keep from harm, preserve, rescue."[103] A Savior is a protector, a rescuer.

Prophecies of a Savior

In Lesson 4 we considered the messianic prophecies that foretold the Messiah who would save his people. There are two prophecies of Jesus' salvation early in Luke. Zechariah prophecies:

"He has raised up **a horn of salvation** for us in the house of his servant David." (Luke 1:69)

The phrase **"horn of salvation"** refers to a mighty act of salvation or deliverance. NRSV translates it, **"Mighty Savior."**[104] A few months later, the angels announce Jesus' birth as a Savior.

"Today in the town of David a **Savior** has been born to you; he is Christ the Lord." (Luke 2:11)

---

[101] For example, we see "God our Savior" in Psalm 18:46; 24:5; 25:5; 27:9; 38:22; 42:11; 43:5; 65:5; 68:19; 79:9; 85:4; 89:26. He is seen as Savior many times in Isaiah and the Minor Prophets.

[102] 1 Timothy 1:1; 2:3; 4:10; Titus 1:3; 2:10; 3:4; Jude 25.

[103] *Sōzō*, BDAG 982, 1.

[104] 'Horn' originally referred to the horn of an animal, but then extended so that "horn" is often used in the Old Testament of military prowess. In the New Testament "horn" could refer to "an exceptional kind of might or power" (*Keras*, BDAG 540).

Friend of Sinners

As we'll see, Jesus' title "the Friend of Sinners," relates to salvation. But on the lips of Jesus' enemies, the title was meant to be an insult.

> "The Son of Man came eating and drinking, and they say, 'Here is a glutton and a drunkard, a **friend of tax collectors and sinners**.'" (Matthew 11:19)

Thank God that he *is* our Friend and will associate with us! We need him so desperately! Jesus went to have dinner at the house of a tax collector named Levi (Matthew):

> "The Pharisees and the teachers of the law ... complained to his disciples, 'Why do you eat and drink with tax collectors and sinners?' Jesus answered them, 'It is not the healthy who need a doctor, but the sick. I have not come to call the righteous, but sinners to repentance.'" (Luke 5:30-32)

When he ate at the home Zacchaeus, the chief tax collector for the region around Jericho, Jesus explained the purpose for the visit. He is a Friend of Sinners, a Friend who saves.

> "For the Son of Man came to seek and to save what was lost." (Luke 19:10)

He came to be a Savior to us who are lost without him.

> **Q1. (Luke 19:10; Matthew 11:19) Jesus came to seek and to save the lost. What does it mean to you personally that Jesus is the Friend of Sinners? How should it affect your relationships with people who are deep in sin?**
> **http://www.joyfulheart.com/forums/topic/1625-q1-friend-of-sinners/**

Rescuer, Deliverer

By and large, the title "Savior" has lost its meaning from overuse in the Christian community. Perhaps a better title for our generation might be Rescuer, which is one of the meanings of the noun *sōtēr* – though the title Rescuer is not found in popular English Bibles. Another Greek word for "rescue, deliver," is *rhyomai*, "to rescue from danger, save, rescue, deliver, preserve someone"[105] It appears once (in participle form) in a title, quoting Isaiah 50:20-21.

> "The **Deliverer** will come from Zion;
> he will turn godlessness away from Jacob.

---

[105] *Rhyomai*, BDAG 908.

And this is my covenant with them
when I take away their sins." (Romans 11:26-27)

When Jesus was in his hometown of Nazareth, he read from a portion of Isaiah's prophecy that laid out his mission as Savior.

"The Spirit of the Lord is on me,
because he has anointed me
to preach good news to the poor.
He has sent me to proclaim freedom for the prisoners
and recovery of sight for the blind,
to release the oppressed,
to proclaim the year of the Lord's favor." (Luke 4:18-19, quoting Isaiah 61:1-2)

There are many examples of *rhyomai*, "rescue," in the New Testament. Zechariah's prophecy of the Messiah included the line:

"... to rescue us from the hand of our enemies." (Luke 1:74a)

Yes, we have enemies, sometimes dangerous ones. But as comic strip character Pogo once said, "We have found the enemy and he is us."[106] We are our own worst enemy. There is in us a deep-rooted bent to sinning that corrupts us. Paul wrote:

"What a wretched man I am! Who will **rescue** me from this body of death? Thanks be to God – through Jesus Christ our Lord!" (Romans 7:24-25a)

"Jesus, who rescues us from the coming wrath." (1 Thessalonians 1:10)

In the context of criticism over eating with sinners, Jesus told the Parable of the Lost Sheep, where the shepherd leaves his flock to search for the lost sheep and doesn't quit until he finds it (Luke 15:1-7). "Rescue" (*rhyomai*) is also found in the Lord's Prayer, "deliver us from evil" (Matthew 6:13).

Jesus is the One Who Rescues us from ourselves, from our sin, and from the evil one. He is our Savior.

Combinations Using Savior

In addition to Luke 2:11 quoted above, Savior is sometimes used absolutely, by itself.

"Our citizenship is in heaven. And we eagerly await a **Savior** from there, the Lord Jesus Christ." (Philippians 3:20)

---

[106] From the *Pogo* daily comic strip for Earth Day, 1971. Pogo was the central character in a comic strip (1948-1975) by cartoonist Walt Kelly.

"Christ is the head of the church, his body, of which he is the **Savior**." (Ephesians 5:23b)

Besides being used by itself, the title Savior occurs in a number of combinations:

- **Lord and Savior Jesus Christ** (2 Peter 1:11; 2:20; 3:18; cf. 3:2).
- **The Savior Jesus** (Acts 13:23).
- **Jesus Christ Our Savior** (Titus 1:4; 3:6; 2 Timothy 1:10).
- **The Savior of the World** (John 4:42; 1 John 4:14).
- **Prince and Savior** (NIV, KJV, Acts 5:31), **Leader and Savior** (NRSV, ESV)
- **Our Great God and Savior, Jesus Christ** (Titus 2:13; 2 Peter 1:1)

A couple of other metaphors relate to Jesus our Savior:

- **Arm of the Lord** (Isaiah 53:1), that is, one who by his might brings about the Lord's salvation. It appears to refer to the Suffering Servant, who, as we saw in Lesson 6, refers to Jesus.
- **Author**[107] **of Salvation** (NIV, NASB), **Pioneer of Salvation** (NRSV), **Founder of Salvation** (ESV), **Captain of Salvation** (KJV; Hebrews 2:10). Jesus is the originator of our salvation.

Finally, when Simeon saw Jesus in the temple at his dedication, the old prophet took him in his arms and said:

"Sovereign Lord, as you have promised,
you now dismiss your servant in peace.
For my eyes have seen your **salvation**,
which you have prepared in the sight of all people...." (Luke 2:29-31a)

It occurs to me that Savior is an active word. The Savior acts whether or not he hears a cry for help. He actively seeks those in need and offers rescue. Christians are sometimes criticized for always trying to evangelize, rather than keep their faith to themselves. Dear friends, we evangelize because the heart of our Savior is to seek and to save the lost. Let's never stop witnessing and evangelizing!

Q2. How are we disciples to assist in Jesus' mission to seek and to save the lost? What is the love-balance between seeking to save our friends and having to back

---

[107] The key word is *archēgos*, "one who has a preeminent position, leader, ruler, prince," as well as, "one who begins or originates, originator, founder" (BDAG 138, 1, 3). This word also occurs in Hebrews 12:2, "the author and finisher of our faith."

off because they feel we are trying to pressure them?
http://www.joyfulheart.com/forums/topic/1626-q2-to-seek-and-save/

Redeemer

Now we move from the Savior, Deliver, to a specific kind of salvation – saving from slavery – redemption.

We begin with Job's famous prophecy of his Redeemer, who will raise him from the dead.

"I know that **my Redeemer** lives,
and that in the end he will stand upon the earth.
And after my skin has been destroyed,
yet in my flesh I will see God;
I myself will see him with my own eyes –
I, and not another.
How my heart yearns within me!" (Job 19:25-27)

The Redeemer who will stand upon the earth is Jesus. Elsewhere, in Isaiah, we see this word connected with another messianic prophecy.

"**The Redeemer** will come to Zion,
to those in Jacob who repent of their sins." (Isaiah 59:20)

The Kinsman-Redeemer

"Redeemer" in the Old Testament is a participle of the verb *gā'al*, "redeem, ransom, do the part of a kinsman."[108] A kinsman had the responsibility to help his relatives in any difficulty or danger.

If a close relative lost his property to a debtor, it was the responsibility of a kinsmen to redeem it. If a relative was murdered, his kinsmen were responsible to avenge his death. If a relative was in prison or in slavery, a kinsman was obligated to pay whatever was necessary to get him released.

The Bible has a number of examples of this. For example, when Abraham's nephew Lot is taken prisoner, Abraham rescues him (Genesis 14). When Lot is threatened by the

---

[108] R. Laird Harris, *gā'al*, TWOT #300. Leon Morris, *The Apostolic Preaching of the Cross* (Eerdmans, 1955), pp. 9-59. Otto Procksch, *luo, ktl.,* TDNT 4:328-335.

destruction of Sodom (Genesis 18-19), Abraham makes it his personal responsibility to intercede and protect his kinsman.

Boaz the Kinsman-Redeemer

Probably the most endearing story in the Bible that illustrates this is the relationship between Ruth, Naomi, and Boaz (Ruth 1-4). Naomi and her husband travel to Moab during a famine. While in Moab, Naomi's husband and both of her sons die. Naomi and her daughter-in-law Ruth return as poverty-stricken widows to Naomi's home in Bethlehem. Ruth is reduced to gleaning behind the harvesters, picking up whatever stray wheat stalks are left.

"It just happens" that she is gleaning in the field of Boaz, a relative of Naomi's husband. In various translations he is called "kinsman-redeemer" (NIV), "near kinsman" (KJV), or "next-of-kin" (NRSV). Boaz loves Ruth, and takes on this role of kinsman-redeemer, not only purchasing back Naomi's dead husband's property, but also marrying Ruth to bear children to continue in his dead kinsman's line, a custom sometimes referred to as levirate marriage.

In the Psalms and the prophets there is a strong theme that God is the Kinsman-Redeemer of his people Israel. When Israel is in bondage in Egypt, God redeems them from slavery and takes them into their own land.[109]

Jesus Our Ransom and Redeemer

Consider the power of this metaphor. The invisible God has so bonded with the people of Israel that he takes on himself the role of their Kinsman. In the New Testament, God sends Jesus to become a human, identify with us and our plight, and redeem us from the power of sin. In the New Testament, Jesus is referred to as the Redeemer, no doubt carrying on the Old Testament understanding of Kinsman-Redeemer.

This was clearly Jesus' own understanding of his mission and destiny. He told his disciples:

> "Whoever wants to become great among you must be your servant, and whoever wants to be first must be slave of all. For even the Son of Man did not come to be served, but to serve, and to give his life as a **ransom** (*lytron*) for many." (Mark 10:43b-45)

---

[109] Especially, Exodus 6:6; Micah 4:10; Psalms 19:14; Isaiah 54:5; 63:16. You can also see the metaphor of Redeemer in Psalm 78:35; Proverbs 23:11; Isaiah 41:14; 43:14; 44:6, 24; 48:17; 59:20; and Jeremiah 50:34.

"For there is one God, and there is one mediator between God and men, the man Christ Jesus, who gave himself as a **ransom** (*antilytron*) for all...." (1 Timothy 2:5-6)

A ransom (*lytron*) is the "price of release, ransom," especially the ransom money for the manumission of slaves.[110] Very similar is the rare word *antilytron*, "ransom."[111] God redeems us with his own Son as the ransom price. Jesus becomes one of us:

"Who, being in very nature God,
did not consider equality with God something to be grasped,
but made himself nothing,
taking the very nature of a servant,
being made in human likeness." (Philippians 2:6-7)

He becomes our kinsman, our brother. And by the surrender of his own flesh and blood he redeems us (Ephesians 1:7; Hebrews 9:12). He buys back his kin who have fallen so far into debt that they cannot redeem themselves – ever.

In most English translations, the actual title Redeemer occurs only in the Old Testament, but the concept of Jesus as our Redeemer appears throughout the New Testament. For example, the men on the road to Emmaus tell their companion,

"We had hoped that he was the one who was going to redeem Israel." (Luke 24:21)

"Christ redeemed us from the curse of the law." (Galatians 3:13; cf. 3:14; 4:5).

"[He] gave himself for us to redeem us from all wickedness and to purify for himself a people that are his very own, eager to do what is good." (Titus 2:13-14)

Paul wrote that Jesus is our Redemption.

"[He] has become for us wisdom from God – that is, our righteousness, holiness and **redemption**." (1 Corinthians 1:30)

The Bible uses many metaphors to convey the truth of our salvation. The metaphor of Lamb of God uses the technical terms associated with temple sacrifice. The metaphor of Redeemer use the technical terms of money paid to free someone, especially one who pays a ransom price. According to the titles from the various metaphors of Scripture, just as Jesus is both our High Priest and Atoning Sacrifice, Jesus is both our Redeemer and our Ransom.

---

[110] *Lytron*, BDAG 605.
[111] *Antilytron*, BDAG 89; "Materially *antilytron* is the same as *lytron*" (Friederich Büchsel, *luō, ktl.*, TDNT 4:349.

Q3. (Mark 10:43-45) How does Jesus serve (like Boaz) as a Kinsman-Redeemer to us? What does the idea of needing a ransom imply about our condition? What was the redemption-price that the Father paid for us?
http://www.joyfulheart.com/forums/topic/1627-q3-kinsman-redeemer/

Jesus Our Shepherd

You may not have looked at it this way, but the title Shepherd is a metaphor for Savior. A shepherd's role was to preserve the sheep by leading them to pasture and water, to protect the sheep by fending off predators, and to rescue the sheep that wandered off.

The title Shepherd is given to Yahweh in the beloved Psalm 23.

"The LORD is my shepherd; I shall not want." (Psalm 23:1; also Psalm 80:1)

Throughout the ancient Near East, rulers and leaders were often spoken of as shepherds of their people. The kings of Judah and Israel, were call shepherds, as well as the priests and religious leaders, who were to care for Yahweh's flock as under-shepherds. But they did not. The religious leaders in Jesus' time ignored the miracles and those who were healed, but rather sought to kill the miracle-worker. As a result, God's people suffered.

Ezekiel prophesies of the Davidic Messiah, that he will rescue Yahweh's flock.

"I will set up over them **one shepherd**, my servant David, and he shall feed them:
he shall feed them and be their shepherd." (Ezekiel 34:23; also 37:24)

Malachi prophesied of this messianic Shepherd who would be born in Bethlehem.

"He will stand and shepherd his flock in the strength of the LORD,
in the majesty of the name of the LORD his God.
And they will live securely,
for then his greatness will reach to the ends of the earth." (Micah 5:4)

In Matthew's quotation of Micah's prophecy he is called, "a ruler who will be **the shepherd of my people Israel**" (Matthew 2:6).

Jesus is that Shepherd.

"When he saw the crowds, he had compassion on them, because they were harassed and helpless, like sheep without a shepherd." (Matthew 9:36)

Jesus cares for his sheep, protects them and calls them by name (John 10:1-16). In contrast to the Jewish leaders, Jesus is the "Good Shepherd."

> "I am **the good shepherd**. The good shepherd lays down his life for the sheep." (John 10:11)

> "I am **the good shepherd**; I know my sheep and my sheep know me – just as the Father knows me and I know the Father – and I lay down my life for the sheep." (John 10:14-15)

Jesus is also, by implication, the shepherd who is "struck" when Jesus is arrested and killed.

> "'You will all fall away,' Jesus told them, 'for it is written: "I will strike **the shepherd**, and the sheep will be scattered."'" (Mark 14:27, cf. Matthew 26:31, quoting Zechariah 3:17)

Later in the New Testament, Shepherd becomes an established title of Jesus.

> "May the God of peace, who through the blood of the eternal covenant brought back from the dead our Lord Jesus, **that great Shepherd of the sheep**...." (Hebrews 13:20)

> "When **the Chief Shepherd** appears, you will receive the crown of glory that will never fade away." (1 Peter 5:4)

Curiously, in Revelation 7:17, the Lamb who is slain also serves as the Shepherd.

> "The Lamb at the center of the throne will be their shepherd;
> he will lead them to springs of living water...." (Revelation 7:17)

Once he is seen as an overseer or bishop of souls.

> "For you were like sheep going astray, but now you have returned to the **Shepherd and Overseer of your souls**." (1 Peter 2:25)

"**Overseer**" (NIV, ESV), "**guardian**" (NRSV, NASB), "**bishop**" (KJV) is *episkopos* (from which we get our word "Episcopal"). In Greek usage it means generally, "one who watches over, guardian," from *epi-*, "over, upon, superintendence[112]" + *skopeō*, "look out for, notice" (from which we get our word "scope"). Of course, the word "bishop" has developed a technical sense in church hierarchy, but in the context of sheep and shepherding, the overseer keeps an eye out for the sheep and their welfare. He lets them

---

[112] *Epi*, Thayer 23, D8.

graze, but when they are threatened or about to run off, he steps in to guide or protect them.

> **Q4. (John 10:11-14) What are the characteristics of the "Good Shepherd"? How do these contrast with the "hired hand"? God calls us to shepherd others as pastors, small group leaders, teachers, mentors, etc. How can we demonstrate that we are "good shepherds" rather than "hired hands"?**
> **http://www.joyfulheart.com/forums/topic/1628-q4-good-shepherd/**

Again and again we are given titles of Jesus that reflect his saving, delivering, caring ministry. They are core to who Jesus is. Thank God that he is the Rescuer and Shepherd who has sought for us until he found us.

Prayer

Thank you, Father, for sending Jesus to be our Savior. You know how much we need saving! I pray that you might put in our hearts a desire to extend your salvation to those around us. Let us never rest, but always be witnesses to your great salvation. We pray in the name of Jesus, the Great Shepherd of the Sheep. Amen.

Names and Titles of Jesus
Horn of Salvation (NIV, ESV, KJV, Luke 1:69)
Mighty Savior (NRSV, Luke 1:69)
Savior (Luke 2:11; Philippians 3:20; Ephesians 5:23)
Friend of Tax Collectors and Sinners (Matthew 11:19)
Deliverer (Romans 11:26)
Lord and Savior Jesus Christ (2 Peter 1:11; 2:20; 3:18; cf. 3:2)
The Savior Jesus (Acts 13:23)
Jesus Christ Our Savior (Titus 1:4; 3:6; 2 Timothy 1:10)
The Savior of the World (John 4:42; 1 John 4:14).
Prince and Savior (NIV, KJV, Acts 5:31)
Leader and Savior (NRSV, ESV, Acts 5:31)
Great God and Savior, Jesus Christ (Titus 2:13; 2 Peter 1:1)
Arm of the Lord (Isaiah 53:1)
Author of Salvation (NIV, NASB, Hebrews 2:10)

Pioneer of Salvation (NRSV, Hebrews 2:10)
Founder of Salvation (ESV, Hebrews 2:10)
Captain of Salvation (KJV; Hebrews 2:10)
Your Salvation (Luke 2:30)
Redeemer (Job 19:25; Isaiah 59:20)
Ransom (Mark 10:45; 1 Timothy 2:6)
Redemption (1 Corinthians 1:30)
One Shepherd (Ezekiel 34:23; 37:24)
Good Shepherd (John 10:11, 14)
Shepherd (Mark 14:27; Revelation 7:17)
Shepherd of my People Israel (Matthew 2:6)
Great Shepherd of the Sheep (Hebrews 13:20)
Shepherd and Overseer of your Souls (NIV, ESV, 1 Peter 2:25)
Shepherd and Guardian of your Souls (NRSV, NASB, 1 Peter 2:25)
Shepherd and Bishop of your Souls (KJV, 1 Peter 2:25)
Chief Shepherd (1 Peter 5:4)

Songs and Hymns

These songs center around Jesus' role as the one who saves and redeems his people. Titles include Savior, Deliverer, Author of Salvation, Redeemer, Ransom, and Shepherd.

"All Glory, Laud and Honor" ("to thee, Redeemer, King ... king of Israel ... David's royal Son ... the King and Blessed One"), words: Theodulph of Orleans (c. 820 AD; translated by John M. Neale (1851), music: St. Theodulph, Melchior Teschner (1615)

"All Things Are Possible" ("My Redeemer"), by Darlene Zschech (© 1997, Hillsong Publishing)

"Be Unto Your Name" ("Jesus, Redeemer, mighty to save"), by Lynn DeShazo and Gary Sadler (© 1998 Integrity's Hosanna! Music)

"Because of Your Love" ("Savior You bore all my shame"), by Phil Wickham (© 2008 Phil Wickham Music)

"Blessed Be the Name" ("Redeemer, Savior, friend of man ... Counselor ... Prince of Peace"), words: William H. Clark, music: Ralph E. Hudson (1888)

"Emmanuel" ("My Shepherd King, you're watching over me"), by Reuben Morgan (© 2005 Hillsong Music Publishing)

"Everlasting God" ("Our Hope, our Strong Deliverer"), by Brenton Brown, Ken Riley (© 2005 Thankyou Music)

"Friend of God," by Israel Houghton and Michael Gungor (© 2003, Integrity's Praise! Music)

"Gentle Shepherd," Gloria and William J. Gaither (© 1974 William J. Gaither, Inc.)

"God With Us" ("Our Deliverer, you are Savior"), by Jason Ingram and Leslie Jordan (© 2012, Integrity's Praise Music)

"Hallelujah! What a Savior," words and music: Philip P. Bliss (1875)

"He Hideth My Soul" ("A wonderful Savior is Jesus my Lord, a Wonderful Savior to me"), words: Fanny Crosby, music: William J. Kirkpatrick

"Here Is Love" ("the Prince of Life our Ransom"), by Matt Redman, Robert Lowry, William Rees (© 2004 Thankyou Music)

"His Name Is Wonderful" ("He's the Great Shepherd"), Audrey Mieir (© 1959 Audrey Mieir. Renewed 1987 Manna Music, Inc.)

"House of God Forever" ("Your shepherd's staff comforts me"), by Jon Foreman (© 2008 Rubadub Publishing)

"I Am Not Skilled to Understand" ("at His right hand is One who is my Savior"), words: Dorothy Greenwell (1873), music: Greenwell, William J. Kirkpatrick (1885)

"I Am" ("Maker of the heavens, Bright and Morning Star ... Fount of Living Water, the Risen Son of Man, the Healer of the Broken .. Savior and Redeemer ... Author and Perfecter, Beginning and the End"), by Mark Schultz (© 2005 Crazy Romaine Music)

"I Know that My Redeemer Lives," words: Charles Wesley (1742), music: Bradford, George F. Handel

"Jesus Paid It All," words: Elvina M. Hall (1965), music: John T. Grape

"Jesus Saves," words: Priscilla J. Owens (1882), music: Salvation, William J. Kirkpatrick

"Jesus, Friend of Sinners," by Mark Hall, Matthew West (© 2011 My Refuge Music)

"Jesus, Name Above All Names" ("Beautiful Savior, Glorious Lord, Emmanuel, God with Us, Blessed Redeemer, Living Word"), by Naida Hearn (1974, 1978 Scripture In Song)

"Jesus, Savior, Pilot Me," words: Edward Hooper (1871), Music: Pilot, John E. Gould (1871)

"Joy to the World" ("the Lord is come ... the Savior reigns"), words: Isaac Watts, music: Antioch, arranged by Lowell Mason (1836)

"Mighty to Save," ("Author of salvation"), by Ben Fielding and Reuben Morgan (© 2006 Hillsong Publishing)

"My Redeemer Lives," by Reuben Morgan (© 1998 Hillsong Music Publishing)

"One Day" ("Living, He loved me; dying, He saved me"), words: J. Wilbur Chapman (1908), music: Charles H. Marsh

"Our God Reigns" ("When we like sheep had gone astray our Shepherd came"), Leonard E. Smith, Jr. (© 1974, 1978 New Jerusalem Music)

"Redeemed, How I Love to Proclaim It," words: Fanny Crosby (1882), Music: William J. Kirkpatrick

"Scandal of Grace" ("Jesus, there's no one besides you"), by Joel Houston, Matt Crocker (© 2012 Hillsong Music Publishing)

"Shepherd of Love," words and music by John W. Peterson (© 1967 John W. Peterson Music Co.)

"Shepherd" ("Good Shepherd of my soul"), by Amanda Cook (© 2013 Bethel Music Publishing)

"Shout for Joy" ("Like a banner high, lift up your grateful heart to the Morning Star ... He's the Saving One"), by Jason Ingram, Lincoln Brewster, Paul Baloche (© 2010 Integrity Worship Music)

"Shout to the Lord" ("My Jesus, my Savior, Lord, there is none like You"), by Darlene Zschech (©
    1993, Darlene Zschech and Hillsong Publishing)

"Shout to the North" ("Jesus is Savior to all, Lord of heaven and earth"), by Martin Smith (© 1995
    Curious? Music)

"Since I Have Been Redeemed," words and music by Edwin O. Excell (1884)

"Strength of My Heart" ("You are unshakable, Mighty Savior, your love's unbreakable"), by Rend
    Collective (© 2014 Thankyou Music)

"Thank You, Jesus" ("Christ my Savior, you rescued me"), by Hannah Hobbs, Matt Crocker (© 2013
    Hillsong Music Publishing)

"There is a Redeemer," by Melody Green (© 1982 Universal Music - Brentwood Benson)

"What a Savior" ("Atoning Sacrifice ... You are the Shepherd King"), Jeremiah Jones (© 2009 Fair Trade
    Global Songs)

Exercises

From Appendix 6. Exercises to Help You Internalize the Names of Jesus, select some
activities that will help you internalize the truths of this lesson's names, titles, descriptors, and metaphors. This week, how can you creatively pray, meditate, write,
worship, consider, draw or paint, compose, picture, and live out these truths in your
community?

Actively participating in these ways will help you grow to be like Christ.

8. Jesus our Head, Cornerstone, and Way

We have looked at titles of Jesus, often formed by verbs of action, like Savior. But many of his titles are based on metaphors, such as Shepherd, that we looked at in Lesson 7. Now we'll examine several further metaphors used as titles to describe who Jesus is.

Jesus is Head

Three New Testament passages give titles of Jesus that include "Head." The first is part of an early hymn to Christ. We'll consider it again in Lesson 10.

> "He is **the head of the body, the church.**
> He is the beginning,
> the firstborn from the dead,
> that in everything he might be preeminent."
>   (Colossians 1:18)

Jesus is the one who calls men and women to follow his Way. Louis Comfort Tiffany, detail from 'Christ and the Apostles' (1890), Richard H. Driehaus Gallery of Stained Glass at Navy Pier, Chicago

Two additional passages speak of Christ as Head.

> "The husband is the head of the wife as Christ is the **head of the church, his body,** of which he is the Savior." (Ephesians 5:23)

> "Now I want you to realize that the **head of every man**[113] is Christ...." (1 Corinthians 11:3)

The question we have is: What did "head" (*kephalē*) mean in first century Greek?

---

[113] *Anēr,* "male."

Head of the Body, the Church

Kephalē means first, the physical head, particularly in the head-body analogy. But then extends to a figurative use as "being of high status, head." With living beings, *kephalē* refers to superior rank. (such as in Colossians 2:10).[114]

Several themes circulate around the word *kephalē*, some of which overlap, as illustrated in Figure 2.

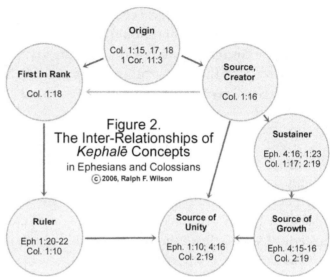

Fig. 2. The Inter-Relationships of *Kephalē* Concepts in Ephesians and Colossians.

1. **Source, Creator** (Colossians 1:16). We derive our idea of "headwaters" from this concept.
2. **Sustainer** (Ephesians 4:16; 1:23; Colossians 1:17; 2:19).
3. **Source of Growth** (Ephesians 4:15-16; Colossians 2:19).
4. **First in Rank** (Colossians 1:18).
5. **Source of Unity**. Christ is the beginning – and the end. All creation finds its right place in him (Ephesians 1:10).
6. **Ruler** (Ephesians 1:20-22; Colossians 1:10). Our "headmaster" carries this idea.

In some circles, people assume that "ruler, authority" is the only real meaning of "head." Not so.

In the title Head, the emphasis is on Christ's vital connection to the body. He is its sustainer, source of growth, origin, and authority. We are Christ's body here on earth and serve "in him" and under his direction. The point is that Christ not only has priority over the principalities and powers; he is the supreme Head of the church itself. We'll consider the titles Beginning and Firstborn from the Dead in Lesson 10.

---

[114] *Kephalē*, BDAG 541-542.

Q1. (Colossians 1:18) How should the assertion that Jesus is the "head of the body, the church" affect the way we conceive of the church? Is he talking about the universal Church or a local congregation, or both? If we believe that Jesus is the head of the church, how should that affect the way we conduct our life and ministry as the church? In what ways does the visible church represent the "head"? How well do we, as the body, follow his leadership?
http://www.joyfulheart.com/forums/topic/1629-q1-head-of-the-church/

God our Rock

Jesus had brought up a couple of messianic passages about stones. And several times in 1 Peter and once in 1 Corinthians, we see the title Rock. We'll examine these. It's important to note, however, that the title of Rock was first applied to God in the Old Testament, especially in the Psalms. For example:

"The LORD is my rock and my fortress and my deliverer,
My God, my rock, in whom I take refuge;
My shield and the horn of my salvation,
my stronghold." (2 Samuel 22:2 = Psalm 18:2)

As we've seen before, in the New Testament, Jesus is given many of the titles of divinity.

Messianic Prophecies Regarding the Stone

The connection between the Rock or Stone in the Old Testament is found in prophecies that were interpreted in Jesus' day as referring to the Messiah. The first uses the vocabulary of masonry construction.

"So this is what the Sovereign LORD says:
'See, I **lay a stone**[115] in Zion,
a tested stone,[116]
a precious cornerstone[117] for a **sure foundation**;

---

[115] "Lay a stone" (NIV), "laid as a foundation" (ESV), "lay for a foundation stone" (KJV, cf. NRSV) is ʾeben, "stone" and mûsād, "foundation, laying, foundation," from yāsad is "to found, to fix firmly" (TWOT #875d).

[116] "Stone" is ʾeben. "Tested" (NIV, NRSV, ESV), "tried" (KJV) is bōḥan, "testing" used as an adjective.

[117] "Precious" is yāqār, from yāqar, "be precious, valuable, costly." "Cornerstone" is pinnâ, "corner." "Cornerstone" in the Greek Septuagint (LXX) translation of Isaiah 28:16 is Greek arkogoniaios, "at the extreme angle, the corner foundation-stone" though some defend the idea of "capstone." BDAG 39-

the one who trusts will never be dismayed.
I will make justice the measuring line
and righteousness the plumb line....'" (Isaiah 28:16-17a)

A **sure foundation** must be constructed with quality materials as well as with accurate tools so that it is totally level and plumb. But the Lord is talking here about a spiritual building, not a physical one. This is clearly a messianic passage prophesying the day of righteousness that the Messiah will usher in, a day of justice and righteousness. Isaiah 28:16 was also interpreted messianically by the Jews, as is clear from its rendering in the Septuagint.

There are also Messianic references in the Rabbinical literature to the plumb line in the hand of Zerubbabel (Zechariah 4:10) and the stones in Isaiah 8:14, which is particularly germane:

"And he will be a sanctuary;
but for both houses of Israel he will be
a stone[118] **that causes men to stumble**
and **a rock**[119] **that makes them fall**.
And for the people of Jerusalem he will be
a **trap**[120] and a **snare**."[121] (Isaiah 8:14)

A third messianic prophecy is found in one of Daniel's visions.

"In the time of those kings, the God of heaven will set up a kingdom that will never be destroyed, nor will it be left to another people. It will **crush** all those kingdoms and bring them to an end, but it will itself endure forever. This is the meaning of the

---

40; *Lidell and Scott's Greek-English Lexicon* (abridged, Oxford Press, 1871), p. 28. The question is whether the cornerstone of Scripture is a foundation stone or a stone which crowns the building. Isaiah 28:16 seems to refer to the former and Psalm 118:22 (*rō' sh pinnâ*) to the latter. By extension, in the NT, Christ is both the foundation on which the church is built, and he is also the coping stone or keystone which crowns the church" (Victor P. Hamilton, TWOT #1738a).

[118] *'Eben*, "stone."

[119] *Ṣûr*. "Rock stands for boulders or formations of stone and for the material which composes mountains" (John E. Harley, TWOT #1901a).

[120] "Trap" (NIV, NRSV, ESV), "gin" (KJV) is *pah*, "bird trap" (see Amos 3:5), from *pāḥah*, "to ensnare" (TWOT #1759a). "Gin" is a Middle English word, short for "engine," which referred to any of various tools or mechanical devices. It is used today mainly in "cotton gin."

[121] "Snare" is *môqēsh*, "snare," from *yāqāsh*, "to lay a snare, set a trap." A fowler (*yāqûsh*) was the one who trapped birds (TWOT #906c). A snare would be used to catch birds, while a trap was used to catch animals, though both words are used of a bird trap (John E. Hartley and Alice Hickcox, "Snare," ISBE 4:556).

vision of **the rock**[122] cut out of a mountain, but not by human hands – **a rock** that broke the iron, the bronze, the clay, the silver and the gold to pieces."(Daniel 2:44-45a)

It has clear messianic implications, for it speaks of the Kingdom of God which will be set up in the Last Days.

A fourth messianic prophecy is found in Psalm 118, one of the Hallel songs that pilgrims sang on their way to worship in Jerusalem at Passover, though it was apparently not interpreted messianically in Jesus' time.

> "**The stone**[123] the builders rejected has become **the capstone;** [124]
> the LORD has done this,
> and it is marvelous in our eyes." (Psalm 118:22-23)

Stone, Cornerstone, Foundation, and Capstone

All four of these are quoted in the New Testament with reference to Jesus. After the Parable of the Tenants in Matthew, Jesus offers this interpretation of Psalm 118:22-23.

> "[42] Jesus said to them, 'Have you never read in the Scriptures:
>
> "The **stone the builders rejected** has become the **capstone**; [125]
> the Lord has done this, and it is marvelous in our eyes"?
>
> [43] "Therefore I tell you that the kingdom of God will be taken away from you and given to a people who will produce its fruit. [44] He who falls on this **stone** will be broken to pieces, but he on whom it falls will be crushed.'" (Matthew 21:42-44)[126]

Jesus takes a passage that wasn't traditionally interpreted messianically with devastating effect. The "builders" are the leaders of Judaism who have become his arch

---

[122] *Eben,* "stone."

[123] *'Eben,* "stone."

[124] *Pinnâ,* "corner."

[125] "Capstone" (NIV), "cornerstone" (ESV, NRSV), "head of the corner" (KJV). The exact role of the stone in this passage has been disputed. KJV translates the Greek literally, "head of the corner," that is, the cornerstone of a building, one of the first building blocks placed in a building. Others consider it to be the capstone above the door or the porch. Jeremias, p. 274, asserts that according to the agreed testimony of the Syriac translation of Psalm 118.22, Symmachus, Testimony of Solomon, Hipp., Tertullian, Aphraates, Prudentius, and Synagogue poetry, the reference is "the stone which crowns the building, or, more precisely, the key stone of the structure probably set above the porch."

[126] Matthew 21:42 quotes Psalm 118:22-23, while verse 44 refers first to Isaiah 8:14, then to Daniel 2:44-45. Luke is similar. In Mark only 118:22-23 is quoted.

enemies.[127] The word "rejected" is *apodokimazō*, "reject (after scrutiny), declare useless."[128] The rulers didn't just make a quick judgment error on the spur of the moment. This word indicates that they had a chance to examine the "stone" carefully and then reject it after reflection.

Whether the stone is "head of the corner" or "capstone," the point is that while this strategic stone was rejected by the builders, it ultimately was placed by God in the key position of the entire building.

Jesus' choice of words concerning the destruction of the Messiah's enemies is a sober one. The word translated twice in this verse as "falls" is the common Greek verb *piptō*. The word translated "broken to pieces" is Greek *synthlaō*, "crush (together), dash to pieces," to crush in such a way that an object is put in pieces.[129] The word translated "crushed" or "grind to powder" is the Greek verb *likmaō*.[130] These words, calling on the rock-crushing imagery of Daniel 2:44-45, portend a terrible fate for the Messiah's enemies – and for the nations of the world that stand against the Kingdom of God.

Peter, speaking to the rulers and elders (the "builders") boldly declares Jesus to be this one whom they rejected.

> "He is '**the stone** you builders rejected,
> which has become the **capstone**.'" (Acts 4:11)

Paul compares the Church to the construction of a holy temple,

> "Built on the foundation of the apostles and prophets,
> with Christ Jesus himself as the **chief cornerstone**." (Ephesians 2:20)

In another passage on building the church, Paul says,

> "No one can lay any **foundation** other than the one already laid,
> which is Jesus Christ." (1 Corinthians 3:11)

Jesus the Living Stone is part of the foundation as well. He is the one who called the apostles, taught them, and commissioned them to pass on his message to us. He is also the Redeemer who brought us salvation. Here he is referred to as the "chief cornerstone"

---

[127] "Builders" is a participle of the Greek verb *oikodomeo*, "build," construct a building. It is also used in a transcendent sense for building up the Christian church (Matthew 16:18; Romans 15:20; 1 Peter 2:5). *Oikodomeo*, BDAG 696.
[128] *Apodokimazo*, BDAG 110.
[129] *Sunthlaō*, BDAG 972.
[130] *Likmaō*, BDAG 596.

(*akrogoniaios*), which means "lying at the extreme corner.[131] It is used of Christ in our passage and also in 1 Peter 2:6, a reference to Isaiah 28:16.

Peter uses the imagery of Jesus the Stone and the temple to teach the unity of the church by interweaving three out of the four messianic prophecies we have identified.

"[4] As you come to him, **the living Stone** – rejected by men but chosen by God and precious to him – [5] you also, like living stones, are being built into a spiritual house to be a holy priesthood, offering spiritual sacrifices acceptable to God through Jesus Christ. [6] For in Scripture it says:

'See, I lay a **stone** in Zion,
  a **chosen and precious cornerstone**,
  and the one who trusts in him will never be put to shame."

[7] Now to you who believe, this **stone** is precious. But to those who do not believe,

'The **stone** the builders rejected has become the **capstone**, [8] and,

'A **stone** that causes men to stumble and a **rock** that makes them fall.'

They stumble because they disobey the message – which is also what they were destined for." (1 Peter 2:4-8)

"**Capstone**" (NIV) is literally "**head of the corner**" (NRSV, KJV). Though the ESV and NASB translate it "**cornerstone**," probably in this instance it refers to a keystone that locks a building together from above. "A stone that causes men to stumble" (NIV, NRSV), is also translated "**stone of stumbling**" (ESV, KJV), and "**stumbling stone**" (NJV). "Rock that makes them fall" (NIV, NRSV), can also be "**rock of offense**" (KJV, ESV).

Now we come to a passage where Paul uses a form of a rabbinical argument to affirm that the pre-existent Christ travelled with the Israelites to meet their needs.[132]

"... They drank from **the spiritual rock** that accompanied them, and that rock was Christ." (1 Corinthians 10:4)

As we reflect on the titles of Jesus as Spiritual Rock, Stumbling Stone, Crushing Stone, and Cornerstone, we see different aspects of Jesus' role. As our Spiritual Rock he is our

---

[131] *Akrogoniaios*, BDAG 39-40. cornerstone," sometimes interpreted as the "capstone."

[132] The reference to "the spiritual rock that accompanied them" (10:4) alludes to a Jewish legend (cf. Pseudo-Philo, *Biblical Antiquities*, 10.7; Tosefta *Sukkāh* 3:11-12) that conceived the idea of a rock which travelled alongside the people during their 40 year journey and supplied them with water as they required it. Paul doesn't endorse this legend, but affirms that Christ travelled with the Israelites to meet their needs (Bruce, *1 and 2 Corinthians*, p. 91).

strength, our might, our sustaining fortress in the midst of conflict. As Stumbling Stone Jesus' divinity and absolute authority highlight the reasons people avoid real discipleship; they are too enamored with their *own* will to surrender to *his* will. As Crushing Stone, Jesus is the one who will come as conquering King to usher in the Kingdom of God – and to destroy with violence all the worldly competitors to his supremacy. As Foundation he is the only one on which we can build a life that will endure. As Cornerstone or Capstone, he is the one who holds our lives together and crowns them with glory.

> **Q2. (1 Peter 2:4-8) In what way are these rock images of Christ attractive to our world? In what way do they repel people? Why? In what ways do you see Jesus as a Rock, Stone, and Foundation in your own life?**
> **http://www.joyfulheart.com/forums/topic/1630-q2-rock-stone-foundation/**

Jesus the Way, the Door, the Gate

We've looked at Jesus as Head and Rock. Now we turn to another metaphor. We find Jesus calling himself the Way and the Door or Gate, all of which point to him as the sole access we humans have to God.

> "Someone asked him, 'Lord, are only a few people going to be saved?' He said to them, 'Make every effort to enter through the narrow door, because many, I tell you, will try to enter and will not be able to.'" (Luke 13:23-24)

> "Enter through the narrow gate. For wide is the gate and broad is the road that leads to destruction, and many enter through it. But small is the gate and narrow the road that leads to life, and only a few find it." (Matthew 7:13-14)

As offensive as it may be to non-believers, Jesus is the Way, the only way, the exclusive way. "Way," of course, refers to a road or pathway.[133]

> "I am **the way** and the truth and the life. No one comes to the Father except through me." (John 14:6)

Jesus declares that he himself is the Way, the "road, highway"[134] to the Father's presence, the Father's house – heaven, if you will.

---

[133] "Way" is *hodos*, generally, an established "way" or "course," such as a road or channel of a river. It is often used as "way, road, highway." Figuratively, it is used of the whole way of life from a moral and spiritual viewpoint, "the way, teaching," in the most comprehensive sense (BDAG 692, 3c).

This shouldn't surprise us. Jesus' characteristic call is, "Follow me!" As we follow him and are obedient to what he teaches us, then he will lead us all the way to the Father's presence.

This phrase, "The Way," is used several places in the Scriptures.

- Isaiah looks forward to "a highway... [that] will be called the Way of Holiness" (Isaiah 35:8).
- Paul testifies that he persecuted "the followers of this Way" (Acts 22:4).
- The writer of Hebrews speaks of "a new and living way" that gives us access into God's very presence (Hebrews 10:19-20).

In a similar way, Jesus is the exclusive **"gate"** (NIV, NRSV) or **"door"** (ESV, KJV) into the sheepfold.

> "I tell you the truth, I am the **gate for the sheep**.... I am the **gate;** whoever enters through me will be saved. He will come in and go out, and find pasture." (John 10:7, 9)

Perhaps Jesus is comparing himself to a gate to protect the sheep, swinging open on hinges to let the sheep through. But there is another possibility, illustrated by a story told about George Adam Smith.

> "[Smith] was one day travelling with a guide and came across a shepherd and his sheep. The man showed him the fold into which the sheep were led at night. It consisted of four walls, with a way in. [Smith] said to him, 'That is where they go at night?' 'Yes,' said the shepherd, 'and when they are there, they are perfectly safe.' 'But there is no door,' said [Smith]. 'I am the door,' said the shepherd. '... When the light has gone and all the sheep are inside, I lie in that open space, and no sheep ever goes out but across my body, and no wolf comes in unless he crosses my body; I am the door.'"[135]

As the Apostle Paul explained,

> "Through him we both [Jew and Gentile] have access to the Father by one Spirit." (Ephesians 2:18)

---

[134] *Hodos*, BDAG 691, 3a.

[135] Morris, *John*, p. 507, n. 30, citing G. Campbell Morgan, *The Gospel According to John* (London and Edinburgh, 1951). In the fuller quote, Smith explains that the shepherd "was not a Christian man, he was not speaking in the language of the New Testament. He was speaking from the Arab shepherd's standpoint."

Jesus' blood shed for us opens up a "new and living way" to the Father (Hebrews 10:20). Because of Jesus, we have full access to the Father.

> "Let us then approach the throne of grace with confidence, so that we may receive mercy and find grace to help us in our time of need." (Hebrews 4:16)

To say that Jesus is "the Way," the only legitimate "Door" into the fold, is to affirm that he is the path to God, the only path. Soon after Jesus' resurrection, Peter affirmed this exclusivity.

> "Salvation is found in no one else, for there is no other name under heaven given to men by which we must be saved." (Acts 4:12)

This offends our world. Our society wants to believe that there are many paths to God in the way that "all roads lead to Rome." That tolerance is the value above all others. But the Scriptures declare that Jesus is the one and only Son of God. He is ultimate truth. Life comes exclusively through him. He is the Way that leads to God.

We can declare this angrily to our corrupt and adulterous generation. Many do so. But I think it is more productive to cast this in a positive light. Many people feel lost and feel like they need guidance. We can assure them that Jesus is the Path that will lead them to joy in this life – in spite of struggles – and to eternal joy in the life to come.

> **Q3. (John 14:6; 10:7, 9) In light of all the world's religions, how can Jesus be the Way to God, the exclusive door or gateway? Why does this offend the world? Since it is true, how can we most winsomely declare this truth to our generation?**
> **http://www.joyfulheart.com/forums/topic/1631-q3-jesus-the-way/**

Banner for the Peoples

Another title is related. Jesus is the Banner, the rallying point for all. In a clear messianic prophecy, Isaiah points to Jesse's descendent as "a banner for the peoples."

> "In that day the Root of Jesse will stand as a **banner** for the peoples;
> the nations will rally to him,
> and his place of rest will be glorious." (Isaiah 11:10)

"**Banner**" (NIV), "**signal**" (NRSV, ESV, NASB), "**ensign**" (KJV) is nēs. "In the OT, nēs generally means a rallying point or standard which drew people together for some common action or for the communication of important information. This usually happened on a high or conspicuous place within the camp or community.[136]

This title recalls Jesus' prophecies of being "lifted up" and becoming the rallying point for all who believe.

> "And as Moses lifted up the serpent in the wilderness, so must the Son of Man be lifted up, that whoever believes in him may have eternal life." (John 3:14-15)

> "'And I, when I am lifted up from the earth, will draw all people to myself.' He said this to show by what kind of death he was going to die." (John 12:32-33)

Jesus being lifted up on the cross has indeed become a rallying place, a source of inspiration, and cause for devotion for his followers. And many have become his followers as they meditated on what he did for them on that cross.

Jesus, the Great Physician

The final title we'll consider in this lesson is a metaphor – that of physician, a healer. Jesus recognized that his enemies would have used this title in a common Jewish proverb to taunt him.

> "Surely you will quote this proverb to me: '**Physician**, heal yourself! Do here in your hometown what we have heard that you did in Capernaum.'" (Luke 4:23-24)

Later, when Levi/Matthew the tax collector was called, Jesus was invited to a banquet in the new convert's home, joined by other tax collectors and those known in the town as "sinners." Jesus was criticized for associating with them.

> "[Jesus] said, 'Those who are well have no need of a **physician**, but those who are sick.'" (Matthew 9:12; Mark 2:17; Luke 5:31)

Though the title "Great Physician" isn't found in the Bible, it has been applied by Jesus' followers since then, since Jesus is the one who heals us. There's an old African American spiritual that sees Jesus in the prophecy of Jeremiah 8:22 concerning the balm or therapeutic aromatic resin or ointment characteristic of the region of Gilead,

> "There is a balm in Gilead, to make the wounded whole,
> There is a balm in Gilead, to heal the sin-sick soul."

Jesus is the one who can make us whole! Physically, emotionally, mentally, spiritually. Whole!

---

[136] People would rally together around a *nēs* for various purposes, one of the most important being the gathering of troops for war. cf. Isaiah 11:12. Marvin R. Wilson, *nēs*, TWOT #1379a.

Q4. (Luke 4:23) How does Jesus as the Great Physician resonate with our broken world? What does it mean to you that Jesus is your Great Physician and Healer?
http://www.joyfulheart.com/forums/topic/1632-q4-great-physician/

Jesus is Supreme. He is the head over the Church and over us also. He is the strong and stable Rock that the Israelites identified with Yahweh in the Wilderness. He is the Tested and Tried Stone that God lays as our Sure Foundation. He is also the Stumbling Stone and ultimately, the Stone that Crushes those who oppose him. Those who sought to be leaders, held onto their positions rather than acknowledge him as the Chief Cornerstone that God had ordained. He is the Living Stone upon which we are built into a living temple.

He is our Way, our Gate, our Door. He is the Banner or Signal that draws us, and he is the Physician who heals us and makes us whole. His name is Jesus, and we love him!

Prayer

Thank you, Jesus, for being our Head, our Rock, our Sure Foundation. We struggle with selfishness and self-rule, rather than submitting willingly to your rule. Forgive us. Let us not stumble over you, but rather live in you. Jesus our Way, lead on and we will follow. In your holy name, we pray with thanks. Amen.

Names and Titles of Jesus

Head (Ephesians 4:15)
Head of the Body (Colossians 1:18)
Head of the Church (Colossians 1:18)
Head of Every Man (1 Corinthians 11:13)
Stone (Isaiah 28:16; Matthew 21:44; Luke 20:18)
Tested Stone (NIV, NRSV, ESV, Isaiah 28:16)
Tried Stone (KJV, Isaiah 28:16)
Precious Cornerstone (Isaiah 28:16)
Sure Foundation (Isaiah 28:16)
Stone that Causes Men to Stumble (NIV, Isaiah 8:14; NIV, NRSV, 1 Peter 2:8)
Stone of Stumbling (KJV, Isaiah 8:14; ESV, KJV, 1 Peter 2:8)
Stone of Offense (ESV, Isaiah 8:14)
Rock of Offense (ESV, KJV, 1 Peter 2:8)

Rock that Makes Men/Them Fall (Isaiah 8:14; NIV, NRSV, 1 Peter 2:8)

Rock of Stumbling (ESV, Isaiah 8:14)

Trap (NIV, NRSV, ESV; Isaiah 8:14; Gin, KJV)

Snare (Isaiah 8:14)

Rock Cut out of a Mountain (Daniel 2:45)

Stone the Builders Rejected (Psalm 118:22; Matthew 21:42; Mark 12:10; Luke 20:17; Acts 4:11; 1 Peter 2:7)

Capstone (NIV, Psalm 118:22; Matthew 21:42; Mark 12:10; Acts 4:11; 1 Peter 2:7)

Cornerstone (ESV, Psalm 118:22; ESV, NRSV, Matthew 21:42; Mark 12:10; Luke 20:17; Acts 4:11; Ephesians 2:20; ESV, 1 Peter 2:7)

Chief Cornerstone (NRSV, Psalm 118:22; NIV, KJV, Ephesians 2:20)

Head Stone of the Corner (KJV, Psalm 118:22)

Head of the Corner (KJV, Matthew 21:42; Mark 12:10; Luke 20:17; Acts 4:11; NRSV, KJV, 1 Peter 2:7)

Foundation (1 Corinthians 3:11)

Living Stone (1 Peter 2:4)

Chosen and Precious Cornerstone (NIV, 1 Peter 2:6)

Cornerstone Chosen and Precious (NRSV, ESV, 1 Peter 2:6)

Chief Cornerstone, Elect, Precious (KJV, 1 Peter 2:6)

Spiritual Rock (1 Corinthians 10:4)

Way (John 14:6)

Gate (NIV, NRSV, John 10:9)

Door (ESV, KJV, John 10: 9)

Gate for the Sheep (NIV, NRSV, John 10:7)

Door of the Sheep (ESV, KJV, John 10:7)

Banner for the Peoples (NIV, Isaiah 11:10)

Signal to/for the Peoples (NRSV, ESV, Isaiah 11:10)

Ensign of the People (KJV, Isaiah 11:10)

Physician (NIV, ESV, KJV, Luke 4:23; also NRSV, Matthew 9:12; Mark 2:17; Luke 5:31)

Doctor (NRSV, Luke 4:23)

Songs and Hymns

These songs relate to various metaphors relating to Jesus, with titles such as Head, Stone, Cornerstone, Foundation, Stone, Rock, Way, Gate, Door, Banner, Ensign, and Physician.

"A Shelter in the Time of Storm" ("Jesus is a rock in a weary land"), words: Vernon J. Charlesworth (1880), music: Ira D. Sankey (1885)

"All the Way My Savior Leads Me," words: Fanny Crosby (1875), music: Robert Lowry (1875)

"Come, O Come, Emmanuel" ("Ensign of thy people, Desire of nations"), words: 12th century; music: 15th century

"Cornerstone" ("On Christ the Solid Rock I stand"), by Edward Mote, Eric Liljero, Jonas Myrin, Reuben Morgan, William Batchelder Bradbury (© 2011 Hillsong Music Publishing)

"Firm Foundation," by Nancy Gordon and Jamie Harvill (© 1994, Integrity's Hosanna! Music)

"His Banner Over Me is Love" ("I am my Beloved's and he is mine"), unknown author.

"His Banner Over Me," by Kevin Prosch (© 1991 Mercy / Vineyard Publishing)

"I Could Sing of Your Love Forever" ("Let the Healer set me free"), by Martin Smith (© 1994, Curious? Music UK)

"I Will Look Up" ("Jesus, Lord of All … Prince of Peace, Perfect Healer, King of Kings, Mighty Savior"), Chris Brown, Jason Ingram, Mack Brock, Matt Redman, Wade Joye (© 2013 Said And Done Music)

"In Christ Alone" ("This Cornerstone, this solid Ground"), by Keith Getty, Stuart Townend (© 2001 Thankyou Music)

"My Hope is Built on Nothing Less" ("on Christ the solid rock I stand"), words: Edward Mote (1834), music: Solid Rock: William B. Bradbury (1863)

"My Redeemer Lives" ("I'll raise a banner") by Reuben Morgan (© 1998 Hillsong Music Publishing)

"Shout for Joy" ("Like a banner high, lift up your grateful heart to the Morning Star … He's the Saving One"), by Jason Ingram, Lincoln Brewster, Paul Baloche (© 2010 Integrity Worship Music)

"The Church's One Foundation" (Is Jesus Christ her Lord"), words: Samuel J. Stone (1866), Music: Aurelia, Samuel S. Wesley (1864)

"The Way," by Ben Cantelon, Nick Herbert, Tim Hughes (© 2014 Ben Cantelon Designee)

"We Want to See Jesus Lifted High" ("A banner that flies across this land"), by Doug Horley (©1993, Thankyou Music)

Exercises

From Appendix 6. Exercises to Help You Internalize the Names of Jesus, select some activities that will help you internalize the truths of this lesson's names, titles, descriptors, and metaphors. This week, how can you creatively pray, meditate, write, worship, consider, draw or paint, compose, picture, and live out these truths in your community?

Actively participating in these ways will help you grow to be like Christ.

9. Jesus our Light, Life, Bread, and Bridegroom

We're still considering metaphors of Jesus. Among the most popular metaphors in the New Testament are Jesus the Light and Jesus the Life and Life-Giver – the Bread of Life, the Vine. Plus, there are a few metaphors and titles that don't seem to find a place elsewhere, that we'll consider at the end of this lesson.

Jesus the Light of the World

John's Gospel begins with a great poem of creation that associates Light and Life.

> "¹ In the beginning was the Word, and the Word was with God, and the Word was God. ² He was with God in the beginning. ³ Through him all things were made; without him nothing was made that has been made. ⁴ In him was **life**, and that life was the **light of men**. ⁵ The **light** shines in the darkness, but the darkness has not understood it." (John 1:1-5)

William Holman Hunt, 'Light of the World' (1851), Manchester Art Gallery

With these verses, John introduces the theme of a war between spiritual light and darkness that runs through his Gospel.[137] Here, Christ's light represents and brings life. Light is brimming with inextinguishable Life. The Light actively attacks the darkness (John 1:5a). As in Genesis 1:3, light is created by God's Word:

> "And God said, 'Let there be light,' and there was light." (Genesis 1:3)

Indeed, light characterizes God's glory, which we'll examine in Lesson 10. Jesus, the Co-Creator is the Bringer of Light to all humankind.

"Darkness" in John 1:5 seems almost to be darkness personified in both the prince of darkness, Satan, as well as all those who live in spiritual darkness. Light is shining but they haven't "understood it" (NIV), "overcome it" (NRSV, ESV), "comprehended it" (KJV). The Greek word *katalambanō*, which has the basic meaning of "to seize, lay hold

---

[137] John 1:4-5, 7-9; 3:19-21; 8:12; 9:5; 11:9-10; 12:35-36, 46.

of," and could refer to gaining a mental or spiritual grasp ("understood" or "comprehend") or it could mean, "seize with hostile intent, overtake, come upon" ("overcome").[138]

Jesus is not only the Bringer of Light. He is Light itself.

> "**The true light** that gives light to every man was coming into the world." (John 1:9)

> "I am the **light of the world**.
> Whoever follows me will never walk in darkness,
> but will have the light of life." (John 8:12)

> "This is the verdict: **Light** has come into the world, but men loved darkness instead of light because their deeds were evil." (John 3:19)

> "While I am in the world, I am the **light of the world**." (John 9:5)

In the Sermon on the Mount, Jesus' disciples are "the light of the world" (Matthew 5:14), called "the people of the light" (Luke 16:8). That light is lit by Jesus.

Messianic Prophecy of the Light

In Isaiah we see several prophecies of the Light. First, a passage that places Messiah's primary ministry in Galilee, quoted in Matthew 4:16.

> "Nevertheless, there will be no more gloom for those who were in distress.
> In the past he humbled the land of Zebulun and the land of Naphtali,
> but in the future he will honor Galilee of the Gentiles,
> by the way of the sea, along the Jordan –
> The people walking in darkness have seen a **great light**;
> on those living in the land of the shadow of death **a light** has dawned." (Isaiah 9:1-2)

Jesus is the Great Light. The Servant (probably here the Messiah, not Israel) is also to be a light.

> "I, the LORD, have called you in righteousness;
> I will take hold of your hand.
> I will keep you and will make you to be **a covenant for the people**
> and **a light for the Gentiles**." (Isaiah 42:6; cf. 49:6)

Finally, a prophecy looking forward to the Days of the Messiah.

> "Arise, shine, for **your light** has come,
> and the glory of the LORD rises upon you.

---

[138] *Katalambanō*, BDAG 520, meanings 1, 2, and 3.

> See, darkness covers the earth
> and thick darkness is over the peoples,
> but the LORD rises upon you
> and his glory appears over you.
> Nations will come to your light,
> and kings to the brightness of your dawn." (Isaiah 60:1-3)

The Sun of Righteousness

In the Old Testament, Yahweh is referred to as "a sun and shield" (Psalm 84:11) and "everlasting light" (Isaiah 60:19-20). In Malachi's prophecy of the last day, this title transfers over to the Messiah.

> "But for you who revere my name,
> the **Sun of righteousness** will rise with healing in its wings.
> And you will go out and leap like calves released from the stall." (Malachi 4:2)

"Healing in his/its wings" (NIV, NRSV, ESV, KJV) should probably be translated, "healing in his rays" (New Jerusalem Bible), since *kānāp*, "wing, winged, border, corner, shirt," is a word that seems to refer to something stretched out, and "rays" fits the imagery of the sun better than "wings." Those upon whom Jesus' light rises will find the healing of truth and his presence.

Rising Sun, Dayspring

In a similar way, the image of the rising sun refers to the Messiah in the prophecy of Zechariah the priest, John the Baptist's father.

> "... Because of the tender mercy of our God,
> by which the **rising sun** will come to us from heaven...." (Luke 1:78, NIV)

"Dayspring" (KJV), "rising sun" (NIV), "sunrise" (ESV, NASB), "the dawn" (NRSV) is *anatolē*, "upward movement of celestial bodies, rising" here, "a change from darkness to light in the early morning, the dawn," figurative of the coming of the Messiah.[139]

Morning Star

But Jesus is not only prefigured by the sun, but by the stars as well. As I write this, just before dawn I have seen three "stars" – planets actually – Jupiter, Mars, and Venus, shining brightly in the early morning sky. It made me think of this passage.

---

[139] *Anatolē*, BDAG 74, 3.

"I, Jesus, have sent my angel to give you this testimony for the churches. I am the Root and the Offspring of David, and **the bright Morning Star.**[140]" (Revelation 22:16)

Peter writes,

"And we have the word of the prophets made more certain, and you will do well to pay attention to it, as to a light shining in a dark place, until the day dawns and the **morning star** (*phōsphoros*) rises in your hearts." (2 Peter 1:19)

KJV translates the word, "**day star.**" In one of Isaiah's prophecies, the title "Day Star, son of Dawn" is claimed by the king of Babylon, whom many see as an antitype of Satan (Isaiah 14:2). But it shouldn't surprise us that kings and fallen angels should claim titles for themselves that are blasphemous and over reaching.

These references probably trace back to Balaam's prophecy of the king that would rise up from Israel to free her from her enemies. In the short term it spoke of David, but ultimately it points to David's successor, Christ the king.

"I see him, but not now;
I behold him, but not near.
A **star will come out of Jacob**;
a scepter will rise out of Israel." (Numbers 24:17)

Q1. (John 1:9; 8:12) In what sense is Jesus the True Light? In what sense is he the Light of the World? In what sense are you the light of the world (Matthew 5:14)? Why do you think people resist Jesus' light, his truth, his view of the Father, our world, and eternal life? How does the world's so-called "light" differ from Jesus' light? What can obstruct Jesus' light in this world? What can obstruct our light? http://www.joyfulheart.com/forums/topic/1633-q1-true-light/

The Life-Giver

Jesus not only brings light, he brings life. The Old Testament, of course, refers life-giving to Yahweh.

"For with you is the fountain of life;
in your light we see light." (Psalm 36:9)

---

[140] "The bright morning star" is two words, each with a definite article: *lampros*, "pertaining to radiating light, bright" (BDAG 585, 1) and *prōinos*, "the one belonging to the morning" (BDAG 892).

Especially in John's writings, Jesus is portrayed as the Life-Giver. As we've seen, this theme is at the very beginning of John's Gospel.

> "In him was **life**, and the life was the light of men." (John 1:4)

Jesus declares that he is the Life. John's Gospel overflows with this theme. Jesus brings eternal life. In fact, he is the very source of life – both physical life as Co-Creator, but eternal life as well. In a number of places in John's Gospel, Jesus asserts his authority to give life.

> "For just as the Father raises the dead and gives them life, even so the Son **gives life** to whom he is pleased to give it." (John 5:21[141])

John's First Epistle declares unequivocally that this eternal life is exclusively in Jesus and in no other.

> "And this is the testimony: God has given us eternal life, and **this life is in his Son**. He who has the Son has **life**; he who does not have the Son of God does not have **life**." (1 John 5:11-12)

We see the same unequivocal declaration on Jesus' lips in John's Gospel:

> "I am the way and the truth and **the life**." (John 14:6)

In Revelation he is revealed as **"the Living One"** (Revelation 1:17b).

The Bread of Life

As the Gospel unfolds, we see Jesus referred to by several titles related to giving life. Following the Feeding of the 5,000, Jesus talks to his disciples about the life-giving qualities of the true Bread, the true Manna.

> "I am the **bread of life**." (John 6:48)

> "I am the **bread of life**; whoever comes to me shall not hunger, and whoever believes in me shall never thirst." (John 6:35)

Of course, the phrase "bread of life" means "bread which brings life."

> "I am the **living bread** that came down from heaven. If anyone eats of this bread, he will live forever. And the bread that I will give for the life of the world is my flesh." (John 6:51)

---

[141] Also John 5:26; 6:33, 57, 68; 10:28a.

"Living bread that came down from heaven" is a comparison with the manna in the Wilderness. Though the title doesn't appear in the Bible, Jesus could be thought of as the Living Manna.

> "For the **bread of God** is he who comes down from heaven and gives life to the world." (John 6:33)

Jesus the Vine

Jesus' parable of the Vine and the Branches in John 15:1-17 is also a parable of the life-giving nature of the vine.

> "I am the **true vine,** and my Father is the gardener." (John 15:1)

> "I am the **vine**; you are the branches." (John 15:5)

Life flows through the vine to the branches and from them to the fruit.

> **Q2. (John 6:51; 15:1-5) What do Jesus' teachings on the Living Bread and the True Vine teach us about drawing from his life? What happens to our vital Life when we rely on ourselves, and stop relying on him? Why is it so hard for us humans to learn the lesson of dependence and trust?**
> **http://www.joyfulheart.com/forums/topic/1634-q2-living-bread-true-vine/**

The Resurrection and the Life

When Jesus hears that Lazarus had died, he comes to Bethany and finds one of Lazarus's grieving sisters. When he assures Martha that her brother will rise again, she points to the final resurrection that was the belief of Pharisees. Jesus doesn't deny this resurrection on the Last Day, but in this case he personalizes it.

> "I am **the resurrection and the life**. He who believes in me will live, even though he dies...." (John 11:25)

Jesus is the key to Lazarus's resurrection; resurrection from the dead starts and completes in Jesus. Jesus himself is the "firstborn from the dead" (Colossians 1:18; Revelation 1:5, which we'll consider in Lesson 10). Yes, others were raised by Jesus and the apostles, but they eventually died. However, when Jesus raises you ultimately, you will never die again. Jesus is the ultimate Life-Giver.

The True God and Eternal Life

John's First Epistle continues the theme.

> "The **life** appeared; we have seen it and testify to it, and we proclaim to you the **eternal life**, which was with the Father and has appeared to us." (1 John 1:2)

> "We know also that the Son of God has come and has given us understanding, so that we may know him who is true. And we are in him who is true – even in his Son Jesus Christ. He is **the true God and eternal life**." (1 John 5:20)

What a statement! John states that Jesus is the True God and Eternal Life!

The Author of Life

This life-giving theme is also picked up by both Peter and Paul. In the preaching of the Gospel in Jerusalem shortly after Jesus' resurrection, Peter declares boldly.

> "You killed **the author**[142] **of life**, but God raised him from the dead. We are witnesses of this." (Acts 3:15)

"Author" (NIV, ESV), "prince" (KJV) is *archēgos*, especially here, "one who begins or originates," hence the recipient of special esteem in the Greco-Roman world, "originator, founder."[143] As we'll see in Lesson 10, there is a similar use of this word in Hebrews, where Jesus is called "**the author and perfecter of our faith**...." (Hebrews 12:2a, NIV, NASB), and as the "**Author of salvation** (NIV, NASB, Hebrews 2:10). Jesus is the originator of our salvation.

Christ Who Is Your Life

We conclude this study of Life-Giving titles with one from Paul. Looking forward to Christ's coming, Paul says:

> "Set your minds on things above, not on earthly things. For you died, and your **life** is now hidden with Christ in God. When **Christ, who is your life**, appears, then you also will appear with him in glory." (Colossians 3:2-4)

Again,

> "I have been crucified with Christ and I no longer live, but Christ lives in me. The life I live in the body, I live by faith in the Son of God, who loved me and gave himself for me." (Galatians 2:20)

---

[142] "Author" (NIV, ESV), "prince" (KJV) is *archēgos*, especially here, "one who begins or originates," hence the recipient of special esteem in the Greco-Roman world, "originator, founder" (BDAG 138, 3).

[143] *Archēgos*, BDAG 138, 3.

Too often, nominal Christians try to live their own life, with them in charge. But that is not the life Jesus was talking about. His life is all consuming. It is in, under, around, and through. He is our Life!

Dear friend, how about you. Is Christ the center, the focus of your life, or have you placed him on the periphery? Now is the time to repent and change that! Let him fill you afresh – or for the first time – with his bubbling, everlasting, joy-filled life.

Q3. (Colossians 3:2-4) To what degree is Christ the center, the focus of your life? If you had to prove to another person that Christ is the center of your life, what evidence would you muster? What evidence would contradict this? What kind of repentance is necessary to reprioritize your life?
http://www.joyfulheart.com/forums/topic/1635-q3-christ-who-is-your-life/

Husband and Bridegroom

Now we'll turn to another sphere of metaphors and titles. Perhaps some of the best known of these to Christians are Husband and Bridegroom.

In the Old Testament, Yahweh is spoken of as the husband, while Israel is his bride.

"For your Maker is your husband,
the LORD of hosts is his name;
and the Holy One of Israel is your Redeemer,
the God of the whole earth he is called." (Isaiah 54:5)

This theme is carried into the New Testament, with Jesus as the Husband and the Church as the Bride of Christ.

"I am jealous for you with a godly jealousy. I promised you to one **husband**, to Christ, so that I might present you as a pure virgin to him." (2 Corinthians 11:2)

"Husbands, love your wives, just as Christ loved the church and gave himself up for her." (Ephesians 5:25)

"Let us rejoice and be glad and give him glory! For the wedding of the Lamb has come, and his bride has made herself ready." (Revelation 19:7)

"I saw the Holy City, the new Jerusalem, coming down out of heaven from God, prepared as a bride beautifully dressed for her **husband**." (Revelation 21:2)

"One of the seven angels who had the seven bowls full of the seven last plagues came and said to me, 'Come, I will show you the bride, the wife of the Lamb.'" (Revelation 21:9)

"The Spirit and the bride say, 'Come!'" (Revelation 22:17a)

Twice in the Gospels we see parables in which the person corresponding to Jesus is the Bridegroom, so I suppose Bridegroom is a legitimate title of Jesus.

John the Baptist: "The bride belongs to **the bridegroom**[144]. The friend who attends the bridegroom waits and listens for him, and is full of joy when he hears the bride-groom's voice. That joy is mine, and it is now complete. He must become greater; I must become less." (John 3:29-30)

Jesus: "How can the guests of **the bridegroom** mourn while he is with them? The time will come when the bridegroom will be taken from them; then they will fast." (Matthew 9:15; Mark 2:19-20; Luke 5:34-35)

According to this analogy, we the Church are presently "betrothed" to him, thus officially (according to Jewish law) he is our Husband. We are to be presented to Christ at his coming as a "pure virgin" (2 Corinthians 11:2) when the "marriage supper of the Lamb takes place (Revelation 19:7). My pastor, Greg Krieger, says that marriage is God's favorite metaphor, one that portrays the wonderful ways we are loved, pursued, protected, and cherished by the One who seeks us to be His own.

> **Q4. (2 Corinthians 11:2) What does it take for us to be presented to Christ as a pure virgin bride? How faithful are we to Christ? To what degree do we partake with the adulterous and sinful generation that Jesus decried? What does the marriage relationship say about love, communication, and intimacy with Christ?**
> **http://www.joyfulheart.com/forums/topic/1636-q4-bridegroom-and-husband/**

The Covenant and Guarantor of the Covenant

Now we look at titles from a completely different set of analogies, those that live in the world of covenants, contracts, and treaties.

---

[144] *Nymphios,* "bridegroom" (BDAG 68).

As we've discussed in Lesson 6, Isaiah alternates between the Servant being Israel and her Messiah. In a passage that seems to point to the Messiah Servant, Isaiah prophesies:

> "I will give you as **a covenant for the people**,
> a light for the nations,
> to open the eyes that are blind,
> to bring out the prisoners from the dungeon,
> from the prison those who sit in darkness." (Isaiah 42:6-7, ESV)

"Covenant" is *berît*. Between nations a *berît* is a treaty, an alliance of friendship. Between individuals, a *berît* is a pledge or agreement, an obligation between a monarch and subjects. Between God and man, a *berît* is a relationship with promises for fulfillment.[145] In his person, Jesus *is* the covenant between Yahweh and his people!

Jesus is also God's guarantee that this covenant will be fulfilled.

> "Jesus has become the **guarantee of a better covenant**." (Hebrews 7:22)

"Guarantee" (NIV, NRSV), **"guarantor"** (ESV), **"surety"** (KJV) is *engyos*, used as an adjective, "pertaining to assurance for the fulfillment of something, under good security," as a noun, "guarantee."[146] Since ancient times people have put forward valuable items, even hostages, to guarantee a treaty, agreement, or payment of an obligation. God put forward his most valuable possession, his own Son, to guarantee that he will keep his word to us. Jesus is the guarantor of a "better covenant" than even Israel experienced.

We have been offered the "new covenant" promised in Jeremiah 31:31-34 (quoted in Hebrews 8:6-13). For Jesus as Mediator of a New Covenant (Hebrews 11:24) see Lesson 3. Jesus' own blood becomes the blood that is shed to seal the new covenant of the Spirit, of forgiveness, and of the knowledge of God. We remember this historical fact by partaking regularly of the Cup of the Lord's Supper, which is, Jesus told his disciples, "the new covenant in my blood" (1 Corinthians 11:25; cf. Matthew 26:28; Mark 14:24; Luke 22:20).

We are so blessed! Jesus is our Light. He is our Life. He is our Bread. He is the Vine from which we draw life itself. He is our Resurrection, he is the original champion of the second chance. He is our Husband, our Bridegroom, our Surety and Guarantor of our relationship with God. And we are thankful!

[145] Elmer B. Smick, *berît*, TWOT #282a.
[146] *Engyos*, BDAG 271.

Prayer

Father, thank you for sending Jesus to us. Thank you for your patience with us, for your offer of Life, even when we don't appreciate it or think we need it. Be the center of our lives. Let us serve well as your Bride. There are not words enough to thank you for your patience and mercy towards us, yet we say thanks. In Jesus' name, we pray. Amen.

Names and Titles of Jesus

Light of Men (John 1:4)

Light (John 1:5; 3:19; Isaiah 9:2)

True Light (John 1:9)

Light of the World (John 8:12; 9:5)

Great Light (Isaiah 9:2)

Light for the Gentiles (Isaiah 42:6; 49:6)

Light for Revelation to the Gentiles (NIV, NRSV, ESV, Luke 2:32)

Light to Lighten the Gentiles (KJV, Luke 2:32)

Your Light (Isaiah 60:1-3)

Sun of Righteousness (Malachi 4:2)

Rising Sun (NIV, Luke 1:78)

Dayspring (KJV, Luke 1:78)

Sunrise (ESV, NASB, Luke 1:78)

Dawn (NRSV, Luke 1:78)

Morning Star (2 Peter 1:19)

Bright Morning Star (Revelation 22:16)

Day Star (2 Peter 1:19)

Star (Numbers 24:17)

Life (John 14:6; 1 John 1:2; Colossians 3:4)

The Living One (Revelation 1:17b)

Bread (John 6:50)

Bread of Life (John 6:35, 48)

Living Bread (John 6:51)

Bread of God (John 6:33)

The Resurrection and the Life (John 11:25)

True Vine (John 15:1)

Vine (John 15:5)

Eternal Life (1 John 1:2; 5:20)

The True God and Eternal Life (1 John 5:20)

Author of Life (NIV, ESV, Acts 3:15)

Prince of Life (KJV, Acts 3:15)

Christ Who Is Your Life (Colossians 3:4)

Husband (2 Corinthians 11:2; Revelation 21:2)

Bridegroom (John 3:29; Matthew 9:15; Mark 2:19-20; Luke 5:34-35)

Covenant for/of/to the People (Isaiah 42:6-7)

Guarantee of a Better Covenant (NIV, NRSV, Hebrews 7:22)

Guarantor of a Better Covenant (ESV, Hebrews 7:22)

Surety of a Better Covenant (KJV, Hebrews 7:22)

Songs and Hymns

The metaphors in this lesson center on the titles of Light of the World, Sun of Righteousness, Dayspring, Morning Star, the Living One, Bread of Life, Resurrection and Life, Vine, Author of Life, Life, Husband, Bridegroom, and Covenant.

"All Hail King Jesus" ("Bright Morning Star") by Dave Moody (1981 Dayspring Music, LLC)

"Because He Lives," by Gloria and William J. Gaither (© 1971 William J. Gaither, Inc.)

"Behold the Lamb" ("So we share in this Bread of Life"), by Keith Getty, Krystyn Getty, Stuart Townend (© 2007 Thankyou Music)

"Break Thou the Bread of Life," words: Mary A. Lathbury (1877), Alexander Groves (1913); music: William F. Sherwin (1877)

"Breathe" ("You are my daily bread"), by Marie Barnett (© 1995, Mercy/Vineyard Publishing)

"Come, O Come, Emmanuel" ("O come, thou Day-spring, come and cheer"), words: 12th century; music: 15th century

"Days of Elijah" ("Behold He comes riding on the clouds, shining like the sun at the trumpet's call"), by Robin Mark (© 1996 Song Solutions Daybreak)

"Forever Reign" ("Light of the world forever reign ... You are Light, You are Light ... You are Hope, You are Hope ... You are Peace, You are Peace"), by Scott Ingram, Reuben Morgan (© 2009 Hillsong Music Publishing)

"Great Are You, Lord" ("You bring light in the darkness"), David Leonard, Jason Ingram, Leslie Jordan (© 2012 Integrity's Alleluia! Music)

"Hark, the Herald Angels Sing" ("Hail the Sun of Righteousness ... risen with healing in his wings"), words: Charles Wesley (1739), music: Felix Mendelssohn (1840)

"He Is Faithful" ("He is freedom, He is healing right now, He is hope and joy, love and peace and life. I have seen a light like the break of dawn"), by Bryan Torwalt, Katie Torwalt (© 2011 Capitol CMG Genesis, Jesus Culture Music)

"Here I Am to Worship" ("Light of the World, you stepped down into darkness"), by Tim Hughes (© 2001, Thankyou Music)

"Here Is Love" ("the Prince of Life our Ransom"), by Matt Redman, Robert Lowry, William Rees (© 2004 Thankyou Music)

"I Am the Light of the World," words and music by Jim Strathdee (© 1969 Desert Flower Music; in Chalice Hymnal, 1995, #469)

"In Christ Alone" ("He is my light, my strength, my song") by Keith Getty, Stuart Townend (© 2001 Thankyou Music)

"Jesus Messiah" ("the Light of the world") by Chris Tomlin, Daniel Carson, Ed Cash, Jesse Reeves (2008 sixsteps Music)

"Jesus, What a Wonder You Are" ("You shine like the morning star"), by Dave Bolton (© 1975, Thankyou Music)

"Light of the World," by Matt Redman (© 1999, Thankyou Music)

"Mighty to Save," ("Shine your light ... we're singing for the glory of the risen King Jesus ... Author of salvation"), by Ben Fielding and Reuben Morgan (© 2006 Hillsong Publishing)

"My Lighthouse," by Rend Collective (© 2013 Thankyou Music)

"Open the Eyes of My Heart" ("To see you high and lifted up, shining in the light of your glory"), by Paul Baloche (© 1997, Integrity's Hosanna! Music)

"Shine, Jesus, Shine" ("Jesus, Light of the world, shine upon us"), by Graham Kendrick (© 1987, Make Way Music)

"Thine Is the Glory" ("Risen conquering Son ... Glorious Prince of life"), words: Edmond L. Budry (1884), translated by Richard B. Hoyle (1923), music: Judas Maccabeaus, George F. Handel (1747)

"This I Believe" ("The Creed": "I believe in the resurrection, that we will rise again ... Our Judge and our Defender"), by Ben Fielding, Matt Crocker (© 2014 Hillsong Music Publishing)

"We All Bow Down" ("He is the love of God ... He's the light of the world and Lord of the cross"), by Lenny LeBlanc (© 2002 Integrity's Hosanna! Music)

"We Will Dance" ("For the Bridegroom will come, the glorious One ... the Risen King, our Groom"), by David Ruis (© 1993 Mercy / Vineyard Publishing)

"You Are the Vine," by Danny Daniels, Randy Rigby (© 1985 Mercy / Vineyard Publishing)

Exercises

From Appendix 6. Exercises to Help You Internalize the Names of Jesus, select some activities that will help you internalize the truths of this lesson's names, titles, descriptors, and metaphors. This week, how can you creatively pray, meditate, write, worship, consider, draw or paint, compose, picture, and live out these truths in your community?

Actively participating in these ways will help you grow to be like Christ.

10. Jesus the Risen King of Glory

As I write this, my wife and I are looking forward to hearing our daughter sing in a great community production of Handel's Messiah, which is full of arias and choruses putting to music the great messianic prophecies of the Old Testament, including most of those we've studied in this series. And I know that I will hear the stirring chorus: "Who Is the King of Glory" taken from the messianic Psalm 24. I can hardly wait!

Detail of 'Resurrection' stained glass window, Co-Cathedral of the Sacred Heart, Houston, 2008, full size is 40ft x 20ft. Designed and constructed by Mellini Art Glass and Mosaics in Florence, Italy. Photo © 2010, Lea McNulty, used by permission.

"7 Lift up your heads, O you gates;
be lifted up, you ancient doors,
that **the King of glory** may come in.
8 Who is this **King of glory**?
The LORD strong and mighty,
the LORD mighty in battle.
9 Lift up your heads, O you gates;
lift them up, you ancient doors,
that **the King of glory** may come in.
10 Who is he, this **King of glory**?
The LORD of Hosts – he is **the King of glory**." (Psalm 24:7-10)

There's a sense in which it was fulfilled when David brought the ark into the city of Jerusalem with shouting and celebration (2 Samuel 6). And then I think of Jesus riding a donkey as he rode into Jerusalem to take his rightful place as Messiah in the City of his God (Matthew 21:1-11). But there is a sense in which it will be ultimately fulfilled in the Last Day, when the Messiah returns to reign at his Second Coming and enters the New Jerusalem, having defeated all his foes (Revelation 11:15). The King of Glory is coming!

We studied Jesus as Messiah, the Son of David. The Jews expected the Messiah to overthrow the Romans and set up the Kingdom of God again in Jerusalem. When they realized that Jesus had no such intentions, they saw him as a threat to *their* power rather than the Romans, and they delivered him up to be crucified. And so Jesus fulfilled part of his Messianic role, to deliver his people from their sin.

But in this final lesson we'll explore Jesus the King of Glory, who conquers all enemies and reigns forever. We've looked at many titles of Jesus, mainly from the perspective of his earthly ministry. Here we see him primarily in his final resurrected state, the Glorified Christ. We'll be looking at eschatological titles, those referring to his role in the Last Day. ("Eschatology" is from *eschatos*, "last," a study of the Last Days.)

God's Shekinah Glory

We'll begin to study the Glorified Christ by reviewing what we know about the Shekinah glory of God.

Throughout the Old Testament we read about the "glory of God," which was sometimes manifested in fire and brightness, what the Jews called the "Shekinah," the dwelling or settling of the divine presence. In Hebrew "glory" is *kābôd*, from *kābēd*—"to be heavy," hence "wealth, honor, dignity, power," etc. In the New Testament, *kābôd* is translated by *doxa*, "reputation."

The concept of glory is first developed in Exodus. God reveals his glory and enhances his reputation in his defeat of Pharaoh in Egypt (Exodus 14:4, 17-18) and in other marvelous deeds (Exodus 15:11). When the Israelites grumble about not having food, God not only provides food, but "they looked toward the desert, and there was the glory of the LORD appearing in the cloud" (Exodus 16:10). The glory appeared as both a cloud and fire:

> "The glory of the LORD settled on Mount Sinai. For six days the cloud covered the mountain... To the Israelites the glory of the LORD looked like a consuming fire on top of the mountain." (Exodus 24:16-17)

One day, Moses asked Yahweh,

> "'Now show me your glory.'
> Then the LORD said, 'There is a place near me where you may stand on a rock. When my glory passes by, I will put you in a cleft in the rock and cover you with my hand until I have passed by. Then I will remove my hand and you will see my back; but my face must not be seen.'" (Exodus 33:18, 21-23)

Moses himself was changed by communing with God.

"When Moses came down from Mount Sinai ... he was not aware that his face was radiant[147] because he had spoken with the LORD. When Aaron and all the Israelites saw Moses, his face was radiant, and they were afraid to come near him." (Exodus 34:29-30)

The Jews call this dwelling presence of God the "Shekinah glory," from the Hebrew root *shakan*, "settle, inhabit, dwell," and is seen in the noun, *mishkān*, "dwelling place, tabernacle."[148]

We see this idea of Shekinah reflected in the Gospel of John.

"The Word became flesh and made his dwelling among us. We have seen his glory, the glory of the One and Only, who came from the Father, full of grace and truth." (John 1:14)

John had seen that very Shekinah glory upon Jesus during the transfiguration, and, with Peter and James, "were eyewitnesses of his majesty" (2 Peter 1:16-18).

"After six days Jesus took with him Peter, James and John the brother of James, and led them up a high mountain by themselves. There he was transfigured before them. His face shone like the sun, and his clothes became as white as the light." (Matthew 17:1-2)

The New Testament uses the same concept in Greek as Hebrew *kāḇôḏ*. The words are based on the Greek root *doxa*, from which we get our word, "doxology," a liturgical expression of praise to God. The noun *doxa* means "the condition of being bright or shining, brightness, splendor, radiance" and the idea, "honor as enhancement or recognition of status or performance, fame, recognition, renown, honor, prestige."[149] The verb *doxazō* means "to influence one's opinion about another so as to enhance the latter's reputation, praise, honor, extol" and "to cause to have splendid greatness, clothe in splendor, glorify," of the glory that comes in the next life.[150]

Now that we've explored the concept of glory in the Old Testament and considered the Greek words in the New Testament, we're ready to look at the glorified Christ.

---

[147] The radiant glory of God was upon Moses. "Radiant" (NIV), "shone" (NRSV, ESV, KJV) is *qāran*, "shine" (TWOT 816).

[148] Willem A. van Gemeren, "Shekinah," ISBE 4:466-468. R. K. Harrison, "Glory," ISBE 2:477-483.

[149] *Doxa*, BDAG 257-258, 1 and 3.

[150] *Doxazō*, BDAG 258, 1 and 2.

Jesus' Glory

As we saw in Lesson 9, John's Gospel speaks of Jesus as Light, evoking the Shekinah glory of God who "dwells in unapproachable light" (1 Timothy 6:16). Three of his disciples saw just a glimpse of it at Jesus' Transfiguration.

Jesus' glory is intended to spill out and be revealed by means of the miraculous signs that he performs. They are sign-posts that point to who he is – the Son of God. At Cana, where Jesus changed the water into wine, John says, "He thus revealed his glory, and his disciples put their faith in him" (John 2:11).[151] Jesus plainly acknowledges that his glory comes directly from his Father, a fact that he does not hide from those who listen to his teachings.[152]

The cross especially – along with his subsequent resurrection and ascension – are seen as the means of his glorification in John's Gospel. After his resurrection, he explained to two men on the road to Emmaus: "Did not the Christ have to suffer these things and then enter his glory?" (Luke 24:26)

Glory at the Coming of the Son of Man

Glory is particularly associated with the Son of Man because of the passage in Daniel:

"One like a son of man ... was given authority, **glory** and sovereign power" (Daniel 7:13-14).

This is fulfilled at the Second Coming of Christ.

"For the Son of Man is going to come **in his Father's glory** with his angels...." (Matthew 16:27)

"For the Son of Man in his day will be **like the lightning**, which flashes and lights up the sky from one end to the other." (Luke 17:24)

"At that time the sign of the Son of Man will appear in the sky, and **all the nations** of the earth will mourn. They will see the Son of Man **coming on the clouds of the sky, with power and great glory**. When the Son of Man comes in his glory, and all the angels with him, he will sit on his throne in heavenly glory." (Matthew 25:30-31)

On that Day we will see fulfilled Isaiah's prophecy:

---

[151] See also John 11:4, 40.
[152] John 8:49-50, 54; 12:28-29; 16:14; 17:1, 4-5.

"And the **glory** of the LORD shall be revealed,
and all flesh shall see it together,
for the mouth of the LORD has spoken." (Isaiah 40:5)

Where is the title in all this, you may ask? Here it is:

"The Son is **the radiance of God's glory**...." (Hebrews 1:3)

"Radiance" (NIV, ESV), "brightness" (KJV) is *apaugasma*. Most translators see it in an active sense: "radiance, effulgence," in the sense of brightness from a source, though some see it as passive: "reflection," that is, brightness shining back.[153]

> **Q1. (Hebrews 1:3; Matthew 17:1-2) In what ways did Jesus show the Father's glory in his ministry? Why do you think Jesus allowed Peter, James, and John to see his Transfiguration? How do you think Jesus will appear in heaven?**
> **http://www.joyfulheart.com/forums/topic/1637-q1-glory/**

While there are few titles related to Jesus' glory, you can see it is a major theme in the Gospels. Now, let's move on to some of the grand, universal titles that apply to the risen, glorified Christ.

Jesus the Beginning and the End, the Alpha and Omega

While Jesus' earthly life was temporal, the glorified Christ is eternal, everlasting. His full glory is revealed when he is exalted on high to where he was before the beginning of time.

Yahweh's name, as mentioned in Lesson 5, seems to be constructed from the Hebrew verb "to be." When Moses asked his name, he revealed himself as "I AM THAT I AM." God *is*! He always was, he is with us now, and he always will be! Hallelujah!

One way this is expressed in the New Testament is God's presence at the beginning and the end. In fact, he *is* the beginning! He *is* the end!

Revelation 1:8 seems to be spoken of God the Father, but there isn't clear separation, since the verse is in the context of the coming of the Son of Man on the clouds (verse 7), and many of the same titles are repeated to make clear reference to the Son later in Revelation.

---

[153] *Apaugasma,* BDAG 99.

"'I am **the Alpha and the Omega**,'
says the **Lord God**,
'**who is, and who was, and who is to come, the Almighty**.'" (Revelation 1:8)

"**Who is, and who was, and who is to come**" (Revelation 1:4, 8) reflects God's eternal nature, the I AM, which is shared by Jesus. Jesus is present in the now; he always was; and he is coming again! Alpha is the first letter of the Greek alphabet; omega is the last letter. We might say the A and the Z.

The one like a Son of Man among the golden lampstands (the seven churches of Revelation), reveals himself with similar titles.

"Do not be afraid.
I am **the First and the Last**.
I am **the Living One**;
I was dead, and behold I am alive for ever and ever!
And I hold the keys of death and Hades." (Revelation 1:17b-18)

He reveals himself to the Church in Smyrna in this way:

"These are the words of him who is the **First and the Last**,
who died and came to life again." (Revelation 2:8)

In the New Jerusalem, the one seated upon the throne says:

"It is done.
I am the **Alpha and the Omega**,
the Beginning and the End.
To him who is thirsty I will give to drink
without cost from the spring of the water of life." (Revelation 21:6)

At the end of Revelation, these titles clearly rest on Jesus Christ:

"Behold, I am coming soon!
My reward is with me,
and I will give to everyone according to what he has done.
I am the Alpha and the Omega,
the First and the Last,
the Beginning and the End." (Revelation 22:12-13)

"Beginning" in these verses is *archē* with the meaning, "the commencement of something as an action, process, or state of being, beginning, that is, a point of time at the beginning of a duration."[154]

Author and Perfecter of Our Faith

The writer of Hebrews picks up this theme in a slightly different way:

"Let us fix our eyes on Jesus, **the author and perfecter of our faith**...." (Hebrews 12:2a, NIV, NASB)

This pair of words can be translated "**the pioneer and perfecter**" (NRSV), "**the founder and perfecter**" (ESV), "**the author and finisher**" (KJV). The first word in the pair is *archēgos*, "one who has a preeminent position – leader, ruler," then "one who begins or originates, originator, founder."[155] The second word in the pair of "pioneer and perfecter" (Hebrews 12:2a) is "one who brings something to a successful conclusion, perfecter," from *telos*, "end, termination," then "goal, outcome."[156]

Archēgos is also found at Hebrews 2:10 as "**author of their salvation**" (NIV) or "**pioneer of their salvation**" (NRSV), "**founder of their salvation**" (ESV), "**captain of their salvation**" (KJV), which we explored in Lesson 7.

> **Q2. (Revelation 1:17-18; Hebrews 12:2) What do the titles First and Last, Alpha and Omega, Beginning and End teach us about Jesus' nature? How does knowing that Jesus is the Author and Perfecter of our faith help build our trust in him? http://www.joyfulheart.com/forums/topic/1638-q2-alpha-and-omega/**

Christ the Firstborn

Christ is not only "first," he is the "firstborn." He was Mary's **firstborn son** (Luke 2:7). One passage at the beginning of Colossians is especially rich in titles and descriptors of Christ's existence both before and after his life on earth. We've examined aspects of this passage before, but here we're looking at the idea of firstborn. We looked

---

[154] *Archē*, BDAG 137, 1.
[155] *Archēgos*, BDAG 138, 3.
[156] *Teleiōtēs*, BDAG 997.

at Christ as Head in Lesson 8 and Image of the Invisible God in Lesson 5. This passage is like an early Christian hymn of Christ.

"[15] He is the image of the invisible God,
the firstborn over all creation.
[16] For by him all things were created:
things in heaven and on earth,
visible and invisible,
whether thrones or powers
or rulers or authorities;
all things were created by him and for him.
[17] He is before all things,
and in him all things hold together.
[18] And he is the **head of the body**, the church;
he is the **beginning and the firstborn from among the dead**,
so that in everything he might have the supremacy.
[19] For God was pleased to have all his fullness dwell in him,
[20] and through him to reconcile to himself all things,
whether things on earth or things in heaven,
by making peace through his blood, shed on the cross." (Colossians 1:15-20)

Verses 15 and 18 use the Near Eastern concept of "firstborn" (*prōtotokos*). "Firstborn" can suggest both birth order (as verse 18b) as well as the special status accorded the firstborn son (as in verse 15[157] and in Exodus 4:22). Thus, "**firstborn over all creation**" (Colossians 1:15) doesn't mean that Jesus is the first created being, but that he is preeminent over all created beings. In the great messianic psalm that looks to the descendent of David, the psalmist says:

"I will also appoint him **my firstborn**,
the most exalted of the kings of the earth." (Psalm 89:27)

It is well known that David himself was not the firstborn, but the eighth son (1 Samuel 16:10-11). Firstborn is used here in the sense of preeminent over all other kings, in somewhat the same sense as "One and Only Son" or "Only Begotten Son," which expresses the supreme honor and uniqueness of the Christ.

---

[157] *Prōtotokos*, BDAG 894, 2a.

In Romans, Paul calls him "**the firstborn among many brothers**" (Romans 8:29). Jesus is referred to as "**the firstborn**" in Hebrews 1:6, to whom the writer attributes the worship of all so-called gods (referring to Deuteronomy 32:43).

Firstborn from among the Dead

In Colossians 1:15-20, in addition to the concept of Christ's preexistence ("he is before all things"), Paul emphasizes Christ as "the beginning" as we saw earlier in this lesson. Here is another nuance of the word "firstborn;" that which relates to birth order.

> "He is the beginning[158] and **the firstborn from among the dead**, so that in everything he might have the supremacy." (Colossians 1:18)

We see this title in Revelation:

> "… Jesus Christ, who is the faithful witness,
> **the firstborn from the dead**,
> and the ruler of the kings of the earth." (Revelation 1:5a)

Jesus is **firstborn from among the dead** in the sense that he is the first to be resurrected from the dead. Jesus, prophets, and apostles raised some from the dead in their mortal bodies, however, they later died a natural death. Jesus' resurrection is the first of a kind since he took on a changed resurrection body.

His resurrection from the dead encourages us that we, too, will be raised at his coming. He is our hope. Jesus told Martha,

> "**I am the resurrection** and the life. He who believes in me will live, even though he dies; and whoever lives and believes in me will never die." (John 11:25-26)

> "The prophets and Moses said … that the Christ would suffer and, as the **first to rise from the dead**, would proclaim light to his own people and to the Gentiles." (Acts 26:22-23)

> "But Christ has indeed been raised from the dead, the **firstfruits of those who have fallen asleep**…." (1 Corinthians 15:20)

> "Christ **the firstfruits**…." (1 Corinthians 15:23)

"Firstfruits" [159] refers to the Jewish religious practice of acknowledging that the land and all its products are a gift of God. It consisted of offering the first portion of the

---

[158] Here, in context with "firstborn," Paul is speaking figuratively of a person, "one with whom a process begins, beginning" (*Archē*, BDAG 137, 2). The idea of ruler or authority derives from the concept of one who begins or initiates.

harvest – cereals, tree fruits, grapes (or prepared oil, flour, dough, etc.) – after which Israelites were at liberty to use the rest.[160] It was used figuratively of first converts in a particular place, etc., and here of Christ, who is the first to rise from the dead.

Heir of All Things

Another title of the glorified, risen Christ is Heir. At the beginning of Hebrews he is called **"Heir of all things"** (Hebrews 1:2). Jesus has all authority, and all things and peoples belong to him. In the great messianic Psalm 2, the psalmist writes:

> "He said to me, 'You are my Son;
> today I have begotten you.
> Ask of me, and I will make the nations your inheritance,
> the ends of the earth your possession.'" (Psalm 2:7-8)

And since you and I are spiritual sons, we too are "heirs of God and co-heirs with Christ" (Romans 8:17). In that sense, all things are ours (1 Corinthians 3:22). This inheritance will be granted at the Last Day.

> "He who overcomes will inherit all this,
> and I will be his God and he will be my son." (Revelation 21:7)

Q3. (Hebrews 1:2; Romans 8:17; 1 Corinthians 3:22) In what sense is Jesus "Heir of All Things"? What does it imply that we are co-heirs with him? In what sense do we possess all things?
http://www.joyfulheart.com/forums/topic/1639-q3-heir-of-all-things/

The Desire of All Nations

Malachi has a powerful passage about Jesus coming, which we'll examine.

> "'Suddenly the Lord you are seeking will come to his temple;
> the messenger of the covenant,
> **whom you desire, will come**,' says the LORD Almighty." (Malachi 3:1b)

---

[159] *Aparchē*, is used here as a cultic technical term, "first fruits, first portion" (BDAG 98), and is a compound word from *apo-*, "from" + *archomai*, "to begin."
[160] Exodus 23:19a; Numbers 15:20; 18:12; Deuteronomy 26:2; Nehemiah 10:35, 37; etc.

This sounds a lot like a prophecy from Haggai.

> "'I will shake all nations,
> and **the desired of all nations** will come,
> and I will fill this house with glory,' says the LORD Almighty." (Haggai 2:7, NIV)

"Desire" (KJV), "desired" (NIV), "treasure" (NRSV, ESV), "wealth" (NASB) is *ḥemdâ*, "desire," also an adjective, "pleasant, precious," from *ḥāmad*, "to desire, delight in." Haggai has been traditionally seen as referring to the Messiah (as he does in Haggai 2:9b).[161]

The Messenger of the Covenant

Now let's look at this Malachi passage further. There are two messengers.

> "[1] 'See, I will send **my messenger,** who will prepare the way before me. Then suddenly the Lord you are seeking will come to his temple; **the messenger of the covenant,** whom you desire, will come,' says the LORD Almighty. [2] But who can endure the day of his coming? Who can stand when he appears? For he will be like a **refiner's fire** or a **launderer's soap**. [3] He will sit as a **refiner and purifier of silver**; he will purify the Levites and refine them like gold and silver. Then the LORD will have men who will bring offerings in righteousness." (Malachi 3:1-3)

"Messenger" (both times in this verse) is *mal'āk*, "messenger, representative, courtier, angel." In the Old Testament there are both human and supernatural messengers, including the Angel of the Lord (the Angel of Yahweh).[162]

In our Malachi passage, John the Baptist is the first messenger, "my messenger, who will prepare the way before me" (Malachi 3:1; Matthew 11:10; Luke 7:27). He is also spoken of in the final chapter of Malachi: "See, I will send you the prophet Elijah before that great and dreadful day of the LORD comes" (Malachi 4:5; Matthew 11:13-14; 17:10-13). His role in preparing the way is also prophesied in Isaiah as: "A voice of one calling: 'In the desert prepare the way for the LORD; make straight in the wilderness a highway for our God'" (Isaiah 40:3).

Jesus is the second messenger, "**the messenger of the covenant**" who "shall suddenly come to his temple" (KJV), immortalized in the great bass solo in Handel's Messiah.

---

[161] However, some see him referring to the contributions of precious things for refurbishing Zerubbabel's temple (2 Chronicles 36:10). We're just not sure.

[162] Andrew Bowling, *mal'āk*, TWOT #1068a.

This coming is initially fulfilled in Jesus coming to the temple in Jerusalem to purify it from the sale of cattle, sheep and doves, as well as the money changers – all of which went to profit the corrupt "sons of Levi," specifically the high priests (John 2:13-16; Matthew 21:12; Mark 11:15-16; Luke 19:45-46).

Refiner and Purifier

In Malachi 3:1-3, there is a sense in which Jesus as Refiner and Purifier also extends to his role as Judge, which we'll consider in a moment. He judges at the end of time, but he also refines and purifies before the Last Day.

> "He will be like a **refiner's fire** or a **launderer's soap**. He will sit as a **refiner and purifier of silver**; he will purify the Levites and refine them like gold and silver. Then the LORD will have men who will bring offerings in righteousness." (Malachi 3:2b-3a)

Jesus is the great "**Refiner.**" The word is the Piel participle of the verb ṣārap, "smelt, refine, test."[163] In ancient days, copper, silver, gold, and iron ores were purified by heating the ore in a pottery crucible or furnace (Psalm 12:6; Proverbs 17:3). Once the contents of the crucible melted, it was possible to separate the purified metal from the slag by differences in melting point, as well as chemical reactions caused by the heat (Proverbs 25:4b). Silver was often found with lead, where the smelting process separated the two by causing the lead to evaporate away (Jeremiah 6:29).[164]

Jesus is also the great "**Purifier.**" The word is the Piel participle of ṭāhēr, "to be pure, clean," used almost exclusively of ritual or moral purity,[165] though the word is sometimes used along with "refine" in the Old Testament (Psalm 12:6; Daniel 11:35; 12:10). Ritual purification of holy things and people in the Old Testament was often achieved by washing, anointing with holy oil, and sacrifice.

In the New Testament, the Word and the Spirit are purifiers.

> "Christ loved the church and gave himself up for her to make her holy, cleansing her by the washing with water through the word, and to present her to himself as a radiant church, without stain or wrinkle or any other blemish, but holy and blameless." (Ephesians 5:25b-27)

---

[163] John E. Hartley, ṣārap, TWOT #1972.
[164] Robert A. Coughenour, "Refine," ISBE 4:64-65.
[165] Edwin Yamauchi, TWOT #792.

[John the Baptist]: "I baptize you with water. But one more powerful than I will come, the thongs of whose sandals I am not worthy to untie. He will baptize you with the Holy Spirit and with fire." (Luke 3:16)

The means Jesus uses on earth to refine us is often "the furnace of affliction" (Isaiah 48:10; Zechariah 13:9) and various kinds of fiery trials (1 Peter 1:6-7). I've often thought that getting married is the first step in training men and women to become less selfish, since they have to live with and care for the needs of someone besides themselves. The second step is becoming a father or mother, forcing men and women to put someone else's needs before their own. Through these processes and our day-to-day struggles, Jesus refines our character.

But there is also a Last Day purifying. Paul tells the Corinthian church in their claims that Apollos was a better apostle, that with regards to a person's work in planting and developing a congregation:

"His work will be shown for what it is, because **the Day** will bring it to light. It will be **revealed with fire**, and the **fire will test the quality** of each man's work. If what he has built survives, he will receive his reward. If it is burned up, he will suffer loss; he himself will be saved, but only as one escaping through the flames." (1 Corinthians 3:13-15)

This is related to the "judgment seat of Christ" (2 Corinthians 5:10), which we'll consider in a moment.

Q4. (Malachi 3:2-3; 1 Corinthians 3:13-15). How does Jesus purify and refine his church? How does he purify and refine us? On the Day that fire will test your deeds, will you have anything that remains, besides your salvation?
http://www.joyfulheart.com/forums/topic/1640-q4-refiner-and-purifier/

Jesus the Judge

We see several titles that refer to the Messiah as Judge. Jesus didn't fulfill this role during his ministry on earth (John 12:47), but when he returns in glory, he will be the Judge of all on Yahweh's behalf (Matthew 25:31-46). As we saw in Lesson 6, in Bible days the king was the supreme court of a nation; he decided all the hard judicial cases. So when we see Jesus as Judge, this is one of his roles as king.

"He has set a day when he will judge the world with justice by the man he has appointed. He has given proof of this to all men by raising him from the dead." (Acts 17:31)

At "the judgment seat of Christ"[166] (2 Corinthians 5:10), Jesus will not only bring condemnation, but reward. In Revelation 20:11-15 we see a vision of a Great White Throne, upon whom sits one who judges men and women by their deeds. He also consults the Lamb's Book of Life, for those whose names are inscribed there will inherit eternal life (Revelation 13:8; 21:27).

Many New Testament passages speak about this, though the titles among these verses are sparse, two in particular stand out.

"He is the one whom God appointed as **judge of the living and the dead**." (Acts 10:42b)

"Now there is in store for me the crown of righteousness, which **the Lord, the righteous Judge**, will award to me on that day – and not only to me, but also to all who have longed for his appearing." (2 Timothy 4:8)

The famous parable where the Son of Man separates the sheep from the goats at his coming also shows Jesus in this role as final Judge (Matthew 25:31-46).

Messiah's Reign Will Have No End

The final part of Jesus' messianic role is to destroy evil and reign forever over his people. As the Bible draws to a close, we increasingly see hints of the time when Jesus will be boldly called King. It was prophesied that he would reign over a never-ending kingdom. Balaam saw this King as a scepter rising.

"I see him, but not now;
I behold him, but not near:
a star shall come out of Jacob,
and **a scepter** shall rise out of Israel." (Numbers 24:17)

"Scepter" is *shēbet*, "rod, staff, scepter." Here it is the symbol of rulership[167] that Jacob prophesied would eventually come to a descendent of the tribe of Judah (Genesis 49:10).

---

[166] I know that some teachers make a distinction between the "the judgment seat of Christ" and the Great White Throne Judgment (Revelation 20:11-15) that is, "the judgment seat of God" (Romans 14:10-11). I believe this is a false distinction. Christ judges on the Father's behalf on that day. They are not separate judgments.

[167] Bruce K. Waltke, *shēbet*, TWOT #2314a.

Isaiah foresaw the Child who is given to reign over us.

"Of the increase of his government and peace there will be **no end**.
He will **reign** on David's throne and over his kingdom,
establishing and upholding it with justice and righteousness
from that time on and forever.
The zeal of the LORD Almighty will accomplish this." (Isaiah 9:7)

In Daniel's vision, the Son of Man is given the Kingdom by the Ancient of Days.

"And to him was given **dominion** and glory and a kingdom,
that all peoples, nations, and languages should serve him;
his dominion is an **everlasting dominion**,
which **shall not pass away**,
and his kingdom one that **shall not be destroyed**." (Daniel 7:14)

Zechariah prophesied at the birth of John the Baptist about this coming Messiah.

"He will be great and will be called the Son of the Most High.
The Lord God will give him the throne of his father David,
and he will **reign** over the house of Jacob **forever**;
his kingdom will never end." (Luke 1:32-33)

At a climax of the Book of Revelation, the Seventh Trumpet is blown.

"The seventh angel sounded his trumpet,
and there were loud voices in heaven, which said:
'The kingdom of the world
has become the kingdom of our Lord and of his Christ,
and **he will reign for ever and ever**.'" (Revelation 11:15)

Jesus will reign forever, and his saints will reign with him (Revelation 22:5).

Commander, Leader, Prince

Throughout the Old Testament, Yahweh is seen as a warrior, though rarely, do we see Christ in this role. Of course, in Revelation the Warrior Messiah appears astride a battle steed to defeat evil in a final battle (Revelation 19:11-18). In this role the Messiah appears in Isaiah's messianic prophecy as a leader and commander.

"I will make an everlasting covenant with you,
my faithful love promised to David.

> See, I have made him a witness to the peoples,[168]
> **a leader**[169] **and commander**[170] **of the peoples**." (Isaiah 55:3-4)

Micah's prophecy of Messiah's birth in Bethlehem calls him a "**ruler**".

> "But you, Bethlehem Ephrathah,
> though you are small among the clans of Judah,
> out of you will come for me one who will be **ruler**[171] over Israel,
> whose origins are from of old,
> from ancient times." (Micah 5:2)

The passage is quoted in Matthew 2:6, using the title "**ruler**" (NIV, NRSV, ESV), "**governor**" (KJV).[172] As we saw in Lesson 7, he is called the **Shepherd and Overseer** (NIV, ESV), **Guardian** (NRSV, NASB) or **Bishop** (KJV) **of your souls**" (1 Peter 2:25).

Several times, as we've seen above, Jesus is referred to as **Prince**, especially in the KJV. In Acts 3:15 he is called the "Author of life" (NIV, NRSV, ESV) or "**Prince of life**" (KJV).[173] In Acts 5:31 he is "**Prince and Savior**" (NIV, KJV) or "**Leader and Savior**" (NRSV, ESV).[174] Revelation 1:5 calls him "**ruler of the kings of the earth**" (NIV, NRSV, ESV), "**Prince of the kings of the earth**" (KJV).[175]

The most famous use of the title Prince is found in the messianic prophecy of Isaiah 9:6. Messiah is "**Prince of Peace**," that is, the leader who brings and maintains peace. In popular speech in our day, "prince" would refer to the son of a reigning king. However, the word in Hebrew can be used of any leader who rules, reigns, or governs.[176]

---

[168] "Peoples" (twice in verse 4) is *le'ōm*, "people," poetic and chiefly found in later Old Testament books. It doesn't refer to the Gentiles, but more generally to any group of people (BDB 52).

[169] "Leader" is *nāgîd*, is "ruler, leader, captain" (TWOT #1298b).

[170] "Commander" is the Piel participle of *ṣāwâ*, "to command" (TWOT #1887). Though it's possible, we just don't have enough evidence to equate "the Commander of the Army of the Lord" in Joshua 5:13-14 with Jesus, since Michael the Archangel seems to have that role in Daniel and Revelation (Daniel 10:13; 12:1, 21; Revelation 12:7).

[171] "Ruler" (NIV, ESV, KJV), "one who is to rule" (NRSV) is the Qal participle of *māshal*, "rule, have dominion, reign" (TWOT #1259).

[172] The word is the present participle of *hēgeomai*, "to be in a supervisory capacity, lead, guide" (BDAG 43, 1).

[173] The word is *archēgos*, "leader, ruler, prince," often "one who begins or originates, originator, founder" (BDAG 13, 1 and 3).

[174] "Prince" (NIV, KJV), "Leader" (NRSV, ESV) is *archēgos*.

[175] The word is *archōn*, "one who is in a position of leadership," especially in a civic capacity, here "one who has eminence in a ruling capacity, ruler, lord, prince" (BDAG 14, 1b).

[176] "Prince" is *śar*, translated variously, "prince, chief, captain, ruler, governor, keeper, chief captain, steward, master," from *śārar*, "rule, reign, act as a prince, govern" (TWOT #2295a).

So Jesus has many titles of governance: leader, commander, ruler, governor, overseer, guardian, bishop, and prince. But the most characteristic title of Jesus in this category is King.

King of Glory Enters Jerusalem

The theme of Yahweh as King of Israel runs throughout the Old Testament. As we began this lesson we read in Psalm 24:

> "Lift up your heads, O you gates;
> be lifted up, you ancient doors,
>   that the **King of glory** may come in." (Psalm 24:7)

The gates mentioned, the ancient doors, are the gates to the Holy City of Jerusalem. The psalm celebrates the entrance of Yahweh into his city. Jesus is the fulfillment of this Psalm. He is the King designated to enter Jerusalem. Jesus is the **King of Glory**. "King of Glory," of course, means the same as "glorious king."[177]

Again and again in the New Testament, Jesus is proclaimed to be King. The Prophet Zechariah foresaw his coming.

> "Rejoice greatly, O Daughter of Zion!
> Shout, Daughter of Jerusalem!
> See, **your king** comes to you,
> righteous and having salvation,
> gentle and riding on a donkey,
> on a colt, the foal of a donkey." (Zechariah 9:9)

This was fulfilled on Palm Sunday, when Jesus deliberately rode into Jerusalem on a donkey to the cries of "Son of David" and "Hosanna!" (that is, "save us"; Matthew 21:4-9; Mark 11:4-10; Luke 19:35-38).

The wise men sought him: "Where is he who has been born **King of the Jews**?" (Matthew 2:2). Nathanael exclaimed: "Rabbi, you are the Son of God! You are the **King of Israel**!" (John 1:49). Over the cross, Pilate's placard declared: "Jesus of Nazareth, the **King of the Jews**." (John 19:19; Matthew 27:37; Mark 15:26; Luke 23:38)

Yes, Jesus *is* the King of the Jews, but he is more than that. He is also king over all other realms and kings. Revelation 15:3 calls him "**King of the nations**" (NRSV, ESV),

---

[177] At Jesus' transfiguration, his disciples saw him in his glory (Matthew 17:2). We examined Jesus' glory extensively earlier in this lesson.

"**King of the ages**" (NIV) or "**King of saints**," KJV. (The differences are due to textual variations in the ancient manuscripts.[178])

Jesus is also proclaimed to be, "**the ruler of the kings of the earth**" or "**prince of the kings of the earth**," (Revelation 1:5).[179] One who rules over other kings is also called an emperor, or "**King of kings**."

Timothy calls him "**The blessed and only Ruler/Sovereign/Potentate**, the **King of kings and Lord of lords**" (1 Timothy 6:15). Jesus is the only true Ruler! "Ruler" (NIV), "sovereign" (NRSV, ESV), "potentate" (KJV) is *dynastēs* (from which we get our word "dynasty"), generally one who is in a position to command others, one who is in relatively high position, ruler, sovereign."[180]

In Revelation, too, Jesus bears this title of the ultimate rule of an Emperor, with kings under his control.

> "They will make war on the Lamb,
> and the Lamb will conquer them,
> for he is **Lord of lords and King of kings**." (Revelation 17:14a)

> "On his robe and on his thigh he has a name written,
> **King of kings and Lord of lords**." (Revelation 19:16)

Q6. (Revelation 11:15; Psalm 24:7) When people think of spending an eternity in heaven, who do they most look forward to being with? Relatives? Jesus? What does it mean that he will reign forever and ever? In what way is he the King of Glory in your life?
http://www.joyfulheart.com/forums/topic/1641-q5-king-of-glory/

We've reached the end of our journey of surveying the many names, titles, descriptors, and metaphors of our Lord and King Jesus. It is my prayer that this study

---

[178] Metzger (*Textual Commentary*, p. 755-756) says that the manuscript evidence for "nations" and "ages" is about equal. However, the Committee felt that "ages" was more likely to be recollected from 1 Timothy 1:17, and "nations" was more in accord with the context. The KJV rendering "King of saints" from the Textus Receptus has only slender support from Greek manuscripts, none early. The Committee preferred "King of the nations," but only gave it a {C} or "considerable degree of doubt" rating.

[179] "Ruler" (NIV, NRSV, ESV), "prince" (KJV) is *archōn*, "one who has eminence in a ruling capacity, ruler, lord, prince" (BDAG 14, 1b).

[180] *Dynastēs*, BDAG 26, 1a.

might continue with you as you spend time in your private worship of Jesus and meditation on him.

When you are in danger, remember him as your Rock, your Savior, your Deliverer. When you are discouraged, recall that he is your Counselor, the Atoning Sacrifice for all your sins, your High Priest, and Advocate before the throne of God. When you long to serve him, he is your Commander, your Master, the Forerunner whose life you can emulate. When you come to the end of your life, know that he is the Way, the Gate, the Door, and it is he who invites you to come into his Father's house. He is Jesus – Yahweh saves – and he will save and deliver you all your life, until that day when he welcomes you into his Kingdom.

My brothers and sisters, we are truly blessed – in Jesus' name. Amen.

Prayer

Jesus, the day will come on earth that is now in heaven when you will appear as the Lord of Glory, the Refiner and Purifier, and the Righteous Judge. Thank you that my name is written in the Lamb's Book of Life, along with my brothers and sisters who count you as their Lord. Purify me. Refine me for your service. Fill me with your grace and glory, now and forever. Amen.

Names and Titles of Jesus

King of Glory (Psalm 24:7-10)
Radiance of God's Glory (Hebrews 1:3)
The First and the Last (Revelation 1:17b; 2:8; 22:13)
The Living One (Revelation 1:17b)
Alpha and Omega (Revelation 1:8; 21:6; 22:13)
Who Is and Was and Is to Come (Revelation 1:4, 8)
Beginning and End (Revelation 21:6, 13)
Author and Perfecter of our Faith (NIV, NASB, Hebrews 12:2a)
Author and Finisher of our Faith (KJV, Hebrews 12:2a)
Founder and Perfecter of our Faith (ESV, Hebrews 12:2a)
Author of Salvation (NIV, Hebrews 2:10)
Pioneer of Salvation (NRSV, Hebrews 2:10)
Founder of Salvation (ESV, Hebrews 2:10)
Captain of Salvation (KJV, Hebrews 2:10)
Prince and Savior (NIV, KJV, Acts 5:31)

Leader and Savior (NRSV, ESV, Acts 5:31)

Firstborn over All Creation (Colossians 1:15)

Firstborn (Psalm 89:27; Hebrews 1:6)

Firstborn Son (Luke 2:7)

Firstborn among Many Brothers (Romans 8:29)

Firstborn from among the Dead (Colossians 1:18)

Firstborn from the Dead (Revelation 1:5a)

The Resurrection and the Life (John 11:25)

First to Rise from the Dead (Acts 26:23)

Firstfruits of Those Who Have Fallen Asleep (1 Corinthians 15:20)

Firstfruits (1 Corinthians 15:23)

Heir of All Things (Hebrews 1:2)

Desire of All Nations (KJV, Haggai 2:7)

Desired of All Nations (NIV, Haggai 2:7)

Messenger of the Covenant (Malachi 3:1)

Refiner's Fire (Malachi 3:2)

Launderer's Soap (NIV, Malachi 3:2)

Fuller's Soap (NRSV, ESV, KJV, Malachi 3:2)

Refiner of Silver (Malachi 3:3)

Purifier of Silver (Malachi 3:3)

Judge of the Living and the Dead (NIV, NRSV, ESV, Acts 10:42b)

Judge of the Quick and the Dead (KJV, Acts 10:42b)

Righteous Judge (2 Timothy 4:8)

Scepter (Numbers 24:17)

Leader and Commander of the Peoples (Isaiah 55:4)

Leader of the Peoples (Isaiah 55:4)

Commander of the Peoples (Isaiah 55:4)

Ruler in/over Israel (Micah 5:2)

Governor (KJV, Matthew 2:6)

Ruler (NIV, NRSV, ESV, Matthew 2:6)

Author of Life (NIV, NRSV, ESV, Acts 3:15)

Prince of Life (KJV, Acts 3:15)

Ruler of the Kings of the Earth (NIV, NRSV, ESV, Revelation 1:5)

Prince of the Kings of the Earth (KJV, Revelation 1:5)

Prince of Peace (Isaiah 9:6)
Your King (Zechariah 9:9; Matthew 21:5)
King of the Jews (Matthew 2:2; John 19:19; Matthew 27:37; Mark 15:26; Luke 23:38)
King of Israel (John 1:49)
King of the Nations (NRSV, ESV, Revelation 15:3)
King of the Ages (NIV, Revelation 15:3)
King of Saints (KJV, Revelation 15:3)
Blessed and Only Ruler (NIV, 1 Timothy 6:15)
Blessed and Only Sovereign (NRSV, ESV, 1 Timothy 6:15)
Blessed and Only Potentate (KJV, 1 Timothy 6:15)
King of Kings and Lord of Lords (1 Timothy 6:15; Revelation 17:14a; 19:16)

Songs and Hymns

Songs in this final lesson center around Jesus the risen, glorified, coming King. Titles include: King of Glory, King, First and Last, Alpha and Omega, Beginning and End, Author and Finisher, Author of Salvation, Firstborn, Firstfruits, Heir of All Things, Desire of All Nations, Messenger of the Covenant, Refiner's Fire, Righteous Judge, Prince of Life, King of kings and Lord of lords.

"All Because of Jesus" ("Maker of Heaven and of Earth ... King over all the universe"), by Steve Fee (© 2007 Sixsteps Songs)

"All Hail King Jesus" ("King of kings, Lord of lords, Bright Morning Star") by Dave Moody (1981 Dayspring Music, LLC)

"All Hail the Power of Jesus' Name" ("And crown him Lord of all"), words: Edward Perronet (1779), music: Coronation, Oliver Holden (1793)

"Alpha and Omega," by Erasmus Mutanbira (© 2005 Integrity's Praise! Music)

"Angels from the Realms of Glory" ("Seek the great Desire of nations ... Suddenly the Lord, descending, In His temple shall appear"), words: James Montgomery (1816), music: Regent Square, Henry T. Smart (1867)

"Be Thou My Vision" ("High King of Heaven"), words attributed to Dallan Forgaill, translated from Gallic to English by Mary E. Byrne (1905), versed by Eleanor H. Hull (1912); music: Slane, Irish folk origin.

"Blessed Be the Name" ("Redeemer, Savior, friend of man ... Counselor ... Prince of Peace"), words: William H. Clark, music: Ralph E. Hudson (1888)

"Celebrate the Child" ("the Child who is the Light ... Godhead and manhood became one ... First born of creation ... Lamb and Lion, God and Man ... Author of Salvation ... Almighty wrapped in swaddling bands"), by Michael Card (© 1989 Birdwing Music)

"Christmas Offering" ("humble Prince of Peace ... I bring an offering of worship to my King"), by Paul Baloche (© 2003 Integrity's Hosanna! Music)

"Come, O Come, Emmanuel" ("Desire of Nations ... King of Peace"), words: 12th century; music: 15th century

"Come, Thou Long Expected Jesus" ("Israel's strength and consolation, Hope of all the earth thou art, dear desire of every nation"), words: Charles Wesley (1745), music: Hyfrydol, Rowland H. Prichard (1830)

"Days of Elijah" ("Behold He comes riding on the clouds, shining like the sun at the trumpet's call"), by Robin Mark (© 1996 Song Solutions Daybreak)

"Famous One" ("Desire of nations and every heart"), by Chris Tomlin, Jesse Reeves (© 2002 sixsteps Music)

"Forever Reign" ("You are Peace, You are Peace"), by Scott Ingram, Reuben Morgan (© 2009 Hillsong Music Publishing)

"Hark, the Herald Angels Sing" ("Come Desire of Nations, come"), words: Charles Wesley (1739), music: Felix Mendelssohn (1740)

"He Is Exalted" ("the King is exalted on high"), by Twila Paris (© 1985, Straightway Music/Word Music (UK))

"He's the Lord of Glory" ("He's the Alpha and Omega, the Beginning and the End ... the Prince of Peace is He"), by Phyllis C. Spiers (© 1950, 1962, Gospel Publishing House)

"Here I Am to Worship" ("King of all days, oh so highly exalted"), by Tim Hughes (© 2001, Thankyou Music)

"Holy" ("Jesus You Are"; "You're the Great I Am ... You will come again in glory to judge the living and the dead"), by Jason Ingram, Jonas Myrin, Matt Redman (© 2011 Atlas Mountain Songs)

"Hosanna" ("I see the King of Glory coming down the clouds with fire"), by Brooke Ligertwood (© 2006 Hillsong Music Publishing)

"How Great Is Our God" ("The splendor of the King ... Beginning and the End ... Lion and the Lamb"), by Chris Tomlin, Ed Cash, Jesse Reeves (© 2004 sixsteps Music)

"How Majestic Is Your Name" ("Prince of Peace, Mighty God"), by Michael W. Smith (© 1981, Meadowgreen Music Co.)

"I Am" ("Maker of the heavens, Bright and Morning Star ... Fount of Living Water, the Risen Son of Man, the Healer of the Broken .. Savior and Redeemer ... Author and Perfecter, Beginning and the End"), by Mark Schultz (© 2005 Crazy Romaine Music)

"I Love You Lord" ("Take joy my King in what you hear"), by Laurie Klein (© 1978, House of Mercy Music)

"I Will Look Up" ("Jesus, Lord of All ... Prince of Peace, Perfect Healer, King of Kings, Mighty Savior"), Chris Brown, Jason Ingram, Mack Brock, Matt Redman, Wade Joye (© 2013 Said And Done Music)

"I Worship You, Almighty God" ("I worship You, O Prince of Peace"), by Sondra Corbett (© 1983 Integrity's Hosanna! Music)

"Isn't He" ("Beautiful, isn't He? Prince of Peace, Son of God"), by John Wimber (© 1980 Mercy / Vineyard Publishing)

"Jesus Lover of My Soul" ("Alpha and Omega, You have loved me"), by Paul Oakley (© 1995 Thankyou Music)

"Jesus Shall Reign Where'er the Sun," words: Isaac Watts (1719), music: Duke Street, attributed to John Hatton (1793)

"Jesus, Lover of My Soul" ("Alpha and Omega, You have loved me"), by John Ezzy, Daniel Grul, and Stephen McPherson (© 1992, John Ezzy, Daniel Grul, Stephen McPherson, and Hillsong Publishing)

"Jesus, Only Jesus" (He is our hope, our righteousness ... Holy, King Almighty Lord"), by Christ Tomlin, Matt Redman, et al. (© 2013 S. D. G. Publishing)

"Love Devine, All Loves Excelling" ("Alpha and Omega be; End of faith, as its Beginning"), words: Charles Wesley (1747); music: Beecher, John Zundel (1870)

"Open the Eyes of My Heart" ("To see you high and lifted up, shining in the light of your glory"), by Paul Baloche (© 1997, Integrity's Hosanna! Music)

"Refiner's Fire," by Brian Doerksen (©1990 Mercy / Vineyard Publishing)

"Rejoice, the Lord Is King" ("Jesus the Savior reigns ... Jesus the Judge shall come"), words: Charles Wesley (1744), music: Darwall's 148th, John Darwall (1770)

"Revelation Song" ("Worthy is the Lamb who was slain ... Lord God Almighty ... King of kings"), Jennie Lee Riddle (© 2004 Gateway Create Publishing)

"This I Believe" ("The Creed": "I believe in the resurrection, that we will rise again ... Our Judge and our Defender"), by Ben Fielding, Matt Crocker (© 2014 Hillsong Music Publishing)

"This Is Amazing Grace" ("the King of Glory, the King of Glory"), by Jeremy Riddle, Josh Farro, Phil Wickham (© 2012 Phil Wickham Music)

"We Bow Down" ("Your are Lord/King of creation and Lord/King of my life ... Lord of all lords you will be ... King of all kings you will be"), by Twila Paris (© 1984, New Spring International)

"We Will Glorify" (We will glorify the King of kings, we will glorify the Lamb"), by Twila Paris (1982 New Spring)

"What Child Is This" ("the King of kings salvation brings"), words: William Chatterton Dix (1865), music: Greensleeves (16th century English melody)

"When I Survey the Wondrous Cross" ("on which the Prince of glory died"), words: Isaac Watts (1707), music: Hamburg, Lowell Mason (1824)

"Worthy, You Are Worthy" ("King of kings, Lord of lords"), by Don Moen (© 1986, Integrity's Hosanna! Music)

"You Are Holy" ("Prince of Peace"), by Marc Imboden and Tammi Rhoton (1994 Imboden Music; Martha Jo Publishing). Many names of Jesus

"You Are My King" ("Amazing Love"), by Billy Fotte (© 1996, worshiptogether.com songs)

"You Are" (Holy ... Faithful ... Savior ... Friend ... Lord on high ... the Way, the Truth, the Life ... the Word made flesh ... the Bright Morning Star ... Alpha and Omega ... Comfort ... Refuge ... Love Personified ... My God and my King"), by Mark Roach (© 2005 Dayspring Music)

Exercises

From Appendix 6. Exercises to Help You Internalize the Names of Jesus, select some activities that will help you internalize the truths of this lesson's names, titles, descriptors, and metaphors. This week, how can you creatively pray, meditate, write, worship, consider, draw or paint, compose, picture, and live out these truths in your community?

Actively participating in these ways will help you grow to be like Christ.

Appendix 1. Participant Handout Guides

If you are working with a class or small group, feel free to duplicate the following handouts at no additional charge. If you'd like to print 8-1/2" x 11" or A4 size pages, you can download the free Participant Guide handout sheets at:

www.jesuswalk.com/names-jesus/names-jesus-lesson-handouts.pdf

Discussion Questions

You'll typically find 4 to 6 questions for each lesson, depending on the topics in each lesson. Each question may include several sub-questions. These are designed to get group members engaged in discussion of the key points of the passage. If you're running short of time, feel free to skip questions or portions of questions.

Suggestions for Classes and Groups

Part of any class should be an attempt to get group members involved in the experience. This could include memory verses, singing songs suggested for each lesson, and getting involved in exercises suggested in Appendix 6 that could involve two or more members in a project.

Be aware that, depending on what translation people use in your group, the exact names and titles could vary. I've used the NIV as the primary text for these lessons, but show variations in the NRSV, ESV, and KJV.

www.jesuswalk.com/names-jesus/names-jesus-lesson-handouts.pdf

Appendix 2. Names, Titles, Metaphors, and Descriptors of Jesus: A Comprehensive List

Abraham, Seed of (Hebrews 2:16), Lesson 3

Abraham, Son of (Matthew 1:1), Lesson 1

Adam, Last (1 Corinthians 15:45), Lesson 3

Advocate with the Father (ESV, NRSV, KJV, 1 John 2:1), Lesson 3

Ages, King of the (NIV, Revelation 15:3), Lesson 10

Almighty, The (Revelation 1:8), Lesson 5

Alpha and Omega (Revelation 1:8; 21:6; 22:13), Lesson 10

Amen (Revelation 3:14b), Lesson 2

Anointed (Psalm 2:2), Lesson 4

Anointed One (NIV, ESV, Daniel 9:25, 26), Lesson 4

Anointed Prince (NRSV, Daniel 9:25, 26), Lesson 4

Apostle (Hebrews 3:1), Lesson 3

Arm of the Lord (Isaiah 53:1), Lesson 7

Atoning Sacrifice (NIV, NRSV, 1 John 2:1-2), Lesson 6

Author and Finisher of our Faith (KJV, Hebrews 12:2a), Lesson 10

Author and Perfecter of our Faith (NIV, NASB, Hebrews 12:2a), Lesson 10

Author of Life (NIV, ESV, Acts 3:15), Lesson 9

Author of Life (NIV, NRSV, ESV, Acts 3:15), Lesson 10

Author of Salvation (NIV, Hebrews 2:10), Lesson 10

Author of Salvation (NIV, NASB, Hebrews 2:10), Lesson 7

Banner for the Peoples (Isaiah 11:10), Lesson 4

Banner for the Peoples (NIV, Isaiah 11:10), Lesson 8

Beginning and End (Revelation 21:6, 13), Lesson 10

Beloved Son (Matthew 3:17; 17:5; Colossians 1:13; Mark 12:6), Lesson 5

Beloved, My (Matthew 12:18, ESV, RSV, KJV), Lesson 5

Beloved, My (Matthew 12:18, ESV, RSV, KJV), Lesson 4

Beloved, The (Ephesians 1:6), Lesson 5

Bishop of your Souls, Shepherd and (KJV, 1 Peter 2:25), Lesson 7

Blemish or Defect, Lamb without (1 Peter 1:19), Lesson 6

Blessed and Only Potentate (KJV, 1 Timothy 6:15), Lesson 10

Blessed and Only Ruler (NIV, 1 Timothy 6:15), Lesson 10

Blessed and Only Sovereign (NRSV, ESV, 1 Timothy 6:15), Lesson 10

Blessed, Christ, Son of the (Mark 14:61), Lesson 4

Blessed, Son of the (Mark 14:61), Lesson 5

Body, Head of the (Colossians 1:18), Lesson 8

Boy Jesus, The (Luke 2:43), Lesson 1

Branch (Isaiah 11:1b; Zechariah 3:8; 6:12), Lesson 4

Branch of the Lord (Isaiah 4:2), Lesson 4

Branch, Righteous (Jeremiah 23:5; 33:15), Lesson 6

Branch, Righteous (Jeremiah 23:5; 33:15), Lesson 4

Bread (John 6:50), Lesson 9

Bread of God (John 6:33), Lesson 9

Bread of Life (John 6:35, 48), Lesson 9

Bread, Living (John 6:51), Lesson 9

Bridegroom (John 3:29; Matthew 9:15; Mark 2:19-20; Luke 5:34-35), Lesson 9

Bright Morning Star (Revelation 22:16), Lesson 9

Brother of James, Joseph, Judas and Simon (Mark 6:3), Lesson 1

Brothers, Firstborn among Many (Romans 8:29), Lesson 10

Builders Rejected, Stone the (Psalm 118:22; Matthew 21:42; Mark 12:10; Luke 20:17; Acts 4:11; 1 Peter 2:7), Lesson 8

Capstone (NIV, Psalm 118:22; Matthew 21:42; Mark 12:10; Acts 4:11; 1 Peter 2:7), Lesson 8

Captain of Salvation (KJV, Hebrews 2:10), Lesson 10

Captain of Salvation (KJV; Hebrews 2:10), Lesson 7

Carpenter (Mark 6:3), Lesson 1

Carpenter's Son (Matthew 13:55), Lesson 1

Chief Cornerstone (NRSV, Psalm 118:22; NIV, KJV, Ephesians 2:20), Lesson 8

Chief Cornerstone, Elect, Precious (KJV, 1 Peter 2:6), Lesson 8

Chief Shepherd (1 Peter 5:4), Lesson 7

Child Jesus, The (Luke 2:27), Lesson 1

Child, Son (Isaiah 9:6), Lesson 1

Chosen and Precious Cornerstone (1 Peter 2:6), Lesson 4

Chosen and Precious Cornerstone (NIV, 1 Peter 2:6), Lesson 8

Chosen One (Isaiah 42:1; Luke 23:35b; 9:35), Lesson 4

Christ (often, especially John 1:41b; Matthew 16:16, 20; 26:63-64; Luke 4:41; etc.), Lesson 4

Christ Jesus (often), Lesson 4

Christ Jesus our Lord (Romans 8:39; 1 Timothy 1:12), Lesson 4

Christ of God (Luke 9:20), Lesson 4

Christ the Lord (Luke 2:11), Lesson 4

Christ Who Is Your Life (Colossians 3:4), Lesson 9

Christ, a King (Luke 23:2), Lesson 4

Christ, Son of the Blessed (Mark 14:61), Lesson 4

Christ, The (used absolutely, Matthew 1:16; 16:20; Mark 14:61), Lesson 4

Christ, the Power of God (1 Corinthians 1:24), Lesson 4

Christ, the Son of God (Acts 9:20), Lesson 4

Christ, the Wisdom of God (1 Corinthians 1:24), Lesson 4

Church, Head of the (Colossians 1:18), Lesson 8

Circumcised, Servant of/to the (NRSV, ESV, Romans 15:8), Lesson 6

Circumcision, Minister of the (KJV, Romans 15:8), Lesson 6

Commander of the Peoples (Isaiah 55:4), Lesson 10

Commander of the Peoples, Leader and (Isaiah 55:4), Lesson 10

Consolation of Israel (Luke 2:25), Lesson 3

Corner, Head of the (KJV, Matthew 21:42; Mark 12:10; Luke 20:17; Acts 4:11; NRSV, KJV, 1 Peter 2:7), Lesson 8

Corner, Head Stone of the (KJV, Psalm 118:22), Lesson 8

Cornerstone (ESV, Psalm 118:22; ESV, NRSV Matthew 21:42; Mark 12:10; Luke 20:17; Acts 4:11; Ephesians 2:20; ESV, 1 Peter 2:7), Lesson 8

Cornerstone Chosen and Precious (NRSV, ESV, 1 Peter 2:6), Lesson 8

Cornerstone, Chief (NRSV, Psalm 118:22; NIV, KJV, Ephesians 2:20), Lesson 8

Cornerstone, Chosen and Precious (1 Peter 2:6), Lesson 4

Cornerstone, Chosen and Precious (NIV, 1 Peter 2:6), Lesson 8

Cornerstone, Elect, Precious Chief (KJV, 1 Peter 2:6), Lesson 8

Cornerstone, Precious (Isaiah 28:16), Lesson 8

Counselor (John 14:16, by implication), Lesson 2

Counselor, Wonderful (Isaiah 9:6), Lesson 2

Covenant for/of/to the People (Isaiah 42:6-7), Lesson 9

Covenant, Guarantee of a Better (NIV, NRSV, Hebrews 7:22), Lesson 9

Covenant, Guarantor of a Better (ESV, Hebrews 7:22), Lesson 9

Covenant, Mediator of a New (Hebrews 11:24), Lesson 3

Covenant, Messenger of the (Malachi 3:1), Lesson 10

Covenant, Surety of a Better (KJV, Hebrews 7:22), Lesson 9

Creation, Firstborn over All (Colossians 1:15), Lesson 10

David (Jeremiah 30:9; Ezekiel 34:23; 37:24-25; Hosea 3:5), Lesson 4

David, Descendant of (NRSV, ESV, Revelation 22:16; NRSV, 2 Timothy 2:8), Lesson 4

David, Offspring of (NIV, KJV, Revelation 22:16; ESV, 2 Timothy 2:8), Lesson 4

David, Root and Offspring of (Revelation 22:16), Lesson 4

David, Root of (Revelation 5:5), Lesson 4

David, Seed of (KJV, 2 Timothy 2:8), Lesson 4

David, Son of (Mark 10:47-48; Luke 18:38-39; Matthew 9:27; 12:23; 15:22; 20:30-31; 21:9, 15), Lesson 4

David, Son of (Matthew 1:1), Lesson 1

Dawn (NRSV, Luke 1:78), Lesson 9

Day Star (2 Peter 1:19), Lesson 9

Dayspring (KJV, Luke 1:78), Lesson 9

Dead and Living, Lord both of the (Romans 14:9), Lesson 5

Dead, First to Rise from the (Acts 26:23), Lesson 10

Dead, Firstborn from among the (Colossians 1:18), Lesson 10

Dead, Firstborn from the (Revelation 1:5a), Lesson 10

Dear Son (KJV, Colossians 1:13), Lesson 5

Deliverer (Romans 11:26), Lesson 7

Descendant of David (NRSV, ESV, Revelation 22:16; NRSV, 2 Timothy 2:8), Lesson 4

Desire of All Nations (KJV, Haggai 2:7), Lesson 10

Desired of All Nations (NIV, Haggai 2:7), Lesson 10

Doctor (NRSV, Luke 4:23), Lesson 8

Door (ESV, KJV, John 10: 9), Lesson 8

Door of the Sheep (ESV, KJV, John 10:7), Lesson 8

Dry Ground, Root out of (Isaiah 53:2a), Lesson 4

Emmanuel, Immanuel (Isaiah 7:14; Matthew 1:23), Lesson 5

End, Beginning and (Revelation 21:6, 13), Lesson 10

Ensign of the People (KJV, Isaiah 11:10), Lesson 8

Eternal Life (1 John 1:2; 5:20), Lesson 9

Everlasting Father (Isaiah 9:6), Lesson 5

Everlasting Father (Isaiah 9:6), Lesson 5

Exact Representation of His Being, The (Hebrews 1:3a), Lesson 5

Faith, Founder and Perfecter of our (ESV, Hebrews 12:2a), Lesson 10

Faithful and True (Revelation 19:11), Lesson 2

Faithful and True Witness (Revelation 3:14b), Lesson 2

Faithful Witness (Revelation 1:5a), Lesson 2

Fall, Rock that Makes Men/Them (Isaiah 8:14; NIV, NRSV, 1 Peter 2:8), Lesson 8

Father, Everlasting (Isaiah 9:6), Lesson 5

Father, Only Begotten of the (KJV, John 1:14), Lesson 5

Father, Son of the (KJV, 2 John 1:3), Lesson 5

Father's Son, The (NIV, NRSV, ESV, 2 John 1:3), Lesson 5

Finisher of our Faith, Author and (KJV, Hebrews 12:2a), Lesson 10

Fire, Refiner's (Malachi 3:2), Lesson 10

First and the Last, The (Revelation 1:17b; 2:8; 22:13), Lesson 10

First to Rise from the Dead (Acts 26:23), Lesson 10

Firstborn (Psalm 89:27; Hebrews 1:6), Lesson 10

Firstborn among Many Brothers (Romans 8:29), Lesson 10

Firstborn from among the Dead (Colossians 1:18), Lesson 10

Firstborn from the Dead (Revelation 1:5a), Lesson 10

Firstborn over All Creation (Colossians 1:15), Lesson 10

Firstborn Son (Luke 2:7), Lesson 10

Firstfruits (1 Corinthians 15:23), Lesson 10

Firstfruits of Those Who Have Fallen Asleep (1 Corinthians 15:20), Lesson 10

Forerunner (Hebrews 6:20), Lesson 6

Foundation (1 Corinthians 3:11), Lesson 8

Foundation, Sure (Isaiah 28:16), Lesson 8

Founder and Perfecter of our Faith (ESV, Hebrews 12:2a), Lesson 10

Founder of Salvation (ESV, Hebrews 2:10), Lesson 10

Founder of Salvation (ESV, Hebrews 2:10), Lesson 7

Fountain (Zechariah 13:1), Lesson 6

Friend of Tax Collectors and Sinners (Matthew 11:19), Lesson 7

Fuller's Soap (NRSV, ESV, KJV, Malachi 3:2), Lesson 10

Gate (NIV, NRSV, John 10:9), Lesson 8

Gate for the Sheep (NIV, NRSV, John 10:7), Lesson 8

Gentiles, Light for Revelation to the (NIV, NRSV, ESV, Luke 2:32), Lesson 9

Gentiles, Light for the (Isaiah 42:6; 49:6), Lesson 9

Gentiles, Light to Lighten the (KJV, Luke 2:32), Lesson 9

Gift, Indescribable (NIV, NRSV, 2 Corinthians 9:15), Lesson 3

Gift, Inexpressible ESV, 2 Corinthians 9:15), Lesson 3

Gift, Unspeakable (KJV, 2 Corinthians 9:15), Lesson 3

Glory, King of (Psalm 24:7-10), Lesson 10

Glory, Lord of (1 Corinthians 2:8; Psalm 24), Lesson 5

Glory, Radiance of God's (Hebrews 1:3), Lesson 10

God (John 1:1), Lesson 5

God and Men, One Mediator between (1 Timothy 2:5), Lesson 3

God and Savior, Jesus Christ, Great (Titus 2:13; 2 Peter 1:1), Lesson 7

God over All (Romans 9:5), Lesson 5

God the One and Only (NIV, John 1:18), Lesson 5

God, Holy One of (Mark 1:24b; Luke 4:34), Lesson 6

God, Lamb of (John 1:29, 36), Lesson 6

God, Lord (Revelation 1:8), Lesson 5

God, Mighty (Isaiah 9:6), Lesson 5

God, My Lord and My (John 20:28), Lesson 5

God, Power of (1 Corinthians 1:24), Lesson 2

God, Son of (many times), Lesson 5

God, Wisdom of (1 Corinthians 1:24), Lesson 2

God, Word of (Revelation 19:13), Lesson 2

God's Glory, Radiance of (Hebrews 1:3), Lesson 10

Good Shepherd (John 10:11, 14), Lesson 7

Good Teacher (Mark 10:17-18; Luke 18:18), Lesson 6

Governor (KJV, Matthew 2:6), Lesson 10

Great God and Savior, Jesus Christ (Titus 2:13; 2 Peter 1:1), Lesson 7

Great Light (Isaiah 9:2), Lesson 9

Great Shepherd of the Sheep (Hebrews 13:20), Lesson 7

Guarantee of a Better Covenant (NIV, NRSV, Hebrews 7:22), Lesson 9

Guarantor of a Better Covenant (ESV, Hebrews 7:22), Lesson 9

Guardian of your Souls, Shepherd and (NRSV, NASB, 1 Peter 2:25), Lesson 7

Head (Ephesians 4:15), Lesson 8

Head of Every Man (1 Corinthians 11:13), Lesson 8

Head of the Body (Colossians 1:18), Lesson 8

Head of the Church (Colossians 1:18), Lesson 8

Head of the Corner (KJV, Matthew 21:42; Mark 12:10; Luke 20:17; Acts 4:11; NRSV, KJV, 1 Peter 2:7), Lesson 8

Head Stone of the Corner (KJV, Psalm 118:22), Lesson 8

Heaven, Lord from (KJV, 1 Corinthians 15:47), Lesson 5

Heaven, Man from/of (1 Corinthians 15:47, 49), Lesson 3

Heir of All Things (Hebrews 1:2), Lesson 10

High Priest (Hebrews 4:15; 7:26; 8:1), Lesson 6

Highest, Son of the (KJV, Luke 1:32), Lesson 5

Holy and Righteous One, The (Acts 3:14), Lesson 6

Holy One (Luke 1:35), Lesson 6

Holy One of God (Mark 1:24b; Luke 4:34), Lesson 6

Holy One, Your (Acts 2:27), Lesson 6

Holy Places, Minister in the (ESV, Hebrews 8:2), Lesson 6

Hope, Our (1 Timothy 1:1), Lesson 3

Horn of Salvation (NIV, ESV, KJV, Luke 1:69), Lesson 7

Husband (2 Corinthians 11:2; Revelation 21:2), Lesson 9

I Am (several times in John), Lesson 5

Image of the Invisible God, The (Colossians 1:15), Lesson 5

Immanuel, Emmanuel (Isaiah 7:14; Matthew 1:23), Lesson 5

Indescribable Gift (NIV, NRSV, 2 Corinthians 9:15), Lesson 3

Inexpressible Gift (ESV, 2 Corinthians 9:15), Lesson 3

Innocent Man (Matthew 27:19, NIV, NRSV), Lesson 6

Instructor (Matthew 23:10), Lesson 2

Israel, Consolation of (Luke 2:25), Lesson 3

Israel, King of (John 1:49), Lesson 10

Israel, Ruler in/over (Micah 5:2), Lesson 10

Israel, Ruler over (Micah 5:2), Lesson 4

Israel, Shepherd of my People (Matthew 2:6), Lesson 7

Jesse, Root of (Isaiah 11:10; Romans 15:12), Lesson 4

Jesus (often), Lesson 1

Jesus Christ (Matthew 1:1; John 1:17; John 17:3; Acts 2:38; Acts 4:10; Acts 9:34; Acts 10:36; Acts 16:18; Romans 1:1, 3, 6; 2:16; 5:15, 17; 6:3; 1 Corinthians 1:1, 4; 2:2; 2 Corinthians 1:19; 4:6; 13:5; Galatians 2:16; Philippians 1:8; 2:11; 1 Timothy 1:15; Hebrews 13:8; 1 John 1:7; 2:1), Lesson 1

Jesus Christ (often), Lesson 4

Jesus Christ our Lord (Romans 1:3; Romans 6:11; Romans 6:23; 1 Corinthians 1:9; 7:25), Lesson 1

Jesus Christ Our Savior (Titus 1:4; 3:6; 2 Timothy 1:10), Lesson 7

Jesus Christ our Savior (Titus 3:6), Lesson 1

Jesus of Nazareth (Mark 1:24; Luke 24:19), Lesson 1

Jesus of Nazareth, King of the Jews (John 19:19), Lesson 1

Jesus the Nazarene (Mark 16:6), Lesson 1

Jesus, the King of the Jews (Matthew 27:37), Lesson 1

Jesus, the Son of God (Hebrews 4:14), Lesson 1

Jews, King of the (Matthew 2:2; John 19:19; Matthew 27:37; Mark 15:26; Luke 23:38), Lesson 10

Jews, Servant of the (NIV, Romans 15:8), Lesson 6

Jonah, One Greater than (Matthew 12:41; Luke 11:32), Lesson 2

Joseph, Son of (Luke 3:23; John 1:45; 6:42), Lesson 1

Judah, Lion of the Tribe of (Revelation 5:5), Lesson 4

Judge of the Living and the Dead (NIV, NRSV, ESV, Acts 10:42b), Lesson 10

Judge of the Quick and the Dead (KJV, Acts 10:42b), Lesson 10

Judge, Righteous (2 Timothy 4:8), Lesson 10

Judge, Righteous (2 Timothy 4:8), Lesson 6

Just Man (Matthew 27:19, KJV), Lesson 6

Just One (KJV, Acts 7:52, 22:14), Lesson 6

King of Glory (Psalm 24:7-10), Lesson 10

King of Israel (John 1:49), Lesson 10

King of Kings and Lord of Lords (1 Timothy 6:15; Revelation 17:14a; 19:16), Lesson 10

King of Saints (KJV, Revelation 15:3), Lesson 10

King of the Ages (NIV, Revelation 15:3), Lesson 10

King of the Jews (Matthew 2:2; John 19:19; Matthew 27:37; Mark 15:26; Luke 23:38), Lesson 10

King of the Jews, Jesus, the (Matthew 27:37), Lesson 1

King of the Nations (NRSV, ESV, Revelation 15:3), Lesson 10

King, Christ, a (Luke 23:2), Lesson 4

King, Your (Zechariah 9:9; Matthew 21:5), Lesson 10

Kings of the Earth, Prince of the (KJV, Revelation 1:5), Lesson 10

Kings of the Earth, Ruler of the (NIV, NRSV, ESV, Revelation 1:5), Lesson 10

Lamb (often in Revelation), Lesson 6

Lamb of God (John 1:29, 36), Lesson 6

Lamb without Blemish or Defect (1 Peter 1:19), Lesson 6

Lamb, Paschal (NRSV, 1 Corinthians 5:7), Lesson 6

Lamb, Passover (NIV, ESV, 1 Corinthians 5:7), Lesson 6

Last Adam (1 Corinthians 15:45), Lesson 3

Launderer's Soap (NIV, Malachi 3:2), Lesson 10

Leader and Commander of the Peoples (Isaiah 55:4), Lesson 10

Leader and Savior (NRSV, ESV, Acts 5:31), Lesson 10

Leader and Savior (NRSV, ESV, Acts 5:31), Lesson 7

Leader of the Peoples (Isaiah 55:4), Lesson 10

Life (John 14:6; 1 John 1:2; Colossians 3:4), Lesson 9

Life, Author of (NIV, ESV, Acts 3:15), Lesson 9

Life, Author of (NIV, NRSV, ESV, Acts 3:15), Lesson 10

Life, Eternal (1 John 1:2; 5:20), Lesson 9

Life, Prince of (KJV, Acts 3:15), Lesson 10

Life, Prince of (KJV, Acts 3:15), Lesson 9

Life, Word of (1 John 1:1), Lesson 2

Life-Giving Spirit (NIV, NRSV, ESV; 1 Corinthians 15:45), Lesson 3

Light (John 1:5; 3:19; Isaiah 9:2), Lesson 9

Light for Revelation to the Gentiles (NIV, NRSV, ESV, Luke 2:32), Lesson 9

Light for the Gentiles (Isaiah 42:6; 49:6), Lesson 9

Light of Men (John 1:4), Lesson 9

Light of the World (John 8:12; 9:5), Lesson 9

Light to Lighten the Gentiles (KJV, Luke 2:32), Lesson 9

Light, Great (Isaiah 9:2), Lesson 9

Light, True (John 1:9), Lesson 9

Light, Your (Isaiah 60:1-3), Lesson 9

Lion of the Tribe of Judah (Revelation 5:5), Lesson 4

Living and the Dead, Judge of the (NIV, NRSV, ESV, Acts 10:42b), Lesson 10

Living Bread (John 6:51), Lesson 9

Living God, Son of the (Matthew 16:16), Lesson 5

Living One, The (Revelation 1:17b), Lesson 10

Living One, The (Revelation 1:17b), Lesson 9

Living Stone (1 Peter 2:4), Lesson 8

Logos, Word (John 1:1-2, 14), Lesson 2

Lord (often), Lesson 5

Lord and Savior Jesus Christ (2 Peter 1:11; 3:18)., Lesson 5

Lord and Savior Jesus Christ (2 Peter 1:11; 2:20; 3:18; cf. 3:2), Lesson 7

Lord both of the Dead and Living (Romans 14:9), Lesson 5

Lord Christ (Colossians 3:24), Lesson 5

Lord from Heaven (KJV, 1 Corinthians 15:47), Lesson 5

Lord God (Revelation 1:8), Lesson 5

Lord Jesus (Acts 7:59), Lesson 4

Lord Jesus (often), Lesson 5

Lord Jesus Christ (often), Lesson 4

Lord Jesus Christ (often), Lesson 5

Lord of All (Acts 10:36), Lesson 5

Lord of All (Romans 10:12), Lesson 5

Lord of Glory (1 Corinthians 2:8; Psalm 24), Lesson 5

Lord of Lords (Revelation 17:14; 19:16; 1 Timothy 6:15), Lesson 5

Lord of Peace (2 Thessalonians 3:16), Lesson 3

Lord of the Sabbath (Matthew 12:8; Mark 2:28; Luke 6:5), Lesson 5

Lord Our Righteousness, The (Jeremiah 23:6), Lesson 5

Lord Our Righteousness, The (Jeremiah 23:6), Lesson 6

Lord, Jesus Christ our (Romans 1:3; Romans 6:11; Romans 6:23; 1 Corinthians 1:9; 7:25), Lesson 1

Lord, One (Ephesians 4:5), Lesson 5

Lord, the God of the Spirits of the Prophets, The (Revelation 22:6), Lesson 5

Lords, Lord of (Revelation 17:14; 19:16; 1 Timothy 6:15), Lesson 5

Man Christ Jesus, The (1 Timothy 2:5-6), Lesson 3

Man from/of Heaven (1 Corinthians 15:47, 49), Lesson 3

Man of Sorrows (Isaiah 53:3), Lesson 3

Man, Head of Every (1 Corinthians 11:13), Lesson 8

Man, Innocent (Matthew 27:19, NIV, NRSV), Lesson 6

Man, Just (Matthew 27:19, KJV), Lesson 6

Man, Righteous (Matthew 27:19, ESV; Luke 23:47), Lesson 6

Man, Second (1 Corinthians 15:47), Lesson 3

Man, Son of (often in the Gospels), Lesson 3

Man, The (John 19:5), Lesson 3

Mary, Son of (NRSV, ESV, KJV, Mark 6:3), Lesson 1

Mary's Son (NIV, Mark 6:3), Lesson 1

Master (*epistatēs*, Luke 5:5; 8:24, 45; 9:33, 49; 17;13), Lesson 2

Master (KJV, often, in the sense of honored teacher), Lesson 2

Mediator between God and Men, One (1 Timothy 2:5), Lesson 3

Mediator of a New Covenant (Hebrews 11:24), Lesson 3

Melchizedek, Priest in the Order of (Hebrews 5:6, 10; 6:19-20; 7:17; Psalm 110:4), Lesson 6

Men, Light of (John 1:4), Lesson 9

Messenger of the Covenant (Malachi 3:1), Lesson 10

Messiah (John 1:41b), Lesson 4

Messiah (KJV, Daniel 9:25, 26), Lesson 4

Mighty God (Isaiah 9:6), Lesson 5

Mighty Savior (NRSV, Luke 1:69), Lesson 7

Minister in the Holy Places (ESV, Hebrews 8:2), Lesson 6

Minister of the Circumcision (KJV, Romans 15:8), Lesson 6

Minister of/in the Sanctuary (KJV, NRSV, Hebrews 8:2), Lesson 6

Morning Star (2 Peter 1:19), Lesson 9

Morning Star, Bright (Revelation 22:16), Lesson 9

Most High God, Son of the (Mark 5:7), Lesson 5

Most High, Son of the (NIV, NRSV, ESV, Luke 1:32), Lesson 5

Mountain, Rock Cut out of a (Daniel 2:45), Lesson 8

My Beloved (Matthew 12:18, ESV, RSV, KJV), Lesson 5

My Beloved (Matthew 12:18, ESV, RSV, KJV), Lesson 4

My God, My Lord and (John 20:28), Lesson 5

My Lord and My God (John 20:28), Lesson 5

My Son (often)., Lesson 5

Nations, Desire of All (KJV, Haggai 2:7), Lesson 10

Nations, Desired of All (NIV, Haggai 2:7), Lesson 10

Nations, King of the (NRSV, ESV, Revelation 15:3), Lesson 10

Nazarene (Matthew 2:23), Lesson 1

Nazarene, Jesus (Mark 14:67), Lesson 1

Nazarene, Jesus the (Mark 16:6), Lesson 1

Nazareth, Jesus of (Mark 1:24; Luke 24:19), Lesson 1

Nazareth, Jesus of, King of the Jews (John 19:19), Lesson 1

Offense, Rock of (ESV, KJV, 1 Peter 2:8), Lesson 8

Offense, Stone of (ESV, Isaiah 8:14), Lesson 8

Offspring of David (NIV, KJV, Revelation 22:16; ESV, 2 Timothy 2:8), Lesson 4

One and Only (NIV, John 1:14), Lesson 5

One and Only Son (NIV, John 3:16, 18; 1 John 4:9), Lesson 5

One and Only, God the (NIV, John 1:18), Lesson 5

One Greater than Jonah (Matthew 12:41; Luke 11:32), Lesson 2

One Greater than Solomon (Matthew 12:42; Luke 11:31), Lesson 2

One Like a Son of Man (Daniel 7:13-14), Lesson 3

One Lord (Ephesians 4:5), Lesson 5

One Mediator between God and Men (1 Timothy 2:5), Lesson 3

One Shepherd (Ezekiel 34:23; 37:24), Lesson 7

Only Begotten of the Father (KJV, John 1:14), Lesson 5

Only Begotten Son (KJV, John 1:18; 3:16, 18; 1 John 4:9), Lesson 5

Only Son (ESV, NRSV; John 3:16, 18; 1 John 4:9), Lesson 5

Only Son, One and (NIV, John 3:16, 18; 1 John 4:9), Lesson 5

Only, One and (NIV, John 1:14), Lesson 5

Our Hope (1 Timothy 1:1), Lesson 9

Our Righteousness (1 Corinthians 1:30), Lesson 5

Our Righteousness (1 Corinthians 1:30), Lesson 6

Overseer of your Souls, Shepherd and (NIV, ESV, 1 Peter 2:25), Lesson 7

Paschal Lamb (NRSV, 1 Corinthians 5:7), Lesson 6

Passover (KJV, 1 Corinthians 5:7), Lesson 6

Passover Lamb (NIV, ESV, 1 Corinthians 5:7), Lesson 6

Peace, Lord of (2 Thessalonians 3:16), Lesson 3

Peace, Prince of (Isaiah 9:6), Lesson 10

Peace, Prince of (Isaiah 9:6), Lesson 3

People Israel, Shepherd of my (Matthew 2:6), Lesson 7

People, Covenant for/of/to the (Isaiah 42:6-7), Lesson 9

People, Ensign of the (KJV, Isaiah 11:10), Lesson 8

Peoples, Commander of the (Isaiah 55:4), Lesson 10

Peoples, Leader and Commander of the (Isaiah 55:4), Lesson 10

Peoples, Leader of the (Isaiah 55:4), Lesson 10

Peoples, Signal to/for the (NRSV, ESV, Isaiah 11:10), Lesson 8

Peoples, Witness to the (Isaiah 55:4), Lesson 2

Perfecter of our Faith, Author and (NIV, NASB, Hebrews 12:2a), Lesson 10

Perfecter of our Faith, Founder and (ESV, Hebrews 12:2a), Lesson 10

Physician (NIV, ESV, KJV, Luke 4:23; also NRSV, Matthew 9:12; Mark 2:17; Luke 5:31), Lesson 8

Pioneer of Salvation (NRSV, Hebrews 2:10), Lesson 10

Pioneer of Salvation (NRSV, Hebrews 2:10), Lesson 7

Potentate, Blessed and Only (KJV, 1 Timothy 6:15), Lesson 10

Power of God (1 Corinthians 1:24), Lesson 2

Power of God, Christ, the (1 Corinthians 1:24), Lesson 4

Precious Cornerstone (Isaiah 28:16), Lesson 8

Priest in the Order of Melchizedek (Hebrews 5:6, 10; 6:19-20; 7:17; Psalm 110:4), Lesson 6

Priest, High (Hebrews 4:15; 7:26; 8:1), Lesson 6

Prince and Savior (NIV, KJV, Acts 5:31), Lesson 7

Prince and Savior (NIV, KJV, Acts 5:31), Lesson 10

Prince of Life (KJV, Acts 3:15), Lesson 10

Prince of Life (KJV, Acts 3:15), Lesson 9

Prince of Peace (Isaiah 9:6), Lesson 10

Prince of Peace (Isaiah 9:6), Lesson 9

Prince of the Kings of the Earth (KJV, Revelation 1:5), Lesson 10

Prince, Anointed (NRSV, Daniel 9:25, 26), Lesson 4

Prophet (Matthew 21:11; Luke 7:16; 24:19; John 6:14; 7:40; cf. John 4:19; 9:17), Lesson 2

Propitiation (KJV, ESV, 1 John 2:1-2), Lesson 6

Purifier of Silver (Malachi 3:3), Lesson 10

Quick and the Dead, Judge of the (KJV, Acts 10:42b), Lesson 10

Quickening Spirit (KJV, 1 Corinthians 15:45), Lesson 3

Rabbi (John 3:2), Lesson 2

Rabbi (John 3:2), Lesson 2

Rabonni (Mark 10:51; John 20:16), Lesson 2

Rabonni (Mark 10:51; John 20:16), Lesson 2

Radiance of God's Glory (Hebrews 1:3), Lesson 10

Radiance of God's Glory (Hebrews 1:3), Lesson 10

Ransom (Mark 10:45; 1 Timothy 2:6), Lesson 7

Redeemer (Job 19:25; Isaiah 59:20), Lesson 7

Redemption (1 Corinthians 1:30), Lesson 7

Refiner of Silver (Malachi 3:3), Lesson 10

Refiner's Fire (Malachi 3:2), Lesson 10

Rejected, Stone the Builders (Psalm 118:22; Matthew 21:42; Mark 12:10; Luke 20:17; Acts 4:11; 1 Peter 2:7), Lesson 8

Renown, Plant of (KJV, Ezekiel 34:29, probably not a messianic title), Lesson 4

Resurrection and the Life, The (John 11:25), Lesson 10

Resurrection and the Life, The (John 11:25), Lesson 9

Righteous Branch (Jeremiah 23:5; 33:15), Lesson 4

Righteous Branch (Jeremiah 23:5; 33:15), Lesson 6

Righteous Judge (2 Timothy 4:8), Lesson 10

Righteous Judge (2 Timothy 4:8), Lesson 6

Righteous Man (Matthew 27:19, ESV; Luke 23:47), Lesson 6

Righteous One (1 John 2:1-2), Lesson 5

Righteous One (NIV, RSV, ESV, Acts 7:52; 22:14; Isaiah 53:11), Lesson 6

Righteous, The (1 Peter 3:18a; 1 John 2:1), Lesson 6

Righteousness of God, The (2 Corinthians 5:21), Lesson 5

Righteousness, Our (1 Corinthians 1:30), Lesson 5

Righteousness, Our (1 Corinthians 1:30), Lesson 6

Righteousness, Sun of (Malachi 4:2), Lesson 9

Righteousness, The Lord Our (Jeremiah 23:6), Lesson 5

Righteousness, The Lord Our (Jeremiah 23:6), Lesson 6

Rising Sun (NIV, Luke 1:78), Lesson 9

Rock Cut out of a Mountain (Daniel 2:45), Lesson 8

Rock of Offense (ESV, KJV, 1 Peter 2:8), Lesson 8

Rock of Stumbling (ESV, Isaiah 8:14), Lesson 8

Rock that Makes Men/Them Fall (Isaiah 8:14; NIV, NRSV, 1 Peter 2:8), Lesson 8

Rock, Spiritual (1 Corinthians 10:4), Lesson 8

Rod (KJV, Isaiah 11:1), Lesson 4

Root and Offspring of David (Revelation 22:16), Lesson 4

Root of David (Revelation 5:5), Lesson 4

Root of Jesse (Isaiah 11:10; Romans 15:12), Lesson 4

Root out of Dry Ground (Isaiah 53:2a), Lesson 4

Ruler (NIV, NRSV, ESV, Matthew 2:6), Lesson 10

Ruler in/over Israel (Micah 5:2), Lesson 10

Ruler of the Kings of the Earth (NIV, NRSV, ESV, Revelation 1:5), Lesson 10

Ruler over Israel (Micah 5:2), Lesson 4

Ruler, Blessed and Only (NIV, 1 Timothy 6:15), Lesson 10

Sabbath, Lord of the (Matthew 12:8; Mark 2:28; Luke 6:5), Lesson 5

Sacrifice, Atoning (NIV, NRSV, 1 John 2:1-2), Lesson 6

Saints, King of (KJV, Revelation 15:3), Lesson 10

Salvation, Author of (NIV, Hebrews 2:10), Lesson 10

Salvation, Author of (NIV, NASB, Hebrews 2:10), Lesson 7

Salvation, Captain of (KJV, Hebrews 2:10), Lesson 10

Salvation, Captain of (KJV; Hebrews 2:10), Lesson 7

Salvation, Founder of (ESV, Hebrews 2:10), Lesson 10

Salvation, Founder of (ESV, Hebrews 2:10), Lesson 7

Salvation, Horn of (NIV, ESV, KJV, Luke 1:69), Lesson 7

Salvation, Pioneer of (NRSV, Hebrews 2:10), Lesson 10

Salvation, Pioneer of (NRSV, Hebrews 2:10), Lesson 7

Salvation, Your (Luke 2:30), Lesson 7

Sanctuary (Isaiah 8:14), Lesson 6

Sanctuary, Minister of/in the (KJV, NRSV, Hebrews 8:2), Lesson 6

Savior (Luke 2:11; Philippians 3:20; Ephesians 5:23), Lesson 7

Savior Jesus, The (Acts 13:23), Lesson 7

Savior of the World, The (John 4:42; 1 John 4:14), Lesson 7

Savior, Jesus Christ Our (Titus 1:4; 3:6; 2 Timothy 1:10), Lesson 7

Savior, Jesus Christ our (Titus 3:6), Lesson 1

Savior, Jesus Christ, Great God and (Titus 2:13; 2 Peter 1:1), Lesson 7

Savior, Leader and (NRSV, ESV, Acts 5:31), Lesson 10

Savior, Leader and (NRSV, ESV, Acts 5:31), Lesson 7

Savior, Mighty (NRSV, Luke 1:69), Lesson 7

Savior, Prince and (NIV, KJV, Acts 5:31), Lesson 7

Savior, Prince and (NIV, KJV, Acts 5:31), Lesson 10

Scepter (Numbers 24:17), Lesson 10

Scepter (Numbers 24:17b), Lesson 4

Second Man (1 Corinthians 15:47), Lesson 3

Seed (Galatians 3:16, 19), Lesson 3

Seed of Abraham (Hebrews 2:16), Lesson 3

Seed of David (KJV, 2 Timothy 2:8), Lesson 4

Seed of Woman (Genesis 3:15), Lesson 3

Servant (Isaiah 42:1; 53:13; Matthew 12:18; NIV, ESV, KJV, Philippians 2:7), Lesson 6

Servant of the Jews (NIV, Romans 15:8), Lesson 6

Servant of/to the Circumcised (NRSV, ESV, Romans 15:8), Lesson 6

Sheep, Door of the (ESV, KJV, John 10:7), Lesson 8

Sheep, Gate for the (NIV, NRSV, John 10:7), Lesson 8

Sheep, Great Shepherd of the (Hebrews 13:20), Lesson 7

Shepherd (Mark 14:27; Revelation 7:17), Lesson 7

Shepherd and Bishop of your Souls (KJV, 1 Peter 2:25), Lesson 7

Shepherd and Guardian of your Souls (NRSV, NASB, 1 Peter 2:25), Lesson 7

Shepherd and Overseer of your Souls (NIV, ESV, 1 Peter 2:25), Lesson 7

Shepherd of my People Israel (Matthew 2:6), Lesson 7

Shepherd of the Sheep, Great (Hebrews 13:20), Lesson 7

Shepherd, Chief (1 Peter 5:4), Lesson 7

Shepherd, Good (John 10:11, 14), Lesson 7

Shepherd, One (Ezekiel 34:23; 37:24), Lesson 7

Shoot (NIV, NRSV, ESV) Isaiah 11:1a), Lesson 4

Shoot, Tender (Isaiah 53:2a), Lesson 4

Signal to/for the Peoples (NRSV, ESV, Isaiah 11:10), Lesson 8

Silver, Purifier of (Malachi 3:3), Lesson 10

Silver, Refiner of (Malachi 3:3), Lesson 10

Slave (NRSV, Philippians 2:7), Lesson 6

Snare (Isaiah 8:14), Lesson 8

Soap, Launderer's (NIV, Malachi 3:2), Lesson 10

Solomon, One Greater than (Matthew 12:42; Luke 11:31), Lesson 2

Son of Abraham (Matthew 1:1), Lesson 1

Son of David (Mark 10:47-48; Luke 18:38-39; Matthew 9:27; 12:23; 15:22; 20:30-31; 21:9, 15), Lesson 4

Son of David (Matthew 1:1), Lesson 1

Son of God (many times), Lesson 5

Son of God, Christ, the (Acts 9:20), Lesson 4

Son of God, Jesus, the (Hebrews 4:14), Lesson 1

Son of Joseph (Luke 3:23; John 1:45; 6:42), Lesson 1

Son of Man (often in the Gospels), Lesson 3

Son of Man, One Like a (Daniel 7:13-14), Lesson 3

Son of Mary (NRSV, ESV, KJV, Mark 6:3), Lesson 1

Son of the Blessed (Mark 14:61), Lesson 5

Son of the Father (KJV, 2 John 1:3), Lesson 5

Son of the Highest (KJV, Luke 1:32), Lesson 5

Son of the Living God (Matthew 16:16), Lesson 5

Son of the Most High (NIV, NRSV, ESV, Luke 1:32), Lesson 5

Son of the Most High God (Mark 5:7), Lesson 5

Son, Beloved (Matthew 3:17; 17:5; Colossians 1:13; Mark 12:6), Lesson 5

Son, Carpenter's (Matthew 13:55), Lesson 1

Son, Dear (KJV, Colossians 1:13), Lesson 5

Son, Firstborn (Luke 2:7), Lesson 10

Son, Mary's (NIV, Mark 6:3), Lesson 1

Son, My (often), Lesson 5

Son, One and Only (NIV, John 3:16, 18; 1 John 4:9), Lesson 5

Son, Only (ESV, NRSV; John 3:16, 18; 1 John 4:9), Lesson 5

Son, Only Begotten (KJV, John 1:18; 3:16, 18; 1 John 4:9), Lesson 5

Son, The (many times in John; also Matthew 11:27; Luke 10:22), Lesson 5

Sorrows, Man of (Isaiah 53:3), Lesson 3

Souls, Shepherd and Bishop of your (KJV, 1 Peter 2:25), Lesson 7

Souls, Shepherd and Guardian of your (NRSV, NASB, 1 Peter 2:25), Lesson 7

Souls, Shepherd and Overseer of your (NIV, ESV, 1 Peter 2:25), Lesson 7

Sovereign, Blessed and Only (NRSV, ESV, 1 Timothy 6:15), Lesson 10

Spirit, Life-Giving (NIV, NRSV, ESV; 1 Corinthians 15:45), Lesson 3

Spirit, Quickening (KJV, 1 Corinthians 15:45), Lesson 3

Spiritual Rock (1 Corinthians 10:4), Lesson 8

Star (Numbers 24:17), Lesson 9

Star (Numbers 24:17b), Lesson 4

Star, Bright Morning (Revelation 22:16), Lesson 9

Star, Morning (2 Peter 1:19), Lesson 9

Stone (Isaiah 28:16; Matthew 21:44; Luke 20:18), Lesson 8

Stone of Offense (ESV, Isaiah 8:14), Lesson 8

Stone of Stumbling (KJV, Isaiah 8:14; ESV, KJV, 1 Peter 2:8), Lesson 8

Stone of the Corner, Head (KJV, Psalm 118:22), Lesson 8

Stone that Causes Men to Stumble (NIV, Isaiah 8:14; NIV, NRSV, 1 Peter 2:8), Lesson 8

Stone the Builders Rejected (Psalm 118:22; Matthew 21:42; Mark 12:10; Luke 20:17; Acts 4:11; 1 Peter 2:7), Lesson 8

Stone, Living (1 Peter 2:4), Lesson 8

Stone, Tested (NIV, NRSV, ESV, Isaiah 28:16), Lesson 8

Stone, Tried (KJV, Isaiah 28:16), Lesson 8

Stumble, Stone that Causes Men to (NIV, Isaiah 8:14; NIV, NRSV, 1 Peter 2:8), Lesson 8

Stumbling, Rock of (ESV, Isaiah 8:14), Lesson 8

Stumbling, Stone of (KJV, Isaiah 8:14; ESV, KJV, 1 Peter 2:8), Lesson 8

Sun of Righteousness (Malachi 4:2), Lesson 9

Sun, Rising (NIV, Luke 1:78), Lesson 9

Sunrise (ESV, NASB, Luke 1:78), Lesson 9

Sure Foundation (Isaiah 28:16), Lesson 8

Surety of a Better Covenant (KJV, Hebrews 7:22), Lesson 9

Teacher (often), Lesson 2

Teacher, Good (Mark 10:17-18; Luke 18:18), Lesson 6

Tender Shoot (Isaiah 53:2a), Lesson 4

Tested Stone (NIV, NRSV, ESV, Isaiah 28:16), Lesson 8

The Almighty (Revelation 1:8), Lesson 5

The Beloved (Ephesians 1:6), Lesson 5

The Boy Jesus (Luke 2:43), Lesson 1

The Child Jesus (Luke 2:27), Lesson 1

The Christ (used absolutely, Matthew 1:16; 16:20; Mark 14:61), Lesson 4

The Exact Representation of His Being (Hebrews 1:3a), Lesson 5

The Father's Son (NIV, NRSV, ESV, 2 John 1:3), Lesson 5

The First and the Last (Revelation 1:17b; 2:8; 22:13), Lesson 10

The Holy and Righteous One (Acts 3:14), Lesson 6

The Image of the Invisible God (Colossians 1:15), Lesson 5

The Living One (Revelation 1:17b), Lesson 10

The Living One (Revelation 1:17b), Lesson 9

The Lord Our Righteousness (Jeremiah 23:6), Lesson 5

The LORD Our Righteousness (Jeremiah 23:6), Lesson 6

The Lord, the God of the Spirits of the Prophets (Revelation 22:6), Lesson 5

The Man (John 19:5), Lesson 3

The Man Christ Jesus (1 Timothy 2:5-6), Lesson 3

The Resurrection and the Life (John 11:25), Lesson 10

The Resurrection and the Life (John 11:25), Lesson 9

The Righteous (1 Peter 3:18a; 1 John 2:1), Lesson 6

The Righteousness of God (2 Corinthians 5:21), Lesson 5

The Savior Jesus (Acts 13:23), Lesson 7

The Savior of the World (John 4:42; 1 John 4:14), Lesson 7

The Son (many times in John; also Matthew 11:27; Luke 10:22), Lesson 5

The True God (1 John 5:20), Lesson 5

The True God and Eternal Life (1 John 5:20), Lesson 9

Trap (NIV, NRSV, ESV; Isaiah 8:14; Gin, KJV), Lesson 8

Tried Stone (KJV, Isaiah 28:16), Lesson 8

True God and Eternal Life, The (1 John 5:20), Lesson 9

True God, The (1 John 5:20), Lesson 5

True Light (John 1:9), Lesson 9

True Vine (John 15:1), Lesson 9

True Witness, Faithful and (Revelation 3:14b), Lesson 2

True, Faithful and (Revelation 19:11), Lesson 2

Truth (John 14:6), Lesson 2

Unspeakable Gift (KJV, 2 Corinthians 9:15), Lesson 3

Vine (John 15:5), Lesson 9

Vine, True (John 15:1), Lesson 9

Way (John 14:6), Lesson 8

Who Is and Was and Is to Come (Revelation 1:4, 8), Lesson 10

Wisdom of God, (1 Corinthians 1:24), Lesson 2

Wisdom of God, Christ, the (1 Corinthians 1:24), Lesson 4
Witness to the Peoples (Isaiah 55:4), Lesson 2
Witness, Faithful (Revelation 1:5a), Lesson 2
Witness, Faithful and True (Revelation 3:14b), Lesson 2
Woman, Seed of (Genesis 3:15), Lesson 3
Wonderful Counselor (Isaiah 9:6), Lesson 2
Word of God (Revelation 19:13), Lesson 2
Word of Life (1 John 1:1), Lesson 2
Word, Logos (John 1:1-2, 14), Lesson 2
World, Light of the (John 8:12; 9:5), Lesson 9
Your Holy One (Acts 2:27), Lesson 6
Your King (Zechariah 9:9; Matthew 21:5), Lesson 10
Your Light (Isaiah 60:1-3), Lesson 9
Your Salvation (Luke 2:30), Lesson 7

Appendix 3. Songs and Hymns Celebrating Names and Titles of Jesus Christ

One of the reasons for this study of the names and titles of Jesus is to know him more fully, in ways that we hadn't explored before. To enter into this takes time in meditation and worship.

Songs and hymns are ways that we use the names and character of Jesus in our worship. To help those designing worship services around the names and titles of Jesus, and to facilitate personal worship, I have tried to include some of the most popular hymns and songs that I could find among the tens of thousands in the CCLI Song Select and Cyber Hymnal databases. I've looked for songs that actually include names and titles somewhat prominently, though that is a judgment call. These are included at the end of every lesson, and for all lessons in Appendix 3 available online. Special thanks in compiling these lists to: Brittney Land, David Pabalate, Darrel Fink, and Jonathan Fink.

If you'd like to learn some of these songs, you'll probably find one or more of them by searching on YouTube.com. It's a great sing-along resource for your personal devotions and will help you learn the songs.

Many songs relate more to the names and titles of God, rather than Jesus. Here, we're focusing on the songs that relate more to Jesus. Songs that focus on God the Father can be found in my companion volume, *Names and Titles of God* (JesusWalk, 2010).

To save space in this book, we include the appropriate songs and hymns at the end of each lesson, but the comprehensive list of all the songs together is available online:

http://www.jesuswalk.com/names-jesus/appendix-3-names-jesus-songs-and-hymns.pdf

Appendix 4. The Title Son of Man in the Gospels

It's instructive to see how Jesus uses the title Son of Man. In the Synoptic Gospels, he uses Son of Man in three primary ways:

1. Earthly Son of Man
2. Suffering Son of Man
3. Apocalyptic or Eschatological Son of Man

He begins his ministry by using Son of Man in a variety of ways. But only after Peter recognizes him as "the Christ, the Son of the living God" at Caesarea Philippi does he begin to share the other aspects of his title, that the Son of Man will suffer and then return in glory. Let's look at each of these uses individually.

The Earthly Son of Man

A number of sayings fall under a category of the earthly Son of Man sayings, those which are not related directly to his death and return:

- Authority to forgive sins (Mark 2:10 = Matthew 9:6 = Luke 5:24)
- **Lord of the Sabbath** (Mark 2:27 = Matthew 12:8 = Luke 6:5)
- Eating and drinking, in contrast to John the Baptist's asceticism (Matthew 11:19 = Luke 7:34)
- Nowhere to lay his head (Matthew 8:20 = Luke 9:58)
- A word against him to be forgiven vs. a word against the Holy Spirit (Matthew 12:32 = Luke 12:10)
- Who do men say the Son of Man is? (Matthew 16:13)
- Sows the good seed (Matthew 13:37)
- Persecution on his account (Luke 6:22)
- Came to seek and save the lost (Luke 19:10)
- Betrayed with a kiss (Luke 22:48)

The Suffering Son of Man

- Must suffer (Mark 8:31 = Luke 9:22)
- Will suffer (Mark 9:12 = Matthew 17:12)
- Risen from the dead (Mark 9:9 = Matthew 17:9)
- Delivered into the hands of men (Mark 9:31 = Matthew 17:22 = Luke 9:44)

- Delivered to the chief priests, condemned to death, rises again (Mark 10:33 = Matthew 20:18 = Luke 18:31)
- Came to serve and give his life as a ransom for many (Mark 10:45 = Matthew 20:28)
- Goes as is written, woe to betrayer (Mark 14:41 = Matthew 26:45)
- Will be three days in the earth (Matthew 12:40 = Luke 11:30)

The Apocalyptic Son of Man

- Comes in glory of Father and holy angels (Mark 8:38 = Matthew 16:27 = Luke 9:26)
- Coming with clouds and great glory (Mark 13:16 = Matthew 24:30 = Luke 21:27)
- Sitting at the right hand of power and coming with clouds of heaven (Mark 14:62 = Matthew 26:64 = Luke 22:69)
- Coming at an hour you don't expect (Luke 12:40 = Matthew 24:44)
- Coming as in the days of Noah (Luke 17:26 = Matthew 24:37)
- Gone through the towns of Israel before he come (Matthew 10:23)
- Send his angels (Mark 13:41)
- Some will not taste death before he comes in his kingdom (Matthew 16:28 = Mark 9:1)
- Sit on his glorious throne (Matthew 19:28)
- Sign of Son of Man appears (Matthew 24:30)
- So will be his coming (Matthew 24:39)
- When he comes in his glory (Matthew 25:31)
- Acknowledges before the angels of God (Luke 12:18)
- Desire to see his days (Luke 17:22)
- The day when he is revealed (Luke 17:30)
- Will he find faith when he comes? (Luke 18:8)
- Stand before him (Luke 21:36)

Jesus' Use of Son of Man in John's Gospel

In John's Gospel, Jesus uses the term Son of Man 12 times. I see three major themes in the Fourth Gospel.

1. Heavenly Son of Man
2. Life-Giving Son of Man

    3.   Glorified Son of Man.

1. Heavenly Son of Man. The first theme of the heavenly Son of Man draws from the passage in Daniel 7:13 where the Son of Man comes on the clouds of heaven and appears before the Ancient of Days. We see angels ascending and descending on him (1:51); the imagery of Jacob's ladder (Genesis 28:12);[181] one who came from heaven (3:13); and one who ascends to heaven (6:62).

2. Life-Giving Son of Man. The second theme is the life-giving Son of Man. This concept doesn't draw directly from Daniel, but from Jesus' teaching in the Gospel of John about him being the source of eternal life. The Son of Man: gives food for eternal life (6:27); must eat his flesh and drink his blood (6:53); and merits belief in him (9:35).

3. Glorified Son of Man. The third theme of the glorified Son of Man is inferred by the Daniel passage, since the Son of Man who "was given authority, glory, and sovereign power" now returns to his glory in heaven, by being lifted up. "Lifted up" points to the cross, of course, but beyond that to God raising him from the dead and exalting Christ to his place of glory at his right hand. Jesus' statement, "the Son of Man must be lifted up" (John 3:14) corresponds to his prediction in the Synoptics that "the Son of Man must suffer many things ... be killed and after three days rise again" (Mark 8:31). All this draws upon the Suffering Servant prophecy:

> "See, my servant will act wisely;
> he will be raised and **lifted up** and highly exalted." (Isaiah 52:13)

John contains six references to the Son of Man who is about to be lifted up and glorified: lifted up as the bronze snake in the wilderness (3:13-14); authority to judge (5:27); lifted up (8:28); his hour to be glorified (12:23); again lifted up (12:34); and now to be glorified (13:31).

From the Gospels we learn that for Jesus, his role as Son of Man was all encompassing. It included his divinity, his suffering, his authority, his glory, and his return at the end of time.

---

[181] Brown (*John* 29A:88-91) discusses the meaning of this passage in "A Detached Saying about the Son of Man."

Appendix 5. Disputed Titles of Jesus

There are some titles that are not unanimously attributed to Jesus. But I'll include them here for the sake of completeness.

Titles from the Song of Solomon

The Song of Solomon has sometimes been interpreted as an allegory of the love between Jesus and his bride. I'm not sure I'm convinced of that, but if you accept this interpretation – *and* see the words as referring to the male lover in this love poem (which can be confusing) – then here are some metaphors and similes that you might include:

- **Rose of Sharon** (Song of Solomon 2:1; probably referring to the female)
- **Lily of the Valleys** (Song of Solomon 2:1; probably referring to the female)
- **Apple Tree** among the trees of the woods (Song of Solomon 2:3)
- **A Gazelle or Young Stag** (Song of Solomon 2:9, 17; 8:14)
- **My lover, my friend** (Song of Solomon 5:16)

The female describes her lover as: Outstanding among ten thousand" (NIV), "distinguished among ten thousand. (NRSV, ESV), "chiefest among ten thousand (KJV, Song of Songs 5:10)

Plant of Renown

"**Plant of Renown**" (KJV, Ezekiel 34:29) isn't recognized as a messianic title by more recent translations. They translate it as "a land renowned for its crops" (NIV); "a splendid vegetation" (NRSV); "renowned plantations" (ESV).

Jesus as the Angel of the Lord

Some teach that the Angel of the Lord in the Old Testament and the angel that appeared in the Fiery Furnace with the three Hebrew young men is actually Jesus. Others see the Captain of the Lord's hosts (Joshua 5:14-15) as the pre-incarnate Jesus. I don't see any compelling argument to support this. In Hebrew, *mal'āk*, can mean "messenger, representative, courtier, angel," depending upon the context. It is true, however, that sometimes in the Old Testament, the angel of the Lord seems to be Yahweh himself, a theophany, and appearance of God. However, Jesus is clearly the one prophesied in Malachi who is "the **Messenger of the Covenant**" (Malachi 3:1).

Appendix 6. Exercises to Help You Internalize the Names of Jesus

It would be sad if studying the names of Jesus were merely an intellectual or academic exercise for you. Beyond your study, here are some exercises that will help internalize what you're learning and let it begin to change you.

Over the several days you are studying a particular lesson, I recommend that you incorporate into your daily life some of the following exercises that will help implant the names in your heart and mind. Try one or more of the exercises listed in Appendix 6, or invent your own.

1. Pray to Jesus using one or more of the names in this lesson. As you pray, call on him in a way that relates to his name.

2. Meditate on one or more of the names in this lesson. Visualize Jesus in the ways suggested by the names in this lesson. Picture him in your mind's eye. See how he is strong for you in these ways.

3. Write down your own answers to the discussion questions in this lesson. Post them to the online forum or read what others have written.

4. Worship him by singing one of the songs suggested above.

5. Consider how you need to change to become like Jesus as reflected by one or more of the names in this lesson, and ask for his help to change you.

6. Draw or paint a scene, figure, or calligraphy related to one of the names.

7. **Make a banner** emblazoned with one of Jesus' titles.

8. Compose a song related to one of the names and then teach it to someone.

9. Community. Find a way to influence your community or church in a way inspired by one of these names, titles, descriptor, or metaphor of Jesus. What project could you help with or initiate that could make a positive difference in the lives of people. For example, if Jesus is the Good Shepherd, what people in your community are "like sheep without a shepherd"? Who are without their basic needs, for example? What project could give feet to being a shepherd to those in need?

10. Picture how a friend or relative of yours could benefit from Jesus' ministry as reflected by one of the names in a particular week's lesson. Pray for that person accordingly and minister to that person yourself when an opportunity presents itself.